KNACK®
MAKE IT EASY

HOME REPAIR & MAINTENANCE

KNACK®

HOME REPAIR & MAINTENANCE

An illustrated problem solver

TERRY MEANY

Guilford, Connecticut
An imprint of The Globe Pequot Press

Copyright © 2008 by Morris Book Publishing, LLC

ALL RIGHTS RESERVED. No part of this book may be reproduced or transmitted in any form by any means, electronic or mechanical, including photocopying and recording, or by any information storage and retrieval system, except as may be expressly permitted in writing from the publisher. Requests for permission should be addressed to The Globe Pequot Press, Attn: Rights and Permissions Department, P.O. Box 480, Guilford, CT 06437.

Knack is a registered trademark of Morris Publishing Group, LLC, and is used with express permission.

Text Design by Paul Beatrice
Illustrations by Jack Tom

Cover photo credits:
Front Cover (left to right): Marilyn Zelinsky-Syarto, © Digitoll | Dreamstime.com, Marilyn Zelinsky-Syarto, © Robert Redelowski/ shutterstock
Back Cover: Marilyn Zelinsky-Syarto, © Don Bayley/ istockphoto, Marilyn Zelinsky-Syarto, © Kelpfish | Dreamstime.com
Photo research by Anna Adesanya
Additional photo research by Marilyn Zelinsky-Syarto

CIP DATA: A catalogue record for this book is available from the British Library

Meany, Terry.
Home repair & maintenance : an illustrated problem solver / Terry Meany.
p. cm.
ISBN 978-0-7627-5693-3
1. Dwellings—Maintenance and repair—Amateurs' manuals. I. Title. II. Title: Home repair & maintenance.
TH4817.3.M3875 2008
643'.7—dc22

Globe Pequot Press International
Footprint Handbooks
6 Riverside Court
Lower Bristol Road
Bath
BA2 3DZ
UK
T+44 (0)1225 469141
F+44 (0)1225 469461

The following manufacturers/names appearing in *Knack Home Repair & Maintenance* are trademarks: 3M™, Porc-a-Fix®, Portland Cement®, Polyfilla®, Velcro®, WD-40®

Printed in India by Replika Press Pvt Ltd

The information in this book is true and complete to the best of our knowledge. All recommendations are made without guarantee on the part of the author or The Globe Pequot Press. The author and The Globe Pequot Press disclaim any liability in connection with the use of this information.

About the author

Terry Meany has the knack! A former contractor, he is the author of *Working Windows (Lyons Press)* and also wrote *The Complete Idiot's Guide to Plumbing* and *The Complete Idiot's Guide to Electrical Repair.* He lives in Seattle, Washington.

CONTENTS

Introduction . . . viii

Chapter 1: Problem Solving
How to Avoid Problems . . . 1
Sizing Up the Problem . . . 2
Water Leaks . . . 4
Gas Leaks . . . 6
Storm Damage . . . 8
Securing a Damaged House . . . 10

Chapter 2: Vital Tools
Tool Ergonomics & Safety . . . 12
Hand Tools . . . 14
Tools to Cut, Scrape & Prise . . . 16
Basic Small Tools . . . 18
Power Tools . . . 20
Tools to Hire . . . 22

Chapter 3: Vital Hardware
Safety Gear . . . 24
Screws & Bolts . . . 26
Nails . . . 28
Gap Fillers & Sealants . . . 30
Tapes & Glues . . . 32
Sandpaper & Steel Wool . . . 34

Chapter 4: Vital Products
Paints & Finishes . . . 36
Stains . . . 38
Clear Finishes . . . 40
Faux Finishes . . . 42
Fillers . . . 44

Chapter 5: Scratches & Chips
Scratched Woodwork . . . 46
Scratched Furniture . . . 48
Wood Floor Scratches . . . 50
Scratched Worktops . . . 52
Repairing & Replacing Tiles . . . 54
Repairing a Chipped Finish . . . 56

Chapter 6: Inside Leaks/Clogs
Taps . . . 58
Toilets . . . 60
Washing Machines . . . 62
Unblocking Sinks & Basins . . . 64
Unblocking Toilets . . . 66
Bath & Shower Wastes . . . 68

Chapter 7: Outside Leaks/Clogs
Roofs . . . 70
Gutters & Downpipes . . . 72
Windows . . . 74
Clearing Gutters . . . 76
Unblocking Downpipes . . . 78
Unblocking Outside Drains . . . 80

Chapter 8: Squeaks/Sticky Issues
Floors: What to Try First . . . 82
Floors: What to Try Next . . . 84
Sticking Doors . . . 86
Sticking Windows . . . 88
Sticking Furniture Drawers . . . 90
Sticking Door Locks . . . 92

Chapter 9: Cracks & Holes
Holes in Plaster . . . 94
Repairing Cracks in Plaster . . . 96
Holes in Plasterboard . . . 98
Cracks in Plasterboard . . . 100
Cracks in Concrete . . . 102
Cracked Glass . . . 104

Chapter 10: Electrical Systems
How Your System Works . . . 106
Fuses & Circuit Breakers . . . 108
Saving Electricity . . . 110
Lamp, Flex & Plug Repair . . . 112
Renewable Energy . . . 114

Chapter 11: Fungal Attack
Know Your Micro-organisms 116
Interior Mould & Mildew 118
Exterior Mould 120
Serious Mould 122
Wood Rot 124

Chapter 12: Pets & Pests
Installing a Pet Door 126
Bird Damage & Repairs 128
Wasps & Bees 130
Pest-Proofing Your Home 132

Chapter 13: Painting
Choosing the Paint & Sheen 134
Interior Preparation 136
Painting Ceilings & Walls 138
Woodwork & Doors 140
Exterior Preparation 142
Exterior Painting 144

Chapter 14: Vital Storage
Putting Up Shelves 146
More Shelving 148
Clothes Storage Solutions 150
Garage Storage 152
Workbench 154
Kitchen Island 156

Chapter 15: Energy Efficiency
Energy Primer 158
Reducing Heat Loss 160
Draught Proofing 162
Adding Insulation 164
Appliances & Energy Savings 166

Chapter 16: Outdoor Repairs
Fence Repairs 168
Fence Repairs (Continued) 170
Decking Repairs 172
Outdoor Lighting 174
Composting 176
Rainwater Butts 178

Chapter 17: Childproofing
Safety Gates 180
Window Precautions 182
Room & Cupboard Doors 184
Electrical Precautions 186
Plumbing Safeguards 188
Other Child Concerns 190

Chapter 18: Appliances
Refrigerator 192
Dishwasher 194
Vacuum Cleaner 196

Chapter 19: Maintenance Timeline
Summer 198
Autumn 200
Winter 202
Spring 204
Monthly 206
Yearly 208

Glossary 210
Photo Credits 214
Index 218

INTRODUCTION

New is very appealing: new clothes, new electronics, or a new car. New usually means shiny clean, everything in working order, no worries or concerns; whatever this new thing is, you can simply use it and enjoy it. Eventually, the new clothes need cleaning or mending, the computer baulks at a strange software program, or that new car's 'check oil light' goes on. The honeymoon isn't completely over, but the relationship is going to require a bit more attention now. In the case of a home, especially if it's an older building, the relationship might require some extensive counselling, as your boiler, roof, plumbing and paint, just to name a few, all demand your attention.

Let's establish one truism up front: no one likes to do home maintenance. We would all prefer our appliances, floor finishes and garage doors to work perfectly and look great forever, despite using (or abusing) them day after day. Without a crew of handy boys and girls discreetly hidden away in the servants' quarters, the maintenance and repair tasks fall on you. And you will not always feel comfortable with the jobs you'll face.

In *The Far Side* cartoon entitled 'An Elephant's Nightmare', an elephant sitting in front of a grand piano in a packed concert hall thinks, 'What am I doing here? I can't play this thing! I'm a flautist, for crying out loud!' If you're unfamiliar with kitchen drains, electrical circuits, entry door locks, and plaster repair, you might feel like this out-of-place pachyderm flautist. Your main tool might be a phone book to call unknown contractors and businesses specializing in repairs to fix your problems.

But this approach prompts other questions. Whom do you call? Do you even need a professional? Do you have the time and money to hire and wait for a plumber? What happens if a sudden freeze bursts a water pipe in the middle of the night? Knowing enough to handle most problems with some skill and success can turn a major predicament into a minor inconvenience.

You don't have to be an expert in plumbing, carpentry, tiling, or any other construction trade to work on your house. Your results don't have to be perfect, but knowing enough to quickly solve or temporarily fix a problem is a major benefit. With nationwide

DIY chains, local and regional hardware stores, books, home repair TV shows, and online help, anyone can find the right tools and materials to tackle painting a bedroom or stop a dripping tap. All you need to get started is a question-and-answer session with yourself.

Is it important to do this repair, or can I put it off?

Chipped paint or scratched wood floors look unsightly, but they can be left alone as long as you're willing to live with their appearances. A loose and overflowing gutter should get attended to before it causes more damage. If you ignore regular boiler maintenance, you'll regret it when the boiler stops running on a freezing winter day. Some jobs, such as touching up the exterior paint, can be left during a warm, dry summer but should be taken care of before the colder weather sets in.

Can I do this job myself?

We might like new things, but we don't always like new experiences that take us outside our comfort zone of skills. Maintaining a home exposes us to a lot of new experiences we might prefer to ignore or even flee from. This book will help you face them with the confidence to figure out how to solve the problems.

Practice leads to improvement and more comfort with tools and techniques. It doesn't have to lead to perfection, unless you find you really enjoy building fences or putting up shelves. Often enough, you'll be surprised at what you can accomplish.

Should I do this job myself?

If you have one bathroom, it's a Friday afternoon, and you're expecting guests for the weekend, it probably isn't the time to replace the inner workings of your only toilet. Call a plumber. Smell gas around your boiler or

stove? Call the gas company. Afraid of heights, and your roof is missing a few tiles after a recent wind storm? Contact a roofer.

Your kitchen has seen better days and needs a new paint job? It might be tedious working around all the cabinets and fixtures, but have a go at it. If nothing else, you'll gain a new appreciation for the painting trade and a different perspective on the notion that 'anyone can paint'. Your tumble dryer suddenly stops drying, but the drum keeps turning? It's probably a heating element and something you can replace and save on an appliance repair technician's call-out charge.

In other words, know your *limitations*, but don't underestimate what you ***can*** do.

Do I have the time to do this?

Even if it's a job you can do, if it doesn't fit your schedule, you might have to hire it out. Some of us believe we should fix everything ourselves, but if it isn't practical, the repair will either go undone or will be done in a hurry, either of which can lead to some regret. Home maintenance is about time and money management as well as the repair work itself. Even people who do repairs contract some of the work in their own homes out to other tradespeople.

Is it worth paying someone to do this work?

Contractors are not inexpensive. Each has to account for overheads, materials, taxes, transportation, losses on some jobs, and profit, the same as you or your employer does in your line of work. Repairs are normally paid for with after-tax income, so that if a contractor is charging you £25 an hour, you would have to earn over £30 an hour to pay the bill. Doing the work yourself keeps the money in your wallet.

However, if it takes you five times as long to do the work and three car trips to a DIY store for materials, and the results are only so-so, then, aside from the learning experience, this job might not be much of a cost saver. In some cases, you won't find this out until you've completed the work. Carefully consider the cost and time advantages and disadvantages before deciding to take on a repair.

Maintenance can be divided into two categories: preventative and immediate

Preventative maintenance is the unexciting, ongoing round of routine tasks that keep your home running smoothly. This includes regular gutter cleanings, paint touch-ups and boiler services. What else falls under preventative maintenance? Checking for broken roof tiles, getting the chimney swept, replacing worn draughtproofing, and sealing off any chinks in walls that could be used by various animals to crawl inside your home are all part of a regular to-do list. You don't have to do anything on this list, but ignoring these tasks can lead to bigger tasks later.

Preventative maintenance helps put off most ***immediate maintenance.*** A broken washing machine hose, a chimney fire, and rats nesting in your attic are examples of immediate or even emergency maintenance. You can't foresee every possible repair, but many can be headed off. An ounce of prevention really is worth a pound of cure when it comes to your home.

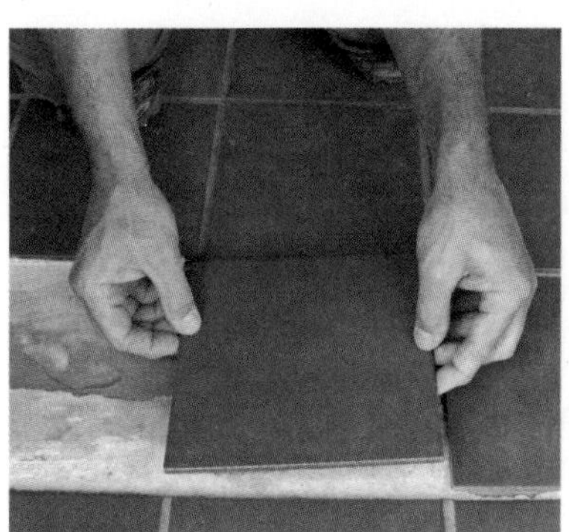

How much time do you need to devote to home maintenance? It depends how many people live in your home and how they behave in it. A single person who is away on business half the year will probably spend more time dusting than cleaning shower drains. A family of six amateur acrobats who practise in the living room and share their home with a small menagerie of animals allowed to run loose inside is a different story! Staying ahead of your maintenance is easier in the long run than falling behind.

This book will give you the tools and guidance to take a crack at many of your home repairs and maintenance tasks without feeling overwhelmed. And when you're not overwhelmed, you'll enjoy your home even more.

HOW TO AVOID PROBLEMS

Schedule regular maintenance check-ups to avoid any problems in the first place

'A stitch in time saves nine' is a traditional proverb that harks back to the days when everyone still repaired their torn clothes instead of throwing them out, but the sentiment remains true. If you catch a problem early, it usually stays manageable. Ignore it, and it becomes a bigger problem at a bigger cost. Most of the systems and parts that make up your home are reliable, at least when they're new. But time passes, and malfunctions show up. They're to be expected. You can run a washing machine or turn a key in a lock only so many times before something gives way. You can't prevent every problem, but you can slow some up, head others off, and be prepared when they happen.

Open Toolbox

- Tools are one of the best investments you can make.
- For the most part, good hand tools will last a lifetime or certainly many years, far more than just about anything else we buy.
- You don't need one of every tool made, just enough of the basics to do most jobs – the rest you can get as and when you need them.
- You also don't need the very best tools – for normal maintenance decent quality is more than adequate.

Measuring the Job

- Accurately measuring can simplify a job, and not measuring can complicate a job – simplifying is better.
- Estimating the size needed for a repair task is fine as a rough guideline, but measuring means fewer trips to the store, a closer cost estimate, and less wasted material.
- If you measure twice and still aren't comfortable cutting or drilling, then measure again until you are comfortable.
- Don't depend on your eye when gauging the size of anything – always use a measuring tape.

Preventative maintenance isn't exactly fun, but it beats the alternatives, such as a leaking roof during a rainstorm or a non-functioning boiler in the dead of winter. Scheduling regular boiler inspections, replacing missing roof tiles, touching up peeling paint, and knowing when to replace a dying dishwasher helps you to control your home environment and keep it safe and inviting. It's best to stay informed and aware and do the work on your terms, knowing it has to be done anyway, rather than having the circumstances dictate work when you least expect them to.

GREEN LIGHT

From an energy and resource standpoint, doing your own repairs using materials to hand defers a contractor's trip to your house and means you don't have to take time off work waiting at home to let them in. You become more capable and save money. And if you have kids, you can pass these skills down to them.

Replacing a Light Fitting

- Be prepared for a few surprises if you have to drill into a wall or ceiling or snoop around in the attic, especially in an older home that may have been worked on by previous owners.
- Changes in building regulations over the years may turn a simple job such as replacing a light fitting into a more complicated job.
- When some of your work involves concealed areas, reckon on spending more time than you expected to; an assistant is always helpful, too.

Home Repairing Is a Learning Process

- Be flexible when approaching your repairs – your one trip to buy materials might turn into several.
- For some jobs, have a contingency plan in case water or heat has to stay off overnight or your painting is taking longer to dry than you expected.
- Know when to walk away from a frustrating repair – it will look different after a meal or some sleep.
- If you're getting in too deep and need expertise, back off and hire help.

SIZING UP THE PROBLEM

Determine which problems need your attention and which ones can wait for professional help

Whether you own or rent your home, problems arise. Drains and roofs leak, often at bad times (is there ever a good time?), the power goes out, the front door won't lock. A slow dripping tap you can live with – forever, if you want – but rain pouring in through a hole in the roof caused by a fallen tree branch can't wait at all. Solving a repair problem is no different from working out a maths problem. First, read and assess the situation. Then try some quick solutions and reassess everything. Try the solutions you thought you could avoid, and if everything fails, do some damage control to stabilize the problem until you have the tools, materials or help to fix it.

You will run into new problems, but you can apply your

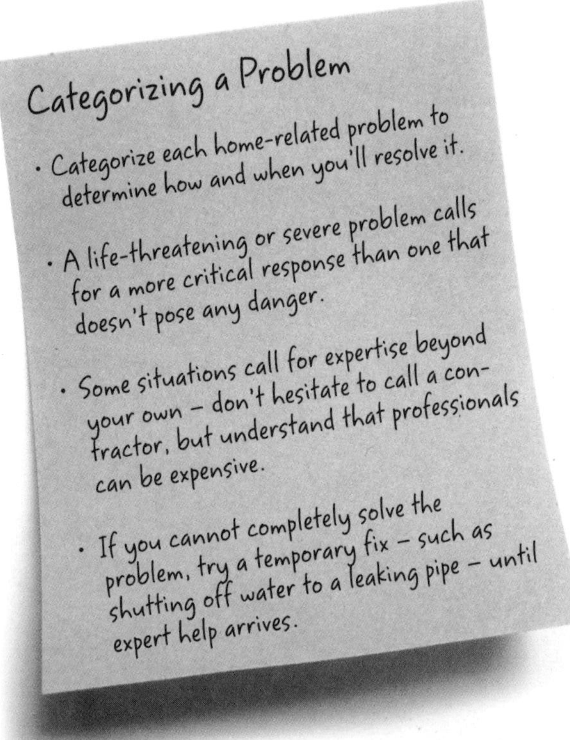

Categorizing a Problem
· Categorize each home-related problem to determine how and when you'll resolve it.
· A life-threatening or severe problem calls for a more critical response than one that doesn't pose any danger.
· Some situations call for expertise beyond your own – don't hesitate to call a contractor, but understand that professionals can be expensive.
· If you cannot completely solve the problem, try a temporary fix – such as shutting off water to a leaking pipe – until expert help arrives.

Basement Flooding

- If the flooding is due to extreme rain, block off any leaking windows and doors as best you can and monitor the situation until the rain stops.
- Broken or backed-up drains are unsanitary and unhealthy; call a plumber who can make repairs and recommend a contractor to clean up the mess.
- If a water pipe breaks, turn off the main stopcock and call your plumber.
- Know where all your stopcocks are located and confirm they're in good working order before you need them.

problem-solving skills to each one and often come up with a reasonable solution. It might not be the fastest or most elegant, but that's not important. Speed and elegance will come later. For now, you took care of it, even if it meant calling someone else to do it. That's a perfectly legitimate solution if you've tried everything you could think of. And remember, online searching dramatically produces more solutions than any one of us can think of.

MAKE IT EASY

If the problem isn't endangering you or causing increasing damage – flooding water, for instance – and you're feeling time pressures to be elsewhere or get something else done, then walk away from it. Fatigue, hunger and time concerns will negatively affect your actions and can make things worse. Some things you can come back to and fix later.

Power Cut

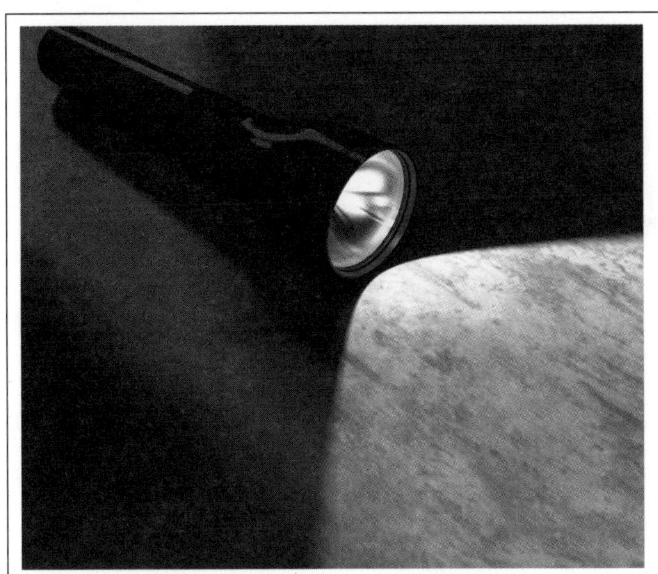

- If your neighbours are also without lights, the power cut isn't isolated to your house but may be weather-related or due to a fault in the main supply.
- If just your house has lost all its power, there is probably a problem with your main power supply.
- When only one area of power goes out, a fuse has burned out or a circuit breaker has tripped.
- When a circuit shuts down, work out what you last turned on – it may have developed a fault or overloaded the circuit.

When to Report an Emergency

- Contractors are available for after-hours emergencies but at a high price, so consider whether your problem really needs an immediate response.
- The time to find 24-hour emergency help is when you don't need it – ask around for personal recommendations of plumbers, electricians, gas engineers, glaziers and locksmiths, and keep their numbers handy.
- Determine what you can hold off on fixing until normal business hours offer a greater range of contractors to call – and better prices, too.

WATER LEAKS

Know which messes should get cleaned up early and which ones can wait for a professional

Water is great when it's clean water in pipes, dirty water in the drains, and rainwater outside. When a pipe or drain leaks, however, or the rain started coming through the ceiling, we panic. Water damages walls, floors, furniture and anything else that gets in its way. Some leaks won't cause much damage – if a pipe bursts in a cellar, say – but they will require the water supply to the house to be shut off until they're repaired. In that sense, such leaks can have a major impact, especially if one occurs in the middle of Christmas dinner. Knowing some quick fixes will get you through until you or a plumber – and not a plumber on holiday rates – can do a permanent repair.

Leaking Pipe

- Shut the water off at the fixture if the leak is coming from a tap.
- Shut off the water supply to the house if a pipe is leaking excessively.
- If the pipe is accessible, wrap it tightly with self-bonding waterproof tape, similar repair tape, or even a bicycle inner tube secured with wire.
- The leaking water can be caught in a bucket, which buys you time until the pipe is repaired.
- Most roof leaks aren't emergencies unless a tree branch crashes on to the roof, leaving a large hole.

Leaking Roof

- In the loft, place a bucket under the leak and time the water dripping into it to determine how often it needs to be emptied.
- A minor, slow leak can even be monitored until repaired as long as the water doesn't damage any exposed timbers on its way into the bucket.
- If you can't get into the loft space, make your best guess as to where the leak originates: you may be able to toss a tarpaulin or plastic sheeting over that area of the roof.

Toilets can leak, too, but if you have more than one, the leaking culprit can be shut off and addressed later.

Roof leaks are problematic and should be considered on a case-by-case basis. An accessible loft space allows you to see where the water is leaking in; a bucket will hold you over until the roof can be repaired. Failing that, a tarpaulin on the roof will do the job. The point is to limit the damage if you can't stop the water itself. Taking interim steps is better than doing nothing at all.

YELLOW LIGHT

You don't want to discover that you don't know where your main stopcock is when you need it. Find it and test it annually; it can be tight if it hasn't been used in some years. Spray it with a lubricant if it's sticking. Show other family members its location as well.

Leaking Toilets

- To temporarily remedy a slow-leaking cistern, catch the water with a bucket or plastic container.
- If the water inlet develops a small leak, place a plastic container under it as well, but address this soon – this valve is important, and you don't want it failing on you.
- If the leak is at the base of the bowl at the floor, shut the water off, flush the water out of the toilet, and stop using it until the toilet can be removed and reset.
- Running water in the cistern wastes water but can be fixed when time permits.

Preparing for Big Leaks

- Big leaks can be very damaging when they show up on floors and worktops instead of staying inside pipes and fixtures.
- Stop the flow of water as quickly as possible, which is at least as important as repairing the leak itself.
- You might have a leak and not even know it – check your water bill for any unexplained increases in water usage.
- Find a plumber now so you're not looking when you do need one.

GAS LEAKS

If you smell gas the situation is dangerous and must be taken seriously and dealt with immediately

The majority of homes are heated with natural gas. In its natural state, it's odourless and colourless. If it was leaking, how would anyone know? The stink made by natural gas comes from an additive called mercaptan. A small amount goes a long way, and it's a good thing. A gas leak in the vicinity of an active pilot light in a boiler or stove can have explosive consequences.

It's difficult to lay down any hard and fast rules regarding how strong a gas smell should drive you out of the house. If a pilot light goes out, and you detect the faint odour of gas, it's probably from the pilot and nothing else.

A gas pipe doesn't suddenly rupture in your house unless it's somehow damaged by a nearby activity. It's critical that

Rules for Gas Leaks

- Whenever you smell a gas leak, turn the gas to that particular appliance off immediately and open doors and windows.
- The problem might be only a pilot light that's gone out, which can be relit after the room has aired.
- If the leak is much more noticeable, shut off the gas to the house immediately, and call the gas company.
- Never try to repair a leaking gas pipe with any kind of temporary patch.

Gas Boilers

- Gas boilers are normally safe and do not present fire hazards, but there are exceptions.
- Some models have been subject to manufacturer recalls – check yours online or talk with your gas company if you're uncertain about it.
- A more probable issue with old or poorly serviced boilers is carbon monoxide poisoning from incomplete gas combustion.
- Regular servicing should pre-empt any carbon monoxide problems.

you know how to shut the gas off at the meter and at each gas appliance.

An overwhelming gas smell sends a clear message: get out immediately and call the gas company from a neighbour's house or a mobile phone. Don't go back inside. If the meter is outside and you can shut the gas off, do so. Otherwise, let the gas company do it. It would prefer that as well.

GREEN LIGHT

The next time you have your gas boiler serviced, ask the engineer to show you how to shut the gas off at the meter if you're uncomfortable doing it yourself. Discuss what emergency measures to take and listen to the recommendations. The gas company wants you to stay safe, too.

Gas Appliances

- Read your appliance owner's manual for proper operation and maintenance.
- Aside from regular servicing, check gas appliances for clean combustion and operation.
- Think twice before having a ventless gas fire installed; it is permissible in certain situations but poses some risk factors not present with vented systems.
- Pilot lights can ignite solvent fumes – turn them off when volatile fumes are present (during floor refinishing, for example).

Your Gas Supply

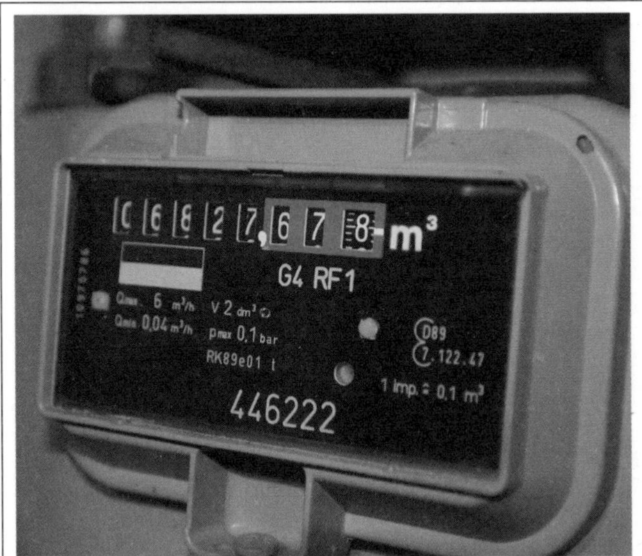

- Your gas shut-off valve is normally located near the gas meter. Find yours or ask your service engineer.
- Should you ever have to turn the gas off completely you must get a qualified gas engineer to check for leaks, turn the gas back on and relight pilot lights.
- If a leak is reported, gas company engineers are authorized to enter your property and inspect the installation and appliances. They will make the leak safe, but you as the home-owner are responsible for replacing faulty appliances.

STORM DAMAGE

Storms and bad weather have plans of their own, so make a game plan for repairs

Weather can be the biggest culprit in causing damage to your home. A harsh freeze can burst a pipe. Ice-laden tree branches can snap off and hit your roof or block your drive. If a strong enough wind blows, there go the phone wires.

One of your best recourses when confronted with severe weather is to be prepared for it, but few people are. A main concern for homeowners is having live power lines go down near their homes. Current can carry across the ground, particularly if it is wet, and could shock or electrocute anyone standing nearby.

Watch out for power lines before tangling with fallen tree branches. Your power company will find them eventually,

Tree Damage

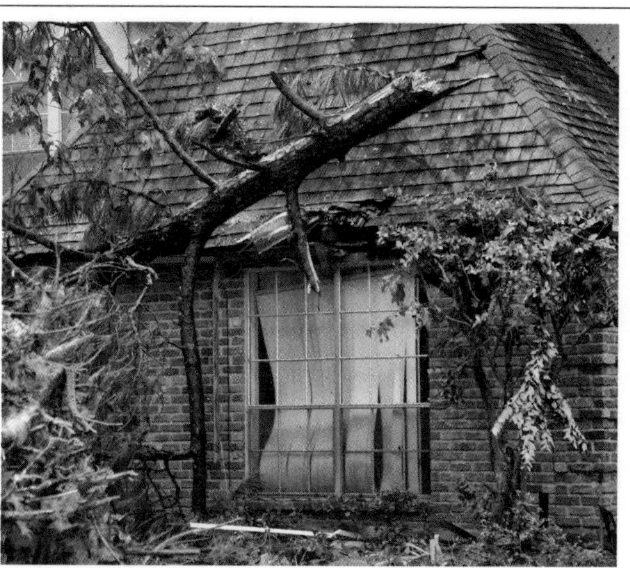

- A fallen tree or branch can render a house uninhabitable and even unsafe for occupation until the damage is evaluated and repaired.
- If you decide to cut away part of the damaged tree yourself, be careful, as this could cause more damage to your home by the remaining section of the tree.
- The best way to avoid tree damage is to keep your trees healthy and remove any that appear problematic; call in a tree surgeon if needed.

Securing Roof Damage

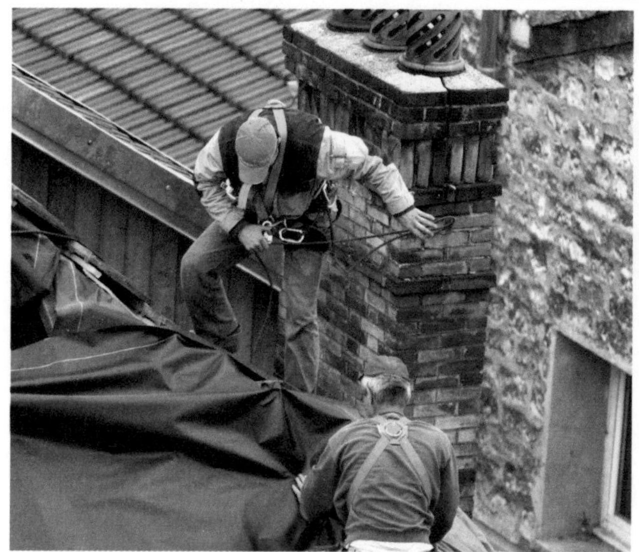

- Clear the damaged area and cover with a tarpaulin as soon as possible.
- If there's a gaping hole in the roof, nail a tarpaulin or tough plastic sheeting over the hole.
- Tuck the tarp under a row of tiles above the opening so water will flow over it and not under it.
- Pull the tarp so it's taut and doesn't allow water to pool in the centre.

but try to report them anyway, especially if they're sparking and endangering you or your neighbours.

What happens if your home is damaged by extreme weather? Act sensibly and evaluate the problem. Assess the risks of walking on a roof to remove debris yourself. If the water main that supplies your house bursts, shut the water off at the meter, notify the water company and find a hotel room, since you're out of water until the pipe is replaced.

MAKE IT EASY

Review your insurance policy for weather-related damage and update it if you're living in an area susceptible to a particular weather problem. Weigh the costs against the chance of ever needing the coverage. In the event of damage, know who to call and follow the claims procedures to the letter. And remember to photograph all damages for the insurance company.

Power Line Dangers

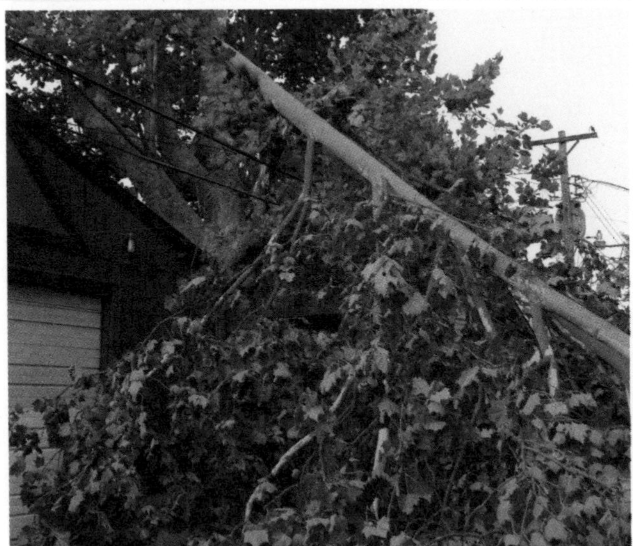

- Stay away from fallen power lines, as current can spread across wet ground.
- Even if the power is shut off and the wires are dead, you should not work around high-voltage wiring.
- Don't be tempted to move a downed power line, even if you're using nonconductive materials such as wood – if they have any moisture on them, they can conduct the current.
- Don't drive over power lines – they can still be energized and can get entangled with your car.

Broken Window Glass

- If you can't get outside to cover a broken window, tape plastic all around the inside as tightly as you can and place a towel at the bottom of the window.
- Exterior-grade plywood will withstand wet weather longer than any interior boards, especially composite products such as chipboard, but for the short term, any wood will do.
- Don't use sheets of plasterboard – they'll deteriorate in the rain.
- Carefully remove any remaining loose glass shards from the window.

SECURING A DAMAGED HOUSE

Secure broken or damaged windows and doors quickly to ensure your safety

Property gets damaged all the time, sometimes by weather, sometimes by other people, sometimes by animals. A kicked-in door or broken window makes for easy entrance into the house and can leave you vulnerable, so you must secure your home until you can effect a complete repair or replacement.

Damaged doors and windows can be secured without scarring the surrounding woodwork too much. Boards can be fastened across them to substitute for broken locks, and plywood can take the place of broken glass. If a door is so badly damaged it can't be closed, use full sheets of plywood to secure the opening.

Securing Your Windows

- A damaged sash window or out-swinging casement can be secured with blocks of wood screwed to the sash and the jamb, or lengths of wood wedged into the window frame to prevent the sash from moving.
- If you have sliding metal windows, insert metal screws in the track to prevent sliding.
- Block sliding uPVC windows with full lengths of wood and avoid screwing anything into any part of the window.

Quick Door Lock Repairs

- Clean out the damaged wood from the jamb; replace the jamb door strike screws with long screws, placing a wood shim behind the strike so it will line up with the door.
- Straighten out and reinforce the lock with longer screws.
- Close the door and screw a 30 cm block of wood into the door frame on the lock side so the wood overlaps the door.
- Screw the block into the door, noting that this door cannot be used for an emergency exit until it's replaced or repaired.

If an automatic garage door has been damaged or won't close, there is often a simple solution – adjusting the sensors, for instance – but if not, modern door openers have release mechanisms for manual operation. Knowing how your door opener works ahead of time will save you some headaches later when it doesn't.

MAKE IT EASY

Check your house insurance policy for damage coverage. Your policy should cover the cost of door replacement plus any damage to the frame, trim and lock, and the follow-up painting, but confirm with your insurance company first.

Garage Door Opener Manual Override

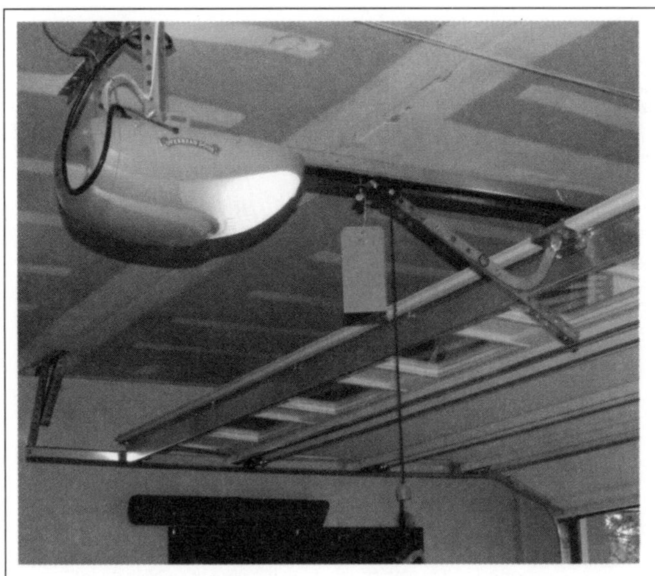

- Automatic garage door openers won't function if the power goes off.
- Pull the release cord or lever on the track near the top of the garage door to release it from the automatic opener and allow you to open and close the door manually until it can be repaired.
- Pulling this release again – follow the manufacturer's instructions – will return the door to machine control and keep it closed and reasonably secure.

Home Security Systems

- The vast majority of calls involving security systems are false alarms, wasting police resources in responding. Many forces will not respond to bell-only alarms unless they also receive a first-hand report of a crime being committed.
- An alarm system can be set up to notify the local police, at a monthly cost, but they will respond only if more than one sensor is activated.
- Even with a monitored service, a succession of false alarms is likely to result in the level of response being lowered, or even stopped.

TOOL ERGONOMICS & SAFETY

Learn the right way to choose and use tools to make your job safe and easy

A good set of comfortable tools used safely can solve all kinds of repair problems. A tool that doesn't fit your grip is not only uncomfortable, but can also be unsafe if it slips during use. It should fit you as close to your dimensions as possible. Given the choice of sizes, weights and grips available, suitable tools are easy to find.

Size adaptations are also possible with existing tools. For instance, tools can be adapted to large hands by wrapping their handles with foam handlebar tubing from a bike shop or by wearing work gloves. Those with small hands will have to test out different brands to find the best fit.

A tool's weight can help it do its job or might mean it's

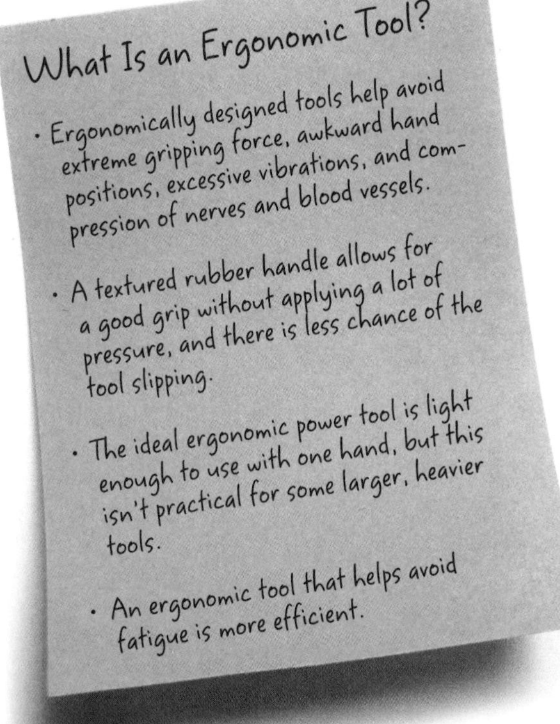

What Is an Ergonomic Tool?
• Ergonomically designed tools help avoid extreme gripping force, awkward hand positions, excessive vibrations, and compression of nerves and blood vessels.
• A textured rubber handle allows for a good grip without applying a lot of pressure, and there is less chance of the tool slipping.
• The ideal ergonomic power tool is light enough to use with one hand, but this isn't practical for some larger, heavier tools.
• An ergonomic tool that helps avoid fatigue is more efficient.

Getting a Good Grip

- For select tools use a power grip – fingers wrapped around the tool and the thumb against it or wrapped around resting on the fingers – for most of your heavy work.
- Short-handled tools may be less stressful than long-handled tools.
- Tools made with compressible grip wrapping are usually easier on the hand than hard plastic.
- You should be able to grip the tool comfortably in either hand while avoiding bending or rotating the wrist.

built for frequent, commercial use. A 'heavy duty' commercial tool lasts longer than a less expensive version, but one that's too heavy for someone in average physical condition causes strain and should be avoided. Most hand tools, with the exception of some hammers, are light enough for comfortable use.

A damaged or worn tool increases the strain on you when using it and should either be repaired or discarded. Most quality hand tools will last for years with little maintenance.

YELLOW LIGHT

A true ergonomic tool design – where the tool fits your hand rather than your hand adapting to the tool – allows for the tool usage and function, not just the grip. Short-handled pliers, for example, will be difficult to use regardless of added padding.

Weight of a Tool

- Proper swinging technique allows the weight of a striking tool (hammer, axe) to do a large amount of the work.
- Some tools (sledgehammers, for instance) must be heavy to do their jobs.
- Overhead work with heavy tools is the most strenuous, so to avoid accidents, take breaks when fatigued.
- If a tool, such as a petrol-powered chain-saw, is too heavy to handle safely, find a smaller, lighter version, even if the job takes longer to do.

Maintaining a Hand Tool

- Be sure all tool handles are secure, blades sharp, and all moving parts shift freely.
- Store tools in a dry location; to avoid corrosion, spray the tool with WD-40 periodically.
- If a tool is beyond repair, discard it (a damaged tool is a liability).
- A wire brush attachment on a bench grinder will clean up the metal parts on any hand tool, removing corrosion and dirt and bringing back a newer appearance.

HAND TOOLS

Collect the must-have tools you need for most small jobs around the house

Hand tools are a bargain – what else can last as long yet cost so little? Each job dictates the tools you need, but a core set will fix most problems. A well-stocked toolbox should contain basic tools that pound, cut, drive and loosen fasteners, measure, grab, pull and scrape. Tools are extensions of your hands and offer clout in the repair world you would never have otherwise.

Must-have tool lists will vary slightly, but most include a hammer, screwdriver, pliers, measuring tape, an adjustable wrench, metal snips, putty knife, spirit level, utility knife, paint scraper, nail punch, and a simple pencil and pad of paper.

As your job list grows, you'll add to your tools, but more isn't necessarily better, nor are multiple copies of the same

Hammers

- Heavier hammers drive nails faster than lighter hammers – use them for nailing joists and other rough work.
- There is a hammer for every purpose, but a curved claw hammer will do most household jobs.
- You might find wood handles more comfortable than steel or fibreglass. (If tool vibrations bother you, search online for 'ergonomic hammers'.)
- To avoid accidents, never use a hammer with a loose or damaged head or a cracked handle.

Screwdrivers

- Screwdrivers fit a number of different screw types, but the most common are slotted (regular) screws and Phillips screws.
- Combination or multi-bit screwdrivers, with both Phillips and slotted drivers, are handy tools; some versions offer other interchangeable bits, which can also be used in electric drills, in a carrying case.
- The tips of cheap screw-drivers will quickly become bent and useless.
- Consider a screwdriver with a magnetized tip for holding steel screws.

tool. You can spend as little as a pound or much more on a tool, but either way you get what you pay for. A good hammer will last a lifetime, but a cheap hammer will bend or break, a dangerous possibility while pounding. Although tools are available to buy online, there's no substitute for handling a tool and getting a feel for it in your hand to be sure it's right for you.

MAKE IT EASY

Combination toolkits group frequently used hand tools in one convenient package and make a great extra set for a kitchen or utility room. These are of moderate quality and are not replacements for higher quality individual tools. Use them for small jobs such as tightening a screw or removing a picture hook.

Pliers

- Pliers grip, bend and sometimes cut, but too often they're used to tighten nuts and bolts – really a job for a wrench.
- A toolbox should include sharp-nosed pliers for doing precision work and handling small objects, slip-joint pliers for plumbing repairs, and a pair of combination pliers for both cutting and gripping.
- Curved sharp-nosed pliers have a bent end for reaching around obstacles.
- Vice-type locking pliers lock in place while gripping, leaving both hands free.

Wrenches

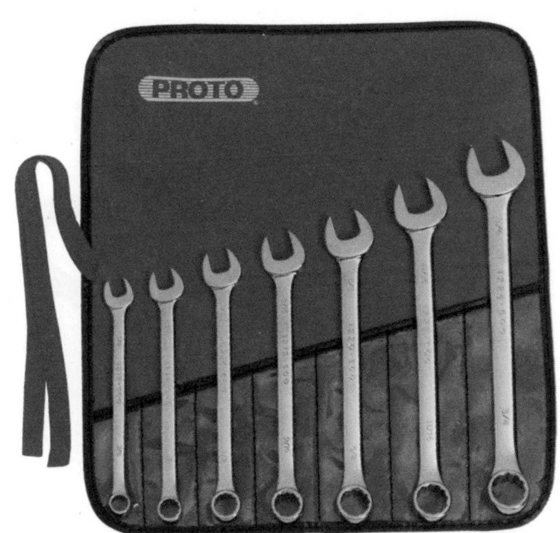

- Fixed wrenches, with an opening at each end, will fit either imperial or metric-sized fasteners – they are not interchangeable, even if they look close in size.
- An adjustable wrench, whose head adjusts to accommodate different sizes of fasteners of any type, can take the place of multiple individual wrenches.
- Hex or Allen keys adjust hex-shaped bolts, which are often found on self-assembly furniture.
- Match the wrench to the fastener for a tight, secure fit.

TOOLS TO CUT, SCRAPE & PRISE

Know what essential sharp, tough tools are needed for cutting a job down to size

When cutting through material, the sharper the tool the better for an easier, more precise and safer job. Dull blades increase a job's difficulty and the time needed to finish, and are more apt to slip and injure you. Blades are made to be sharpened, although most are eventually replaced. It takes some practice to get a good edge on a scraper or knife blade using a file or sharpening stone, but sharpening when a blade begins going dull increases the life of the tool and is a worthwhile skill.

Handsaws can rip through rough timber or make the most delicate cuts in wood trim and moulding. Although power saws are used for most cutting now, there are times when only

Cutting Tools

- Quality tools use harder steel and maintain their sharp edges longer than less expensive cutting tools.
- A retractable utility knife, which comes with extra blades in its handle, strips sheathing from wire and cuts cardboard, softboard, carpet and some plastics – it's a must for your toolbox.
- Tin snips or tinner's shears are used to shape sheet metal and can cut rope, cardboard, metal insulation strip and thin wires.
- Longer-handled tin snips offer more leverage but might be less comfortable for smaller hands.

Crowbars

- You should need only one crowbar of any given size as they last forever and almost never break.
- Some very flat and thin crowbars can also be used as scrapers.
- A crowbar that fits in a toolbox is as big as you need for most jobs.
- Woodwork always has more nails than you might expect – prise carefully to avoid splitting the wood.

a handsaw will do. Besides, why drag out a power mitre saw when a handsaw can make quick work of a single cut?

Crowbars range from mild-mannered to aggressive. Some remove lost-head nails, and others pull up entire floors. Most home use calls for flat crowbars, including a 12–15-cm mini bar. Flat bars are thin enough to slip behind wood mouldings and skirting boards and remove them with limited damage.

Scrapers are highly versatile. They can be used to remove paint and floor finishes or shave down wood. A 4-cm-wide hook scraper is a traditional choice.

ZOOM

Crowbars are all about leverage. A long bar has more than a short bar, but not every job needs so much. Use a block of wood under whichever end of the bar presses against a finished surface to avoid damage. Prise slowly and steadily.

Saws and Files

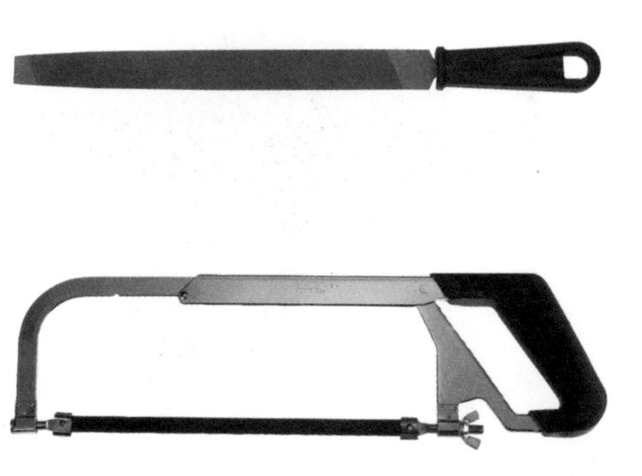

- It's worth spending a little extra on a carpenter-quality handsaw, which will keep sharp cutting teeth much longer than cheaper saws.
- Crosscut saws have teeth that cut across wood grain, ripsaws cut with the grain, and a bow saw is used for garden trimming, although a crosscut saw can cut through branches.
- Japanese saws have thin blades and are ideal for precise cutting.
- Hacksaws, normally used on metal, also offer precision cutting on thin sections of wood.

Scrapers

- It's a good idea to buy extra blades when buying a scraper so you always have sharp replacements on hand.
- The simplest scraper is a rectangular cabinet scraper, used for scraping wood smooth prior to finishing; it also removes varnish.
- A 4-cm-wide hook scraper is simple, versatile, and easy to handle, while scraper kits offer multiple, changeable blades for different shapes and cuts of wood moulding.
- Carbide scrapers have the longest-lasting blades.

BASIC SMALL TOOLS

These seemingly insignificant tools play a big role in many home repair jobs

Many repair jobs require measuring. You need to know the size of a room before buying paint or the dimensions of a window to order a blind. A number of tools are available for measuring, but a tape measure is the simplest and most compact. A longer tape measure is more versatile than a short one – look for an 8-m metal retractable-tape model with a locking mechanism. Most longer tape measures display measurements down to 1mm, more than enough precision for home repairs.

Chisels are used for removing small sections of wood, stone, concrete or mortar. Practise using a wood chisel on a piece of scrap wood first. Stone chisels are heavier and look less

Tape Measure

- It's worth having one or two small tape measures around the house for impromptu measuring jobs in addition to an 8-m model.
- Take your time reading your measurements – you don't want to order window blinds based on the wrong dimensions.
- Laser measurers are capable of calculating distance, area and volume, depending on the model.
- Wipe a metal tape with a clean cloth, lightly coat with spray silicone, don't allow the tape to retract too quickly, and replace a tape measure that has cracked tape.

Heat Gun

- Heat guns produce extremely hot air of varying temperatures for removing paint, drying out wet wood, speeding up paint drying, softening adhesives and thawing frozen pipes.
- Heat guns are safer than blow torches, but still require caution.
- The materials being heated can produce disagreeable if not toxic fumes, requiring you to wear an appropriate respirator.
- Lead-based paint will vaporize at temperatures over 600°C – use a heat gun with a lower setting for this job.

refined than wood chisels, but there's no other hand tool as effective for attacking concrete cracks that need widening or cleaning out.

Nail punches are metal punches used to force lost-head nails below the surface of wood. This allows the space above the head to be filled for a smooth finish. Individual nail punches are available, but buy a set of three in a range of sizes.

A basic circuit tester indicates if electricity is present at a socket or other device. It's an inexpensive but critical safety device that every electrician uses and depends on.

MAKE IT EASY

Use a large round wire nail as a nail punch. File the sharp end down a bit first. This is not as sturdy as a normal nail punch, but it will do at a pinch. Using a screwdriver as a chisel, however, is a great way to ruin the screwdriver.

Chisels

- You're better off buying one or two good wood chisels than a larger set of poor quality tools.
- Using a wood chisel is an art requiring practice and patience – try it on a piece of scrap wood first until you're comfortable with it.
- Inexpensive chisels are not easy to maintain, get nicked easily, and eventually become useless for precision work, so keep in mind value when assessing cost.
- Protect the sharp ends of chisels when stored so they don't get dull.

Nail Punches

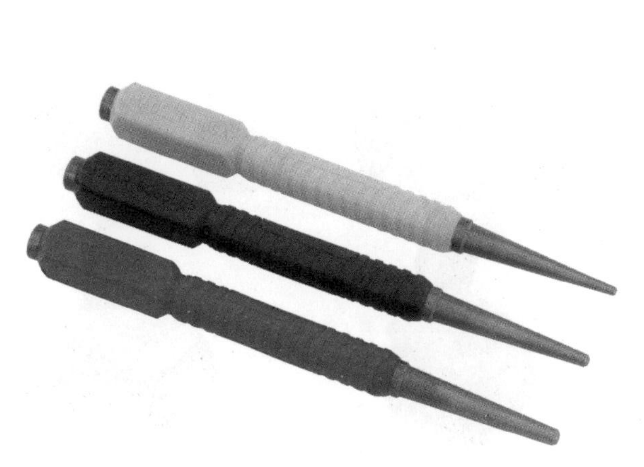

- If you buy a kit of three different-sized nail punches, you shouldn't have any trouble matching a nail with the correct punch.
- Don't treat a nail punch as a chisel to chip away at stone or concrete – this will ruin the finish end.
- You can use a nail punch to make a starter or pilot hole for a large screw if a drill isn't handy.
- Nail punches can punch holes in sheet metal and leather as well as wood.

POWER TOOLS

These tools perform with a speed and accuracy you can't match by hand

Imagine mixing a smoothie by hand. You can do it, but will you match the consistency and texture you get with a blender in the same amount of time? The same holds true for power tools. They will outcut, outdrill and outsand their hand counterparts every time. There is no reason not to use them and no virtue in avoiding them, although they can be more bother than they're worth for very small jobs, especially if it means dragging out extension leads.

Some power tools do multiple jobs. A drill makes holes, but it also buffs, sands and grinds with the right attachments. Power tools are loud, so ear protection is a must, even for quick jobs. They are also dangerous. It's one thing to slip while

Drills

- Drills perform multiple tasks such as making holes, driving screws, and running buffing pads and sandpaper discs, but you're better off using a buffer/polisher or sander for these two tasks.
- A medium-duty, 13-mm variable-speed drill will be able to handle most household jobs.
- Cordless drills are convenient, but require regular battery recharging.
- The material you drill through determines the type of bit you'll need – one type does not work for all jobs.

Sanders

- Sanders throw out a lot of dust, but make quick work of tedious jobs.
- A belt sander removes material quickly, while a random-orbit disc sander is less aggressive, leaving a smoother finish. Use palm sanders for finish work.
- Dust bags will not collect all the dust produced by a power sander, so be prepared for some additional cleaning up with a vacuum cleaner or broom.
- Practise sanding scrap wood, applying light pressure until you're comfortable with the tool.

using a handsaw, quite another to slip while running an electric circular saw – probably the most dangerous power tool commonly used. Caution and care must accompany power tool use, but the advantages they bring more than outweigh the extra vigilance on your part.

Power tools create dust just as hand tools do, but it spreads out over a larger area. There is more to clean up, but a vacuum cleaner solves that problem faster than a dustpan and brush.

YELLOW LIGHT

Sanders are loud, so wear ear protection as well as a dust mask. Do not wear work gloves with either belt or disc sanders – they can get caught in the moving parts and pull your fingers into the tool. Sandals are for the beach; wear stout work shoes around power tools.

Saws

- An electric saw is as dangerous as it is useful – always treat it with respect and care.
- Use a circular saw to cut timber and board or a modestly priced power mitre saw (an excellent choice for non-professionals) to safely cut lengths of timber and mouldings.
- Match the saw blade to the type of cutting you're doing – plywood, rough timber, wood mouldings or metal.
- Don't force the saw; move it only as it makes its cut.

Vacuum Cleaners and Blowers

- Inexpensive cylinder vacuum cleaners, which are fairly portable, are convenient and durable ways to clean up a mess.
- If your vacuum uses disposable bags, buy plenty of extras when you purchase the vacuum cleaner.
- HEPA vacuums trap finer dust and allergen particles than standard vacuum cleaners.
- Electric blowers are good tools for blowing dust out of standard household vacuum cleaners, especially the hoses.

TOOLS TO HIRE

Some tools are impractical to own but perfect to hire for occasional use

There is little point in owning a tool you rarely need or will use only once. A good hire shop offers a range of tools at affordable prices along with the additional necessities: extension leads, sandpaper, drill bits, saw blades and so on.

If possible, reserve the tool in advance. You and most other homeowner customers will be out in force at the weekend, all looking for the same tools. Commercial users do most of their hiring during the working week.

Hire shops vary from single-owner shops to chain stores. A good shop has a policy of checking all tools upon their return, before hiring them out to another customer. Power cords should be intact and not taped or patched, and the

Wallpaper Steamers

- Wallpaper steamers are simple and foolproof: just add water, heat it up and steam off multiple layers of wallpaper, being careful to cover the floor area completely with plastic dust sheets.
- Follow the manufacturer's instructions for topping up with more water – the unit becomes extremely hot, and you can be exposed to scalding water.
- Hire units are larger and more robust than many consumer models.

Chainsaws

- A petrol chainsaw is a good tool to hire for major tree work and is also a heavy tool that must be used carefully.
- Electric chainsaws are lighter and safer than petrol-powered models, but not as powerful. They are cheap enough to consider buying for regular pruning.
- Never use a chainsaw when you're tired – it's too dangerous.
- Chainsaws can also cut through wooden posts and beams, but check first that they're free of nails and other metal objects.

assistant should give you a run-through on each tool's operation and explain your liability (be sure to read the hire contract so you understand your obligations).

Depending on the tool and the length of the hire period, you might be better off purchasing some tools. Compare the costs before deciding either way. If the shop is closed on a Sunday, you may be able to negotiate a reduced rate if you pick the tool up at closing time on Saturday and return it first thing Monday morning.

YELLOW LIGHT

If you have problems with your hired tool (say the motor slows down or is otherwise malfunctioning), stop immediately and call the shop. These tools are heavily used and even with inspection can break down unexpectedly. If you're not at fault, the shop should credit you for lost time and replace the tool.

Pressure Washers

- A pressure washer is rated by pressure (bar) and the volume of water (litres per hour) that flows through it.
- Pressure that's too low won't clean well and too high can damage some surfaces (a pressure of around 150 bar will do most jobs).
- When washing wood surfaces, start from 1m away and gradually move forward to test the pressure.
- Pressure washing will not remove all dirt and grime – some additional scrubbing may be required.

Nail Guns

- Nail guns allow carpenters to avoid hand nailing and the fatigue that comes with it.
- Pneumatic nail guns, which require an air compressor, make short work of big nailing jobs; gas-powered guns are available for finish work and construction, but they're expensive and it's better to hire them.
- For strictly light finish nailing, a cheaper electric nail gun is worth purchasing.
- Nails for nail guns are sold by the box – buy extra when hiring just in case, as you can always return them.

SAFETY GEAR

Doing a job properly means taking the precautions to protect yourself, too

Using tools means dust, noise, nicks, scrapes and flying debris, with the user on the receiving end. It's easy to discount safety, but for a few minutes and a few pounds you can protect your sight, hearing, skin and lungs. Both power tools and excessive hammering assault your hearing. Once it's damaged, it doesn't come back. Even occasional power tool usage calls for hearing protection. Consider this: while normal conversation registers at 60 decibels, a power saw – probably the worst power tool offender – registers at over 100. Ear protection is simple and inexpensive and using it quickly becomes second nature. Protection ranges from disposable ear plugs to state-of-the-art earmuff-style devices with built-in AM/FM radios.

Ear Protection

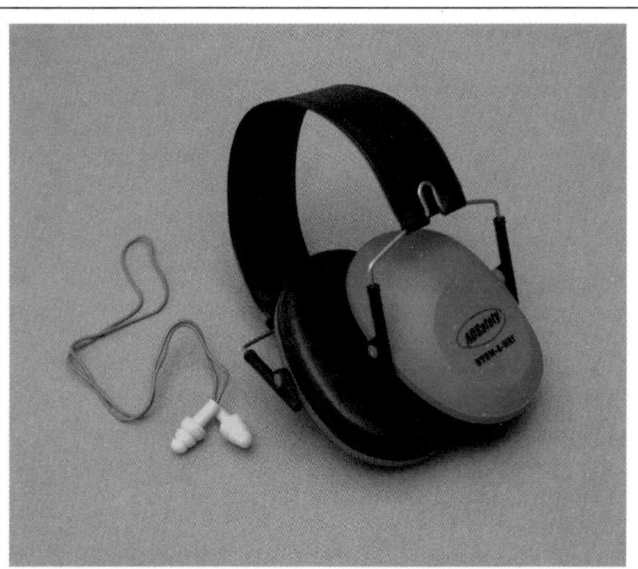

- Loudness is represented by decibels – the higher the decibels, the harder it is on your hearing – whether the noise source is from power tools or excessive hammering.
- Earmuff protectors are the most comfortable form of hearing protection.
- Disposable foam ear plugs can be washed and reused – just soak them in warm, soapy water and keep extra pairs on hand.
- Always keep a pair of disposable ear plugs with you – you never know when you'll run into prolonged noise exposure.

Eye Protection

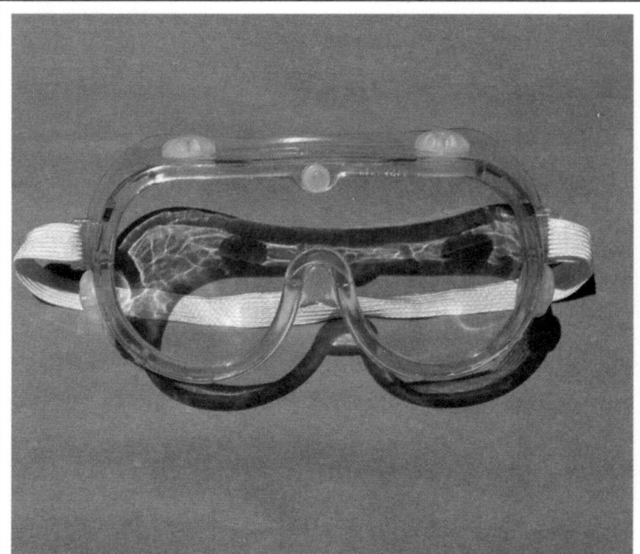

- Safety glasses are available in both clear and tinted lenses for working outdoors in direct sunlight.
- Hammering, grinding, sawing, sanding and power washing all have eye-damaging potential.
- Wear safety glasses when working with chemicals overhead, such as paint remover.
- Store safety glasses in an old sock to prevent scratching the lenses, and always replace cracked safety glasses.

Vision is priceless, while eye protection costs next to nothing. Inexpensive safety glasses, which also fit over regular spectacles if you wear them, should be worn when chipping, chiselling, sawing or doing any overhead work that blows dust or debris into your eyes.

Dust, smoke and chemical vapours can also affect your health. Dust masks and appropriate respirators are a must when sanding or handling noxious solvents and paints.

Even tough hands need protection. Gloves are a bargain compared with damaged hands.

YELLOW LIGHT

Be sure to match the level of protection to the hazard produced by your work. Overkill wastes money, and too little protection doesn't keep you healthy. This is especially true when picking out the right respiratory protection.

Respiratory Protection

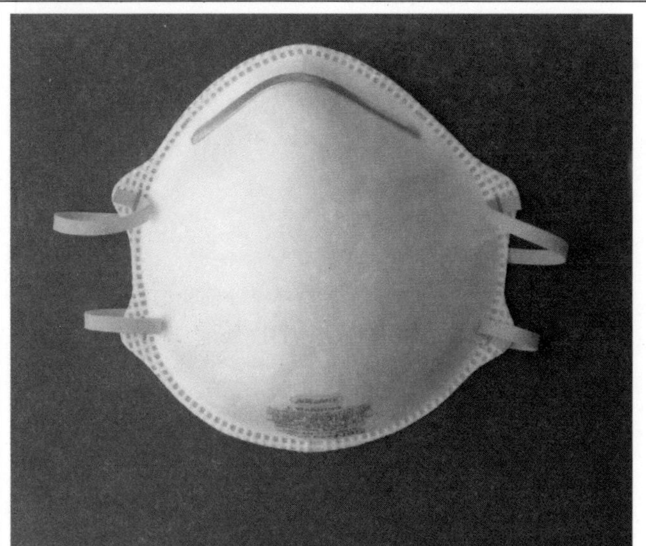

- Respiratory protection is available as disposable masks and full- and half-face rubber/plastic reusable respirators that use disposable filters.
- Respirators are not particularly comfortable, although the disposable style is more tolerable to wear.
- Buy dust masks (3M 8200 series is recommended) by the box so you don't run short; avoid light paper dust masks, which provide little protection.
- Protection from smoke calls for HEPA filters, and for vapours you need charcoal-activated filters.

Hand Protection

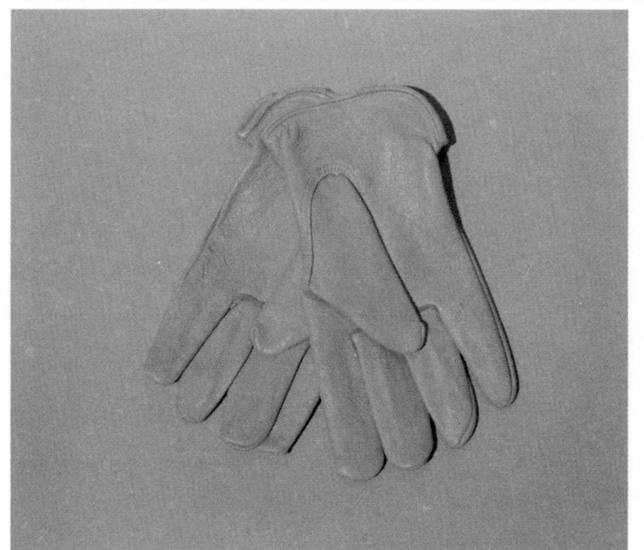

- Gloves wear out often – keep an extra pair or two as replacements.
- For painting, wear lightweight cotton neoprene, and PVC gloves when working with paint stripper, solvents or washing solutions.
- Leather gloves protect against rough timber and nails and offer some shock absorption when hammering.
- Never wear work gloves when using power tools with spinning blades, shafts, or similar moving parts – the gloves can get caught and can pull your hands into the tool.

SCREWS & BOLTS

An ancient and great invention, screws of every type and size keep it all together

Screws and bolts are necessities for putting projects together. A screw is a threaded fastener. Threads give a screw both penetrating and holding power. When screwing into wood, most screws require a pilot hole to be drilled first; otherwise, you risk splitting the wood, jamming the screw and often stripping its head. Some screws, notably plasterboard and sheet metal screws, are self-tapping, which means they do not require a pilot hole before being inserted and driven in. One advantage of screws over nails is that they can be removed and reinserted any number of times without damaging the material they are fastening.

Screws vary by thickness, length, finish and head type

Wood Screws

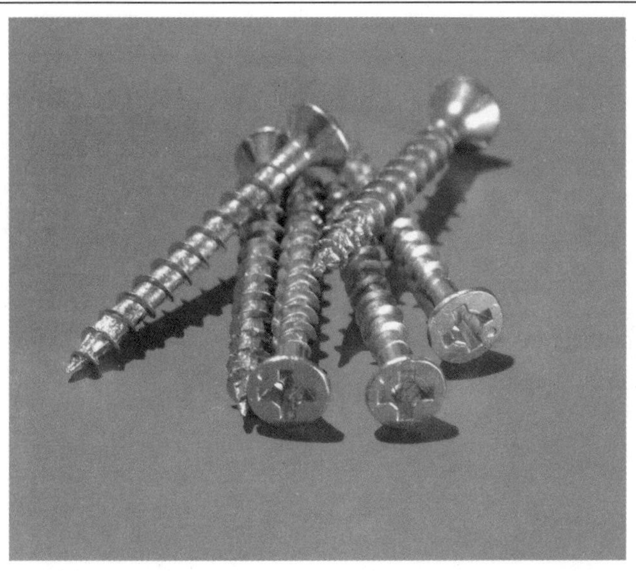

- Drill a pilot hole or starter hole – narrower than the shaft of the screw – to avoid splitting wood with a screw.
- A screw thread forms an inclined plane that, when inserted into wood, forms a corresponding plane that holds the screw in place more tightly than a nail.
- Rubbing the screw thread on a bar of soap can make a screw easier to turn, while overtightening can snap its head off.
- Phillips head screws are easier to install and remove than slotted.

Drywall Screws

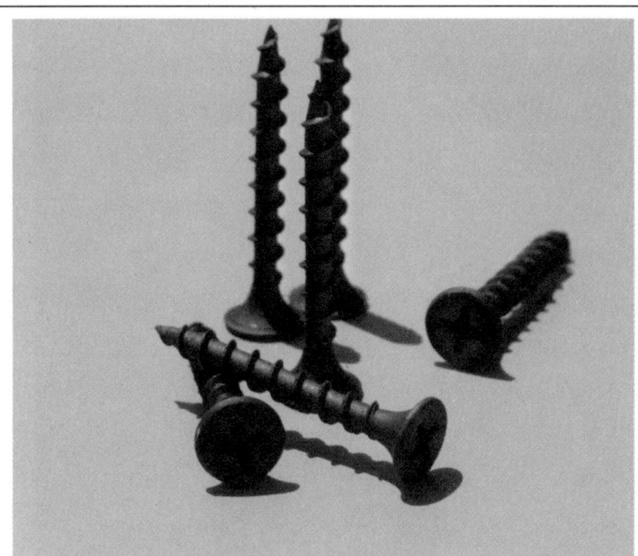

- Drywall screws are the universal fastener for non-metals; case-hardened, they're inexpensive, self-tapping in most materials, and screw in fast.
- These screws are sold by the hundred; buy several sizes for various jobs.
- Do not use them for structural applications or outside – even coated drywall screws will rust.
- They are available in lengths from 25 mm to 100 mm, in both fine and coarse threads.

(slotted and Phillips being the most common) and are sold by the box, by weight or singly. Flat-head screws lie flush, while oval and round-headed screws protrude from the surface. Overwhelmingly, screws are made from some type of steel. Brass screws are used to attach visible hardware such as cabinet hinges and drawer pulls.

A bolt resembles a screw, but the thread is narrower and does not cut through the material it's attached to. A bolt normally requires a threaded nut at the end of it to secure it. Bolts and nuts are sold in similar quantities as screws.

RED LIGHT

If you drill a pilot hole too small, you won't get the screw all the way in. If you get too much resistance, back the screw out and drill a slightly larger hole. Overtightening a screw can snap off its head. Be especially careful when using a drill to tighten a screw.

Sheet Metal Screws

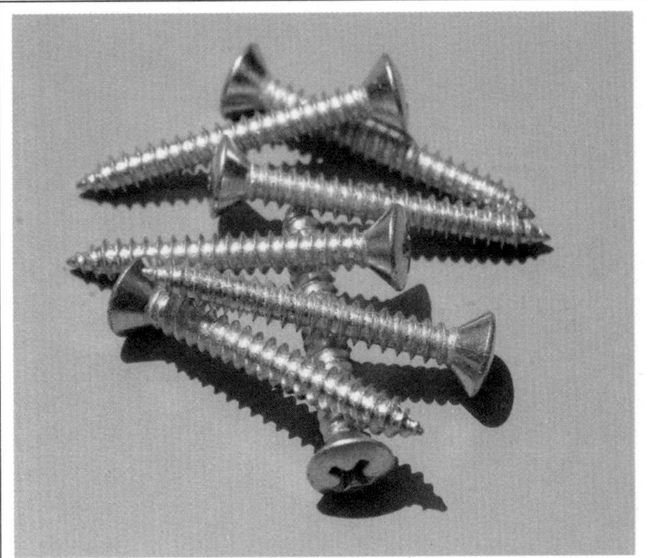

- Sheet metal screws are self-tapping – they cut their way through metal, plastic and fibreglass – and are harder than wood screws.
- Small, flat-head sheet metal screws can be used to install metal draughtproofing strips when nailing isn't practical.
- Use these screws when replacing corroded metal guttering or aluminium venting; attach old sections to new with sheet metal screws.
- You can also use metal screws in wood, but you should not use a wood screw in sheet metal.

Nuts and Bolts

- Bolts and nuts come in metric and imperial sizes – don't mix them together.
- To replace a bolt and nut, take both old ones to your hardware store and match each with its new counterpart.
- If either the bolt or nut threads are stripped – meaning they're worn smooth and no longer tighten – replace both bolt and nut.
- To keep track of bolts/nuts/washers during a disassembly, loosely connect them together so they stay in a grouping.

NAILS

For fastening wood to wood, nails are quick, fast, and cheap

Nails range in size and shape from the tiniest finishing brads to 300mm spiral spikes. They have round heads for when their appearance isn't important or distracting, and they have no head at all other than a dimpled end for finish work. These nails are driven below the surface of the wood so they won't be seen. Nails are manufactured for all purposes and applications, from withstanding exterior weather exposure to assembling wooden fruit boxes. It's best to use specific types of nails for specific jobs, but in some instances, you can substitute, for example, a longer nail for a shorter one.

However, you must pay attention to a nail's size. If you use one that is too long, you may drive it all the way through a board, leaving the sharp end sticking out where you don't want it. Use too thick a nail too close to the end of a board,

Buying and Using Nails

- Nails are cheap, so buy common sizes by the box.
- Variety packs of small nails and fasteners work as a back-up to a regular nail supply.
- Drill a pilot hole in hardwood before nailing to avoid splitting the wood.
- Be aware that the plating on brass-plated wire nails doesn't always prevent corrosion when exposed to moisture.
- Nail gun nails, which are slightly blunt-ended and square in shape, will shoot through soft and hard woods without splitting either. These pass through wood more easily than rounded nails.

Round Wire Nails

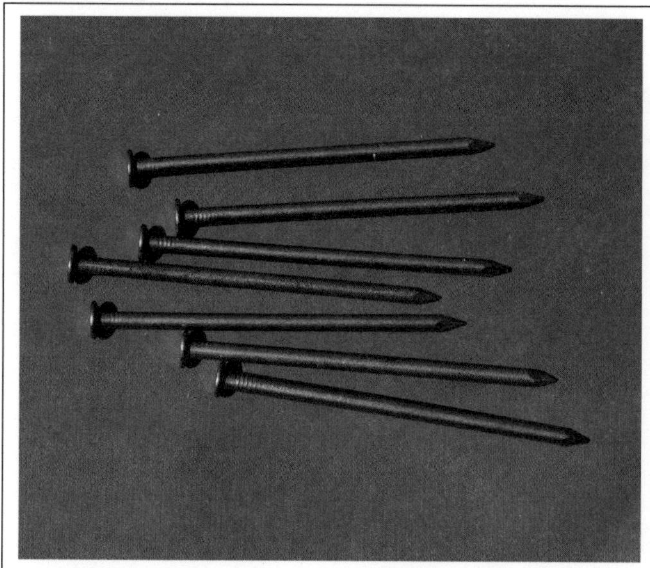

- Round-head nails are used when the nail heads can remain visible.
- Common nails are used with sawn timber, and box nails, which have narrower shafts, are used with thin pieces of wood.
- Bigger isn't always better – a large nail driven into thin wood will split it.
- Use nails about two times longer than the thickness of the wood being driven through.

and you can split the wood. Not certain what you need? Buy several sizes by the box. They store easily and always come in handy for other jobs.

For exterior work, always use galvanized nails to withstand moisture. Paint alone can't protect the head of an exterior nail from rust.

Lost-head Nails

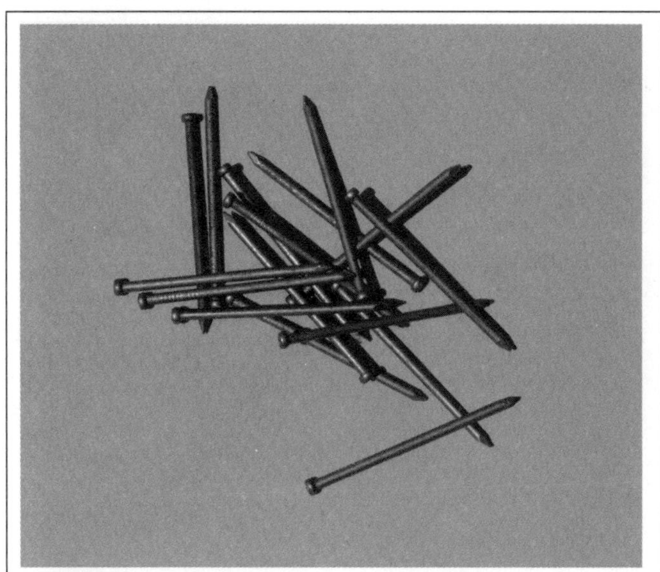

- A lost-head nail can often be used in place of a round wire nail, but you don't want to use a round wire nail for finishing work.
- Lost-head nails can sometimes replace common nails if necessary – just use more of them.
- Oval wire nails can also be punched below the surface of wood. They are less likely to split wood if they are used with the longer sides parallel with the grain.
- Panel pins are very small finishing nails, used for fixing small mouldings.

How to Nail

- Even experienced carpenters bend nails and hit thumbs. A few guidelines will keep your nails straight:
- To avoid splitting wood, blunt the sharp end of your nails. Place the head of the nail on a hard surface and tap the sharp end with a hammer.
- If your nails are a little long for the job, nail them in at an angle.
- Hammer with a few long, steady blows, keeping an eye on the head of the nail. Hold on to the nail only as long as you need to get it started.

GAP FILLERS & SEALANTS

Wood, metal, brick, concrete and tiling – there's a filler for every gap

Flexible fillers and sealants keep rain, wind and insects out when they're used outside, and provide a more finished appearance to woodwork and seal plumbing fixtures inside. There are dozens of types of filler, suitable for an equal number of applications; acrylic and silicone fillers are the most common. Each type comes in a long tube or cartridge, which fits inside a cartridge gun. The gun has a moveable pressure rod that presses against the bottom of the tube and forces the filler out of the nozzle at a controlled rate.

Some are tedious to apply, but with practice you'll get smooth results. Go slowly; it's easy to run too much filler out and make a mess. Guns range from mediocre to excellent,

Filler

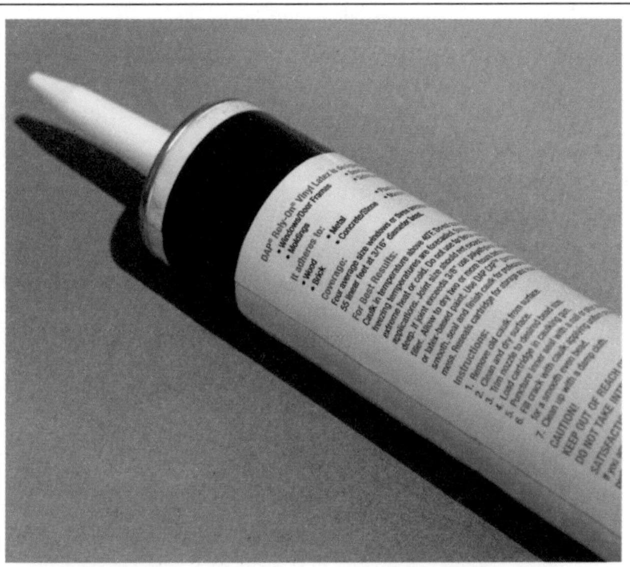

- Always read the label and technical information on a tube before using filler to assure you have the best material for your job.
- Most filler will last for years after it has been applied, but exterior filler is more likely to need renewing from time to time.
- Standard acrylic filler, used by painters, comes in multiple colours, is used on wood, can be painted, and cleans up with water.
- All-silicone sealant is used on non-porous surfaces – tile, glass, metal – is very durable but not paintable, and cleans up with solvent.

Cartridge Guns

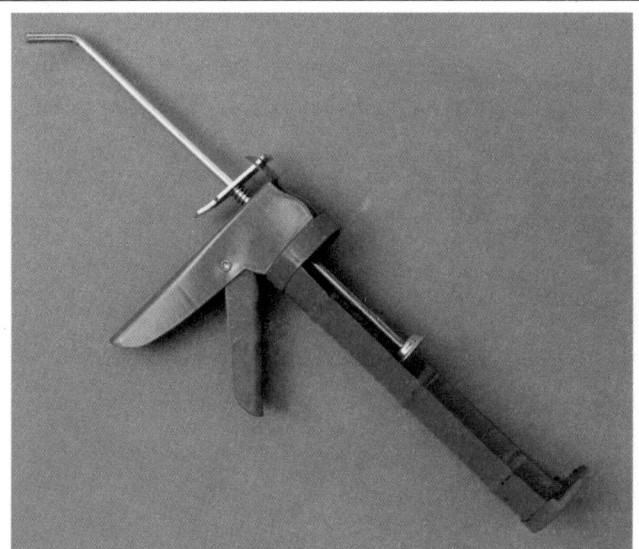

- Paint stores that supply the trade will normally have a good range of professional quality cartridge guns.
- Better quality guns have a swing-out narrow metal cutter for puncturing the end of the cartridge nozzle and a thumb-operated lever release that stops the flow of filler.
- When you have finished, remove the cartridge and wipe down the gun.
- Some bathroom sealant comes in small, squeezable tubes for quick repair jobs.

depending on their make and style. Look for an open-style gun in at least the mid-price range at a home improvement, paint or hardware store. The least expensive guns are the hardest to use and not worth the small savings.

Before you start, the surface must be clean, mildew free, and dry. Remove any old, loose filler. Cut the end of the cartridge nozzle at a 45° angle and just smaller than the opening you're filling. Apply filler in warm, dry conditions.

YELLOW LIGHT

Old filler past its expiration date should be discarded if it has started to dry out. Test any filler from a part-used cartridge on a piece of scrap wood for flow, colour and drying time before using it.

Applying Filler

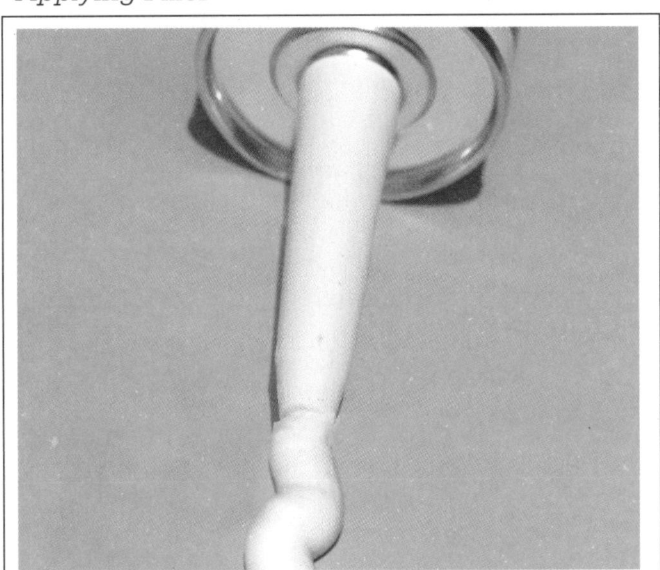

- Cut away any old filler with a utility knife or putty knife before applying.
- Apply in warm, dry conditions, starting slowly while maintaining steady pressure as you move the gun, releasing the trigger near the end of the run.
- Run a finger or spreader over acrylic filler to smooth it, followed by a sponge to wipe up any excess.
- When you have finished, wipe the cartridge tip clean and press a long nail into it to prevent the remaining filler from drying out.

Painting Filler

- Acrylic filler can be painted after it dries and cures. Siliconized acrylic sealant can be painted; pure silicone sealant cannot.
- Use paintable filler for woodwork and next to most painted surfaces. Follow the curing times on the tube before painting.
- Clear filler goes on white and dries clear, and can be used when a sealant is needed that does not require paint.
- Applying paint to uncured filler can cause the paint film to pull away and wrinkle as the filler continues to dry.

TAPES & GLUES

Look beyond duct tape and PVA glue to secure your projects

In home repair projects, tape has many uses. It can secure plastic sheeting over a door opening to keep dust out, mask woodwork when painting, hold glued sections together until the glue dries, temporarily repair electric flex and broken tool grips, and be used for marking just about anything when written on with a felt marker. A well-equipped toolbox will have rolls of masking, insulating and duct tape in it for those odds-and-ends jobs that occur when you least expect them.

Paper tapes, primarily masking tape, have a limited life before the glue dries out and removing the tape becomes difficult. Low-tack masking tape is designed as a painter's tool to mask off painted areas; it lasts longer than standard masking tape because paint jobs can span several days, and it's less likely to pull off dried paint.

Wood Glue

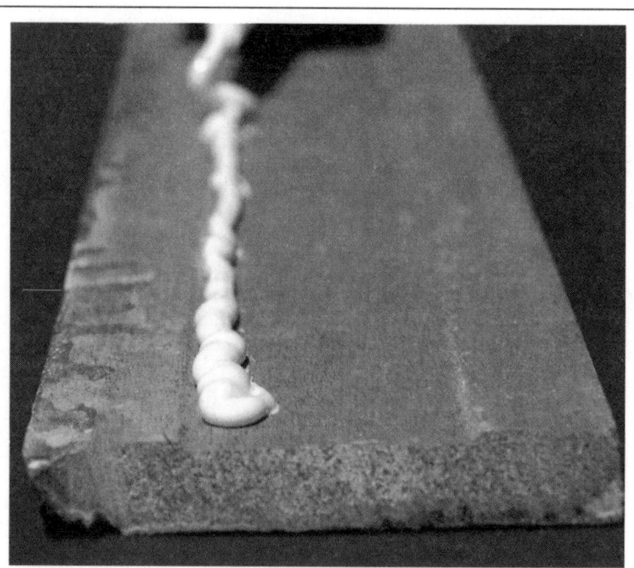

- PVA glue works well on porous materials not exposed to moisture, non-structural repairs and arts and crafts; it's non-toxic and dries clear.
- Use glue in addition to screws when repairing split doors or other woodwork for a tight, long-lasting fix.
- Yellow wood glue offers more water resistance than PVA glue; apply a modest amount to both surfaces and secure them together with a clamp or tape until the glue has hardened.
- Too much glue can actually weaken a glued joint.

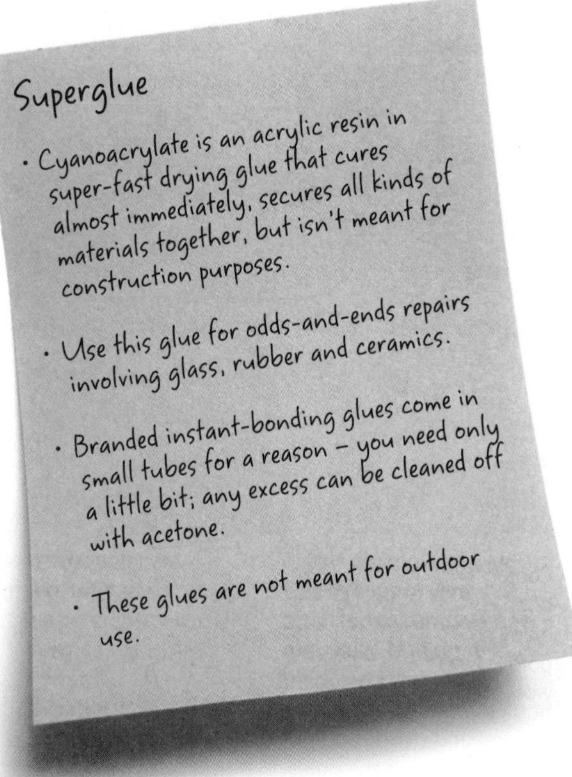

Superglue
· Cyanoacrylate is an acrylic resin in super-fast drying glue that cures almost immediately, secures all kinds of materials together, but isn't meant for construction purposes.
· Use this glue for odds-and-ends repairs involving glass, rubber and ceramics.
· Branded instant-bonding glues come in small tubes for a reason – you need only a little bit; any excess can be cleaned off with acetone.
· These glues are not meant for outdoor use.

Glue isn't a mechanical fastener like a nail or a screw. It's a chemical compound that holds things together. Some glues are designed to bind porous materials such as wood and paper, while others work best on non-porous ceramics. Water-resistant glue is a must on any surfaces near moisture. For many woodworking projects, standard yellow wood glue does the trick.

As a rule, less glue forms a better bond than more glue.

RED LIGHT

Superglue can accidentally stick your fingers together. Remove it with acetone, as found in nail varnish remover. Apply a small amount on a cotton bud and wash off immediately the glue is released. An alternative is to soak the affected area in warm, soapy water until the skin can be rolled apart.

Contact Adhesive

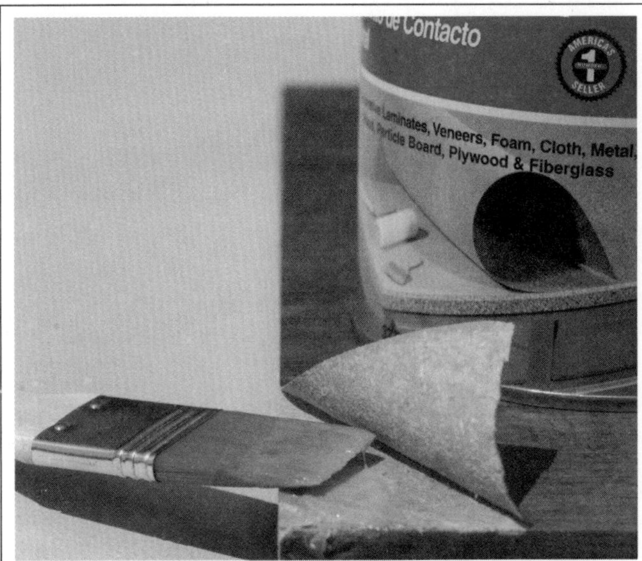

- Contact adhesive is used to bond plastic laminate and many porous and non-porous materials, but not wood.
- Contact adhesive is available in (flammable) solvent and water-based versions; use the flammable version in a well-ventilated area.
- Coat both surfaces with adhesive and leave to become tacky before pressing together.

Tape

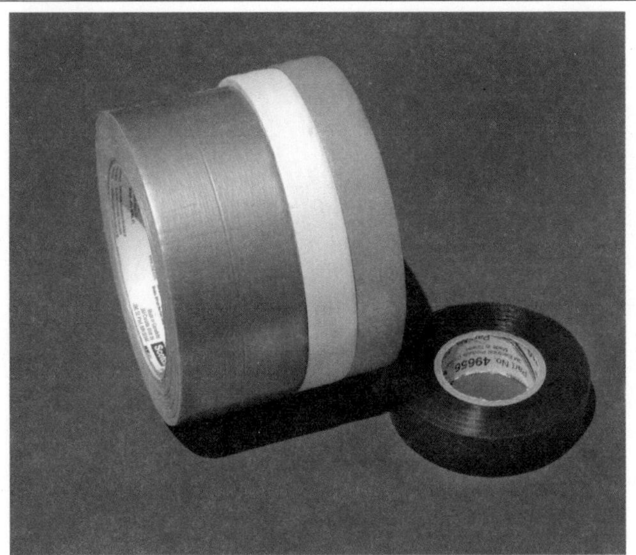

- Repair jobs often call for a specific tape for a reason: each is designed for a certain purpose and they are not always interchangeable.
- Vinyl or plastic insulation tape prevents the conduction of electricity, but it isn't meant to secure or strengthen anything.
- Masking tape is regularly used to tape off areas to keep paint off them.
- Duct tape is often used as a sealant for heating and ventilation ductwork, even though research suggests it's not effective for this use.

SANDPAPER & STEEL WOOL

Get familiar with abrasive materials that smooth, clean, grind and polish wood and metal

Woodwork, floors and furniture are normally sanded smooth before being finished, or the finish itself is sanded to remove any imperfections and to allow the next coat to stick better. When picking out your materials, be aware that sandpaper comes in many forms, sizes and grades, which are distinguished by their grit (the small cutting particles glued to the paper). The higher the number – 220, 280, 360 – the finer the paper and the less abrasive it is.

Hand-sanding is appropriate for scuffing a finish, minor, quick smoothing, or for areas where dust is a consideration. Otherwise, power sanding with a sander is a far better way to go. You cannot duplicate the speed or movements of a

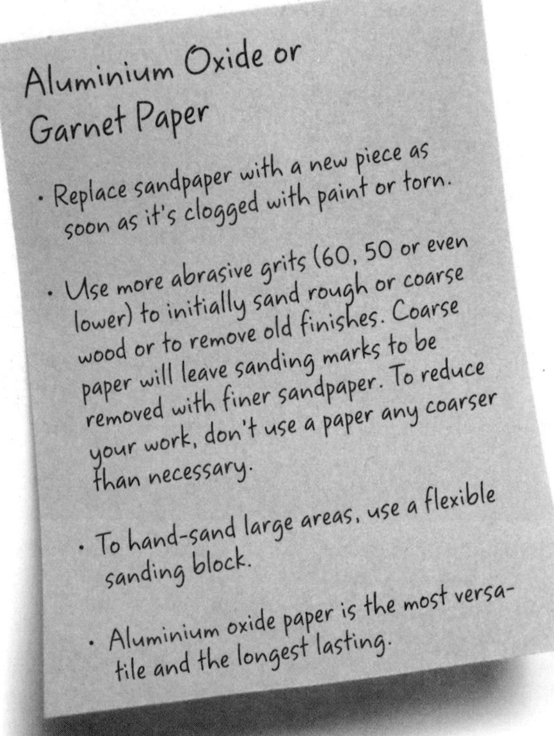

Aluminium Oxide or Garnet Paper

- Replace sandpaper with a new piece as soon as it's clogged with paint or torn.
- Use more abrasive grits (60, 50 or even lower) to initially sand rough or coarse wood or to remove old finishes. Coarse paper will leave sanding marks to be removed with finer sandpaper. To reduce your work, don't use a paper any coarser than necessary.
- To hand-sand large areas, use a flexible sanding block.
- Aluminium oxide paper is the most versatile and the longest lasting.

Sanding Sheets

- Sandpaper is sold in a variety of sheet sizes and packaging, from mixed packs of different grits to 50- and 100-sheet sleeves or 5-m rolls.
- Full sheets of sandpaper commonly measure 230 x 280 mm and can be folded and cut or torn into smaller sizes to fit sanders and sanding blocks.
- Some imported sheets are undersized and do not fold or cut evenly into smaller sections – avoid these.
- You can also buy paper pre-sized for sanders, but it's more expensive.

power sander with hand-sanding any more than you can outrun a car.

The material being sanded determines the grit of paper used. Tough jobs such as sanding off varnish call for coarser, heavier grits. If you use a grit that's too coarse, you can usually remove the sanding marks with finer grades of sandpaper.

For metal work, steel wool is manufactured in grades like sandpaper, but its coarseness is measured by the thickness of its steel strands.

MAKE IT EASY

Mixed packets of sandpaper or sandpaper by the sheet are fine for small sanding projects. For large jobs or ongoing jobs, such as sanding rooms full of woodwork and doors or floor sanding, consider buying by the roll in the grit(s) you know you'll need.

Discs and Belts

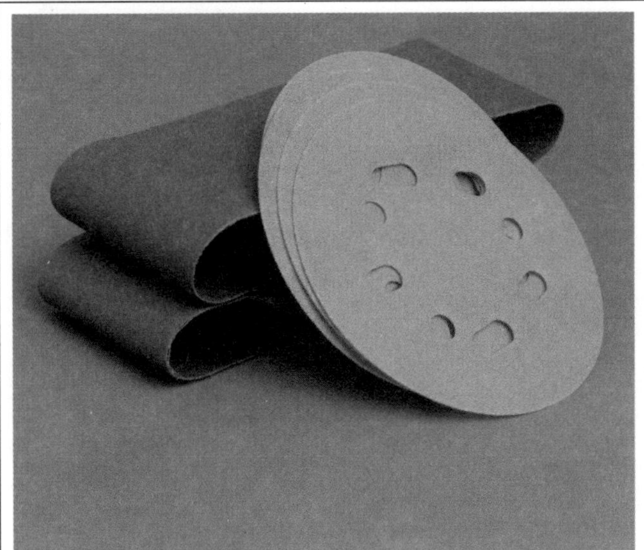

- Sanding discs are available in all grades. Some attach to a sander via hook and loop (Velcro), the most convenient to change, while others secure with a nut attached to the sanding pad.
- Be sure the discs you purchase will fit your sander – the wrong type won't work properly.
- Disc sanders cut fast – try a very light grit disc first to get used to the machine.
- Sanding belts range from 10–100 mm wide for commonly available belt sanders.

Steel and Brass Wool

- Steel wool comes in grades; its coarseness is measured by the thickness of its steel strands.
- Extra coarse grade 4 removes some rust and corrosion, while extra fine 0000 can polish furniture with wax or bring a shine to brass.
- Less common brass wool is more resistant to corrosion when wet.
- Wear gloves to keep shards of steel strands out of your fingers. Discard wet steel wool when finished – it will corrode if you save it for another use.

PAINTS & FINISHES

Know your coatings: emulsion, oil paint and primer each have a different purpose

To protect wood, plasterboard and plaster surfaces and make them washable, a coating of some kind must be applied. Unprotected wood exposed to the weather will deteriorate, and possibly rot. Paint and other finishes seal these surfaces as well as adding colour. A paint store can be a very confusing place. Do you get matt emulsion or eggshell? Polyurethane or marine varnish? Fast-drying or oil-based primer? Any number of finishes can work on different projects, but you must decide on the degree of gloss or shine, the type of finish, and the ease or difficulty in applying the finish.

Most household paints are either water-based or oil-based. Water-based paint has been the overwhelming choice for

Primers

- Primer prepares a surface for paint; it is not a finish coat, nor is diluted paint a substitute for primer.
- Use acrylic primer with arylic paint and oil primer with oil paint for the best results. On exterior surfaces, oil primer is recommended with acrylic paint.
- Use fast-drying primer for spot priming, not large areas.
- If exterior primer sits too long without being painted, the paint may not bond properly – follow the manufacturer's directions for curing times.

Paints

- Oil paint has a harder film, takes longer to dry, and fades faster than acrylic paint, and while it adheres well to different surfaces, it becomes brittle on exteriors and yellows with age.
- Acrylic dries quickly, remains flexible and allows moisture to pass through, but is less hard-wearing than oil-based paint.
- Oil works well on interior woodwork but less so on exterior woodwork unless all previous coats of paint are oil-based.
- Oil-based paint is less sensitive to cold temperatures.

homeowners. It's easier to apply and clean up, dries quickly, and forms a flexible film on exteriors where paint has to give a little and 'breathe' as temperatures change and moisture passes through it.

Paint gloss reflects its solids content: the higher the gloss, the more solids and the tougher the finish. Primer is applied first on unpainted surfaces: it seals and provides a faintly rough surface to help paint adhesion.

ZOOM

Oil paint sticks to most surfaces, is harder to apply than water-based paint, has a more offensive smell, and a much longer drying time. Oil works well on interior woodwork but not on exteriors unless all previous paint coats are oil-based. Water-based paint can be used over oil after thorough preparation and priming.

Different Glosses

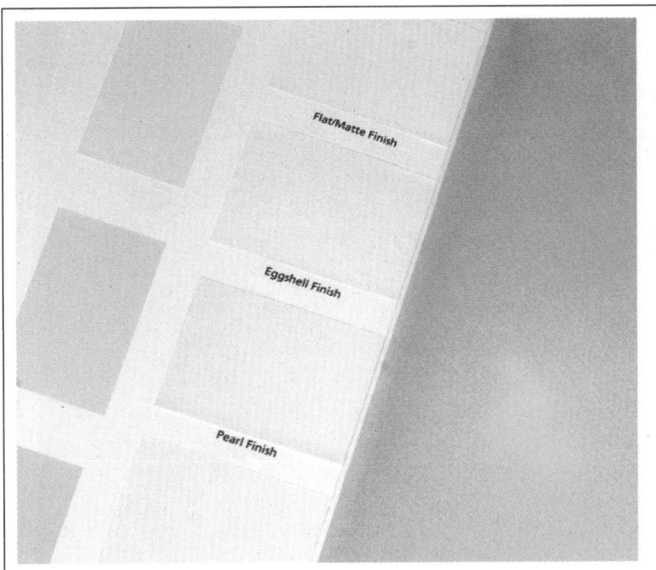

- Paint gloss indicates the solids content: the more solids, the tougher – and more washable – the finish.
- Semigloss paint was traditionally used on woodwork and shows imperfections easily, while high-gloss paint is used in marine applications and on furniture.
- Matt paint absorbs light and hides wall and ceiling defects.
- Satin or eggshell paint's soft sheen is washable, making it appropriate for bathrooms, kitchens and children's rooms.

Exterior Paints

- Exterior paint with tougher resins and additional pigment withstands any weather conditions and covers all types of surfaces, including wood, stucco, brick and existing paint.
- Interior paint resists wear but can be used only on interior surfaces.
- The highest quality exterior paint will be the least expensive in the long run, but even this paint will not hold up on a badly prepared surface.
- Dark exterior colours will fade more noticeably, and faster, than light colours.

STAINS

Stain colours surfaces and offers some protection but not as much as paint

Paint is loaded with solids, which obscure surfaces when it is applied. Stain has a lower solids content and both penetrates and colours wood, while allowing much of the grain to show through. Stain alone offers much less protection than paint, especially in an exterior application. It's common to see deteriorated exterior woodwork and fences after one forlorn and long-gone application of stain that goes for years without a recoat. You should expect to recoat exterior stains twice as often or more than paint. On the plus side, exterior semi-transparent and transparent stains don't require a primer coat and are easy and quick to apply. They do not build up a surface film and never blister or peel as paint can.

Interior Stain

- A small amount of stain goes a long way – you can somewhat control stain colour by how much you apply and how fast you wipe the excess off.
- Stain colour looks different on different woods.
- Test your stain colour in both daylight and night-time lighting conditions to be sure the colour is what you're looking for.
- Apply stain to wood scraps before using in your project.

Exterior Stain

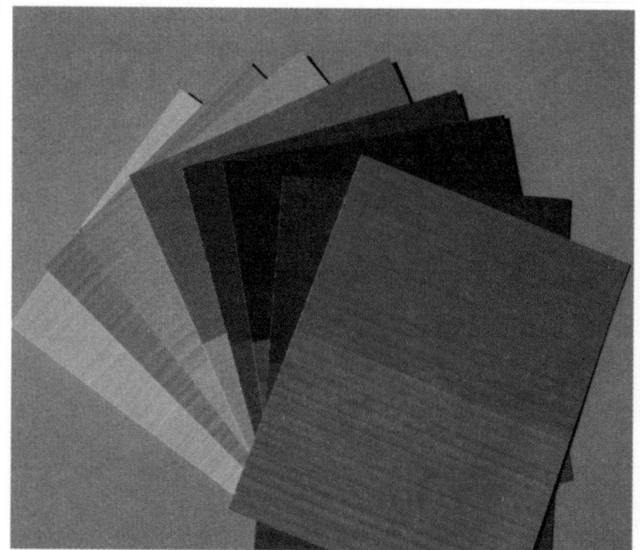

- Semitransparent or transparent exterior stains require more frequent recoating than paint (every 3–5 years depending on weather exposure).
- Solid-body exterior stain is like a light-bodied paint but without the holding power.
- Solid-body stains spread more easily than paint but don't form as strong a film.
- Stains contain fungicides to fight exterior mildew.
- Oil-based stains penetrate more deeply than acrylic stains. Clean brushes with paint thinner.

Interior stains are always followed by some type of clear coating to protect and seal them. Otherwise, the stains will wear off after foot traffic or other use. Pre-mixed interior stains are easy to apply with a brush, rag, or combination of the two and come in a variety of colours. Oil stains are considered to penetrate more deeply than acrylic and have sharper colour.

A clear exterior water-repellent preservative offers limited protection for about a year. Some painters apply this before applying an exterior stain, but not all clear preservative manufacturers recommend this.

MAKE IT EASY

Always test softwood such as fir and pine for stain absorption. It's often necessary to seal interior softwoods first so the stain goes on evenly. After testing your stain colour, consider going one shade lighter. Stain selection can be more problematic than paint colour, and going lighter is often the right choice.

Applying Stain

- Interior stains are brushed on to woodwork or applied with a rag to furniture, and both are wiped down with clean rags to remove any excess.
- Exterior stain is brushed, rolled, or sprayed and is absorbed quickly into raw wood.
- Stain the entire length of board or section of a piece of furniture without stopping, otherwise it will have an irregular appearance.
- Maintain a wet edge as you stain, brushing from a dry area into the previously stained wet material.

Clear Water Repellents

- Clear water repellents contain polymers or wax and offer some protection, but an extra coat of stain probably provides more.
- Always follow the manufacturer's application instructions – these products can become tacky and not dry properly if misapplied.
- Don't mix a water repellent with an exterior stain – apply each separately.
- Water repellents also protect and help seal masonry but are not normally recommended on historic structures and can discolour brick (always test first).

CLEAR FINISHES

From traditional varnish to modern lacquer, clear coats protect and shine through

Clear finishes are divided into two broad categories: those that form tough surface films and those that form weaker films. These categories include oils derived from plants, varnishes, polyurethane, lacquer, shellac and modified oils. Pure oils penetrate and form a soft film, which offers mild resistance to wear and tear but is easily recoated with a clean rag. Varnishes and polyurethane also penetrate, form a harder film, and are not as easily renewed or reapplied.

Oil-based and acrylic clear finishes protect both stained and unstained wood, allowing the wood grain to show. Flat, satin and higher gloss clear finishes are available, although the softer-appearing satin is most commonly used in homes.

Varnish and Polyurethane

- Polyurethane and varnish each form a clear, durable film, although water-based polyurethane will appear milky when first applied.
- Apply in temperatures of 18°C or higher to avoid drying problems, especially with oil-based products.
- Clear exterior finishes, sometimes seen on front doors, need recoating more often than a painted finish.
- Apply at least three coats of these finishes over raw wood for complete coverage and penetration, carefully following the manufacturer's drying time requirements.

Oils

- Pure and modified oil finishes require more frequent application than varnish and polyurethane, depending on the application, because they form weaker films.
- Pure tung oil is expensive, requires a lot of rubbing, is easily repaired and maintained, and is slow drying.
- Modified oils, also known as oil/varnish blends, are sold under a variety of brand names and are usually applied with a rag.
- Wiping varnish, another finish, forms more of a film than modified oil.

Pure oils include tung and linseed. Both are used as ingredients in other finishes, including varnish and modified oils. Tung oil takes some effort to apply and is very slow drying. Popular modified oils have added resin and paint thinner, are easy to apply, offer moderate protection and require multiple coats.

Shellac is a favourite with some antique restorers. It offers little resistance to moisture and comes in various colours. However, it dries very quickly, so it can be difficult to apply. Shellac can be an undercoat for varnish and sticks to all kinds of surfaces.

ZOOM

Lacquer, another clear finish, dries extremely fast and is often used as a furniture finish on interior woodwork and prefinished doors. Brushing lacquer is also available, but varnishes and polyurethane offer harder finishes. Spray cans of lacquer work well for small art projects but are inappropriate for larger jobs.

Shellac

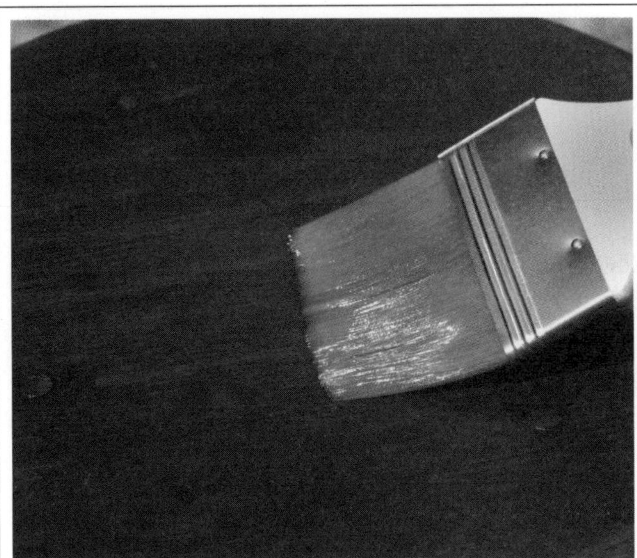

- Shellac or button polish is a specialized finish used by restorers and hobbyists.
- Shellac-based primer/sealers make excellent stain blockers.
- Shellac has no petroleum-based ingredients and no paint thinner odour.
- Water will leave a white mark on a shellac finish that has added wax.
- Note the expiration date on any can of shellac before buying.

Wax Finish

- Wax alone is not effective as a final finish, but it maintains furniture finishes as a top coat, brightens metal, and offers some stain protection to worn kitchen sinks.
- Liquid wax is easier to apply but offers less protection than paste wax.
- Apply wax sparingly – otherwise, too much is wiped off and wasted.
- After applying, wax solvent begins evaporating, and the wax turns hazy. If the wax sits too long and is hard to rub off, apply fresh wax to resoften.

FAUX FINISHES

Create a stone, marble or wood-grain finish using paint and a few simple tools

A faux finish is a disguise that turns a plain interior wall or woodwork into an exciting and enticing surface. Trompe l'œil, or 'trick of the eye' is a type of faux finish that creates the optical illusion of depth in a painted image.

Faux finishes can range from techniques in applying ordinary house paint to the use of special glazes, plaster and associated finishes to obtain a range of traditional faux looks. Like many decorating techniques, faux finishes, which date back thousands of years, go through periods of popularity and rejection. After a resurgence in the early 1990s, faux finish materials and tools are readily available for all levels of skill and creativity.

Wood Graining

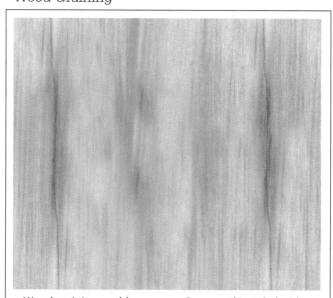

- Wood graining enables a softwood or less expensive wood to resemble a hardwood. For instance, pine can be grained to resemble oak.
- It can be hard to distinguish a successful graining job from real wood.
- Raw wood is sealed with a base coat, such as shellac or paint, and then a glaze finish is applied and worked with a series of tools to produce the desired wood grain appearance.
- When dry, the grained finish is coated with a clear finish for protection.

Ragging and Marbling

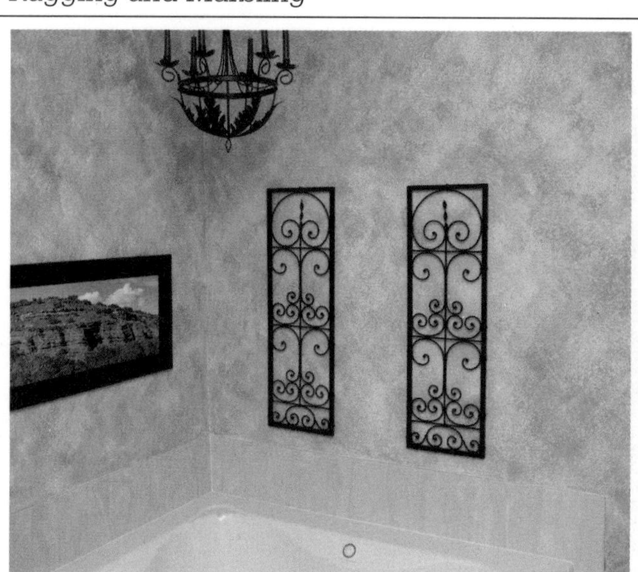

- These techniques can be used on any woodwork or walls, but too much can overwhelm a room.
- Subtle colour mixing and patterns are critical to successful marbling, ragging and rag-rolling – expect to practise first before doing your final work.
- To get a realistic effect of marble, the different shapes and addition of veins in the finish are multiple tasks that can't all be done at once.
- Some protective clear coats will yellow with age, affecting the appearance of the paint.

The beauty of a faux finish, aside from its intrinsic appearance, is the ease with which you can change or paint over a project that just didn't work out. With practice, an amateur can get very presentable results. One approach for this practice is to do the inside of a cupboard or utility room until you're satisfied with your technique and tool selection.

Virtually anything can be used to tool a faux finish: rags, sponges, paint rollers, common and special brushes, combing tools, and feathers for marbling. A small investment in time and money can yield surprising results.

MAKE IT EASY

Internet sites are fine as an introduction to faux finish techniques, but a book offers far more information, detail and photos of sample finishes all in one place. There are plenty of titles available: look in your local bookshop or public library.

Common Graining Tools

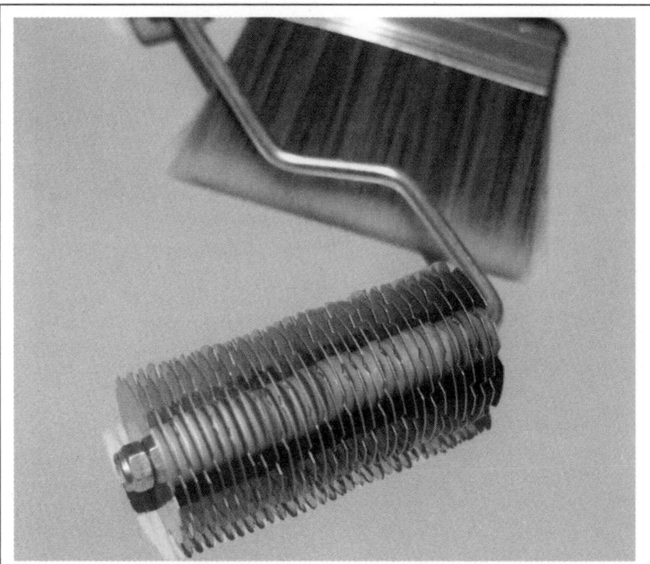

- A professional faux finish specialist has an array of brushes and hand tools for specific effects, but you can get by with fewer.
- Sea sponges, cotton rags, small pieces of hessian, chamois and muslin are all used to produce marbled and wood grain effects.
- Aside from brushes to apply and spread the basecoat, use separate brushes with both coarse and fine bristles for drawing out wood grain, creating marble veins, and dragging a finish.
- Steel combs are used for creating wood grain.

Faux Finishing with Basic Tools

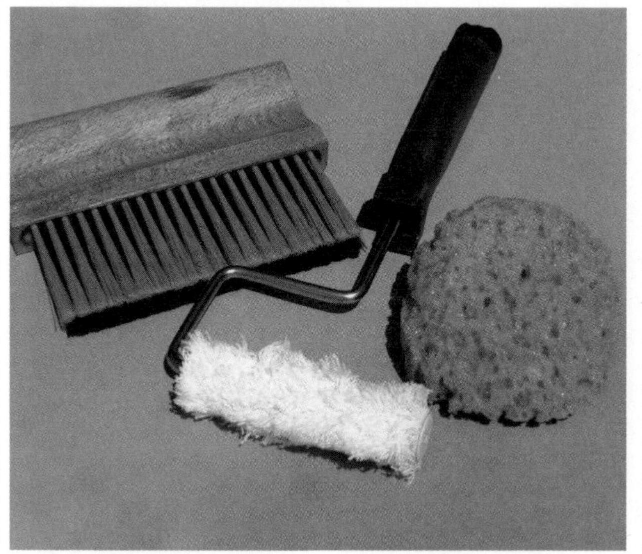

- There are plenty of online and other suppliers of faux finish tools and materials, but you can also create some interesting finishes with what you have.
- Kitchen sponges, wool socks, plastic pot scrubbers, and damp wash cloths can duplicate various faux effects.
- Branches from shrubs, especially evergreens, can be dragged through a wet glaze finish for interesting results.
- Children's paint sets have the ideal-size paintbrushes for some veining techniques.

FILLERS

Holes, cracks and damaged surfaces all need fillers to complete their repairs

Fillers, like so many other materials, come in all forms, but they all do the same thing: they fix imperfections in surfaces before painting. Some are very dense and strong, while others are softer and more pliable. Some dry very fast, which means you have only a short time to work with them, while others are more forgiving. The most common filler for small holes is Polyfilla, which despite being a brand name has become so universally used it's become a generic term.

Some fillers have migrated from their original purpose to home repairs. Car body filler can fill large holes if applied in several applications. It does not shrink and can be shaped and sanded to replace missing corners or decorative plaster.

Ready-mixed filler

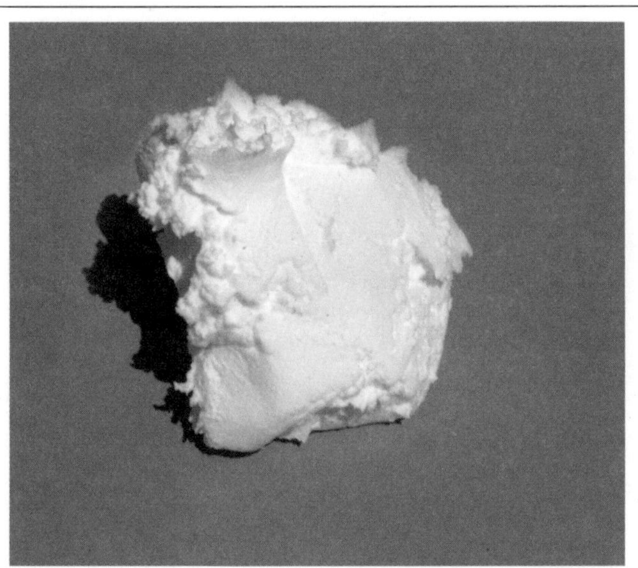

- Pre-mixed, ready-to-use pliable plaster-like paste filler is sold in interior and exterior versions.
- It is suitable for only small holes and should not be used for large repairs – it won't dry properly, and the repair will fail.
- Keep unused filler sealed in its container and discard if it dries out.
- Once dry, the filler can be sanded smooth and painted with the rest of the wall. It will take nails and screws.

Car Body Filler

- Car body filler is a two-part mix that dries hard in minutes, holds paint well, and should be used sparingly in finish work.
- It comes with a separate hardening agent, but buy an extra tube of hardener because it often runs out before all the filler is used.
- Car body fillers come with or without reinforcing fibreglass strands for extra strength and can be shaped and sanded to replace missing corners or decorative plaster.
- Do not nail or screw into car body filler.

Traditional plasterwork consists of three coats of different types of plaster. Interior filler repairs all three layers with an easy-to-mix compound that must be worked quickly before it dries. For deep holes, apply it in multiple, thin coats.

Wood filler or wood putty fills holes and pores in unpainted wood. It's formulated to match the appearance of wood so it won't stand out too much when stained or clear-coated. Wood fillers dry quickly and sand easily.

MAKE IT EASY

Buy a larger box of patching plaster than you think you'll need for one job because you'll always need more later. Until you're used to mixing the correct amount for the job and working it before it dries out, you'll experience some wasted material.

Interior filler

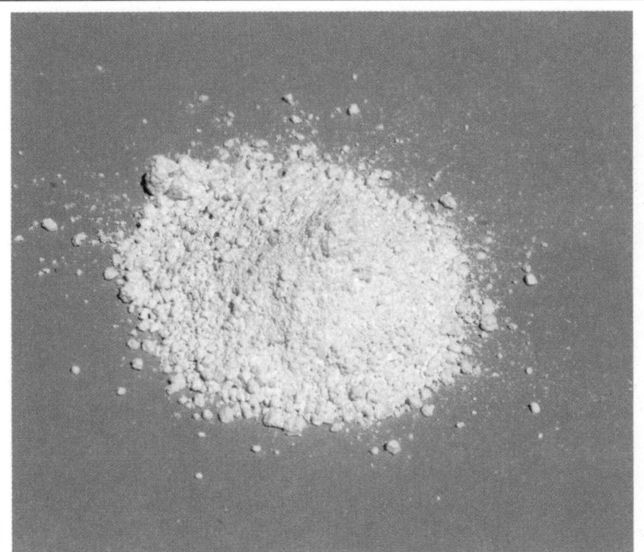

- Interior fillers are packaged in powder form. They are mixed with cold water and set to a stiff consistency in a few minutes, and dry hard shortly thereafter.
- Use just enough to do a smooth job, removing any excess with a filling knife.
- Use pre-mixed or other soft filler as a final finish coat over small repairs.
- Powder filler can also be used to repair and fill wood holes and cracks, and can be painted over.

Wood Filler

- Most wood filler, a combination of a binder and wood flour or similar fine material, is sold pre-mixed in cans in both solvent and water-based formulas.
- A little goes a long way – use it sparingly.
- Wood filler comes in a variety of colours to mimic the natural appearance of some woods, although no match will ever be perfect.
- Open cans dry out quickly – keep the lid on except when removing the filler.

SCRATCHED WOODWORK

Love your pets but hate their scratches on your furniture? Here's the fix you need

As much as they would like to, cats and dogs can't open doors, but they can scratch at them and at other woodwork. Several of the fillers previously mentioned can be used to repair these scratches.

Your choice of filler depends on the depth and number of scratches, the detailing of the woodwork, whether it's painted or stained and clear-coated, and the amount of dust you're willing to put up with.

Light scratches can be filled with the door in place – use a dust sheet or piece of plastic on the floor – or removed and placed on sawhorses elsewhere. Heavy scratching calls for more filler and sanding, which is most easily done with a

Scratched Door

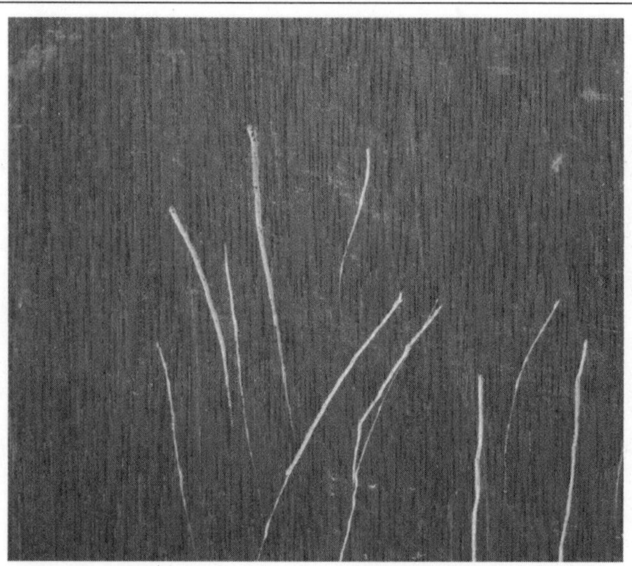

- Pre-mixed filler covers cracks up to 2 mm or so and is easy to sand.
- Car body filler (see previous page) can fill almost any size opening but is difficult to hand-sand if applied excessively.
- Don't waste wood filler on painted wood – it's meant for unpainted wood repairs and is too expensive for repairs that will be painted over.
- Powder filler is fine for wood repairs if the surface will be painted.

Filling the Scratches

- Lightly sand the scratched area, wipe off the dust, press the filler in with a clean putty knife, and allow it to dry completely.
- Keep the amount of filler to a minimum to avoid extra sanding.
- Wipe the putty knife clean when finished to keep built-up filler from drying on the edge.
- Stained woodwork and doors can be touched up with a matching wax stick if the scratches aren't too deep.

power sander on the removed door. Usually the surrounding woodwork is less scratched and requires less filling. Hand-sanding filler throws out the least dust. Machine-sanding removes excess filler faster, but cleaning up can be a real problem, especially if the door and woodwork are sanded in place.

The condition of the repaired and surrounding areas determines how much work is required. Paint a complete section, even on recently painted wood, rather than trying to touch up just the damaged area, so that the repairs blend in well.

RED LIGHT

If the door or woodwork is painted with old, lead-based paint, you must take precautions against spreading contaminated dust, especially if children, pregnant women, or pets live in the house. Avoid using a power sander and strip paint using a heat gun at a low temperature.

Sanding Fillers

- Wear a dust mask and start with 80-grit sandpaper to sand most fillers smooth.
- Sand in the direction of the wood grain if sanding by hand.
- If the door is removed, sand the patched area with a palm sander or a random-orbit sander until the area is smooth; follow up with 100-grit paper.
- Consider a final sanding with a finer-grit paper – 120 or 150 – and wipe off all dust before applying the finish.

Priming and Painting

- The repaired and surrounding areas determine how much repainting or staining/varnishing is required.
- As a minimum, coat the complete section of a door containing the damaged area and recoat the entire section when woodwork is repaired.
- Recoat a logical area – the whole of a door frame, for instance – if one section is damaged but recoating it alone will stand out too much.
- Sometimes a stained door can be touched up acceptably; otherwise, sand the whole section and refinish.

SCRATCHED FURNITURE

Repair a few scratches without refinishing the entire piece of furniture

Wood furniture is subject to nicks, scratches and spills. Some can be repaired without stripping and refinishing. Because furniture has so many distinct sections – legs, individual drawers, tops – you can repair any one of them individually to match the rest of the piece. This is what good antique restorers do all the time to repair minor damage.

Start with the least invasive approach – in some cases, cleaning and polishing the affected area with a polish/wax combination and very fine steel wool. In others, a wax filler stick, which is like a specialized wax crayon for filling scratches on stained furniture, produces an acceptable repair.

The furniture finish will influence the repair. Refinishing a

Scratched Furniture

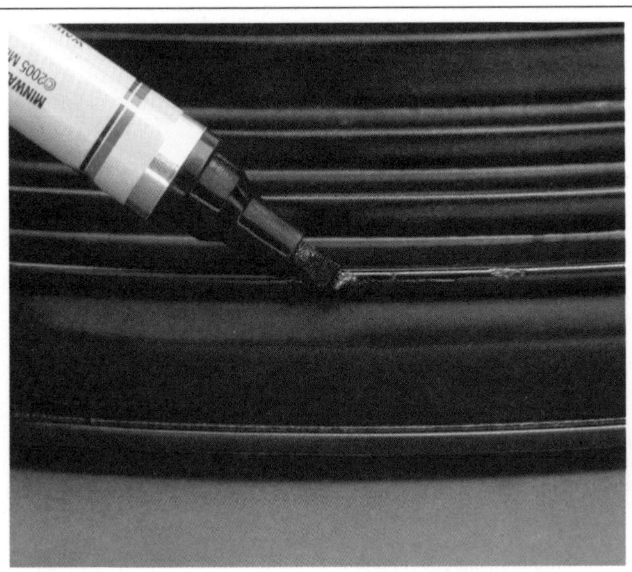

- Fill small cracks, nicks, and scratches with a wax stick, available in a range of colours to match different woods.
- Touch-up pens, available from some fine furniture stores, contain dyes for blending in scuffs and scratches.
- White rings can often be removed with denatured rubbing alcohol on a clean rag – go easy, you don't want to dissolve the old finish – followed by an application of furniture wax.
- Minor chips in a clear finish can be carefully touched up with clear nail polish.

Damaged Finishes

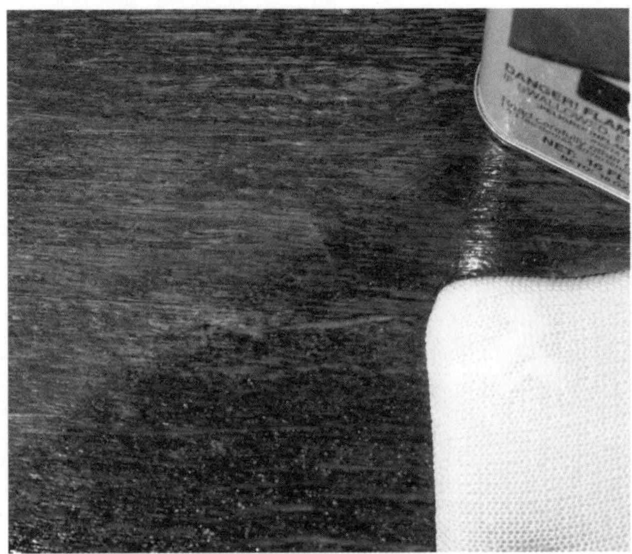

- Sunlight can cause a clear finish to shrink and crack, and it can leave furniture with a bleached-out look.
- Many pieces of furniture have veneered sections – thin sheets of expensive hardwood glued to less expensive woods.
- Veneer can be carefully and lightly sanded with fine sandpaper to remove an old finish, but furniture reviver is safer.
- Furniture reviver is available anywhere paint is sold and at many antique shops.

table top with a lacquer finish over stain requires scrubbing all the lacquer out of the wood before restaining. Otherwise, the new stain can appear splotchy. A wax finish over oil is simpler to work with.

Sunlight also damages furniture finishes, especially on top. If the rest of the piece looks acceptable or can be buffed up a bit, the top alone can be refinished.

Whenever any of the old finish is completely removed, replace it with new stain and a clear top coat to match the rest of the piece and protect the wood.

MAKE IT EASY

Furniture revivers and burnishing creams, which combine solvents and oils, are suitable for spot refinishing on furniture, but for extensive damage you may need to strip the surface using gel paint remover and renew the finish completely. The simplest repair is to cover a damaged top with something decorative.

Staining Furniture

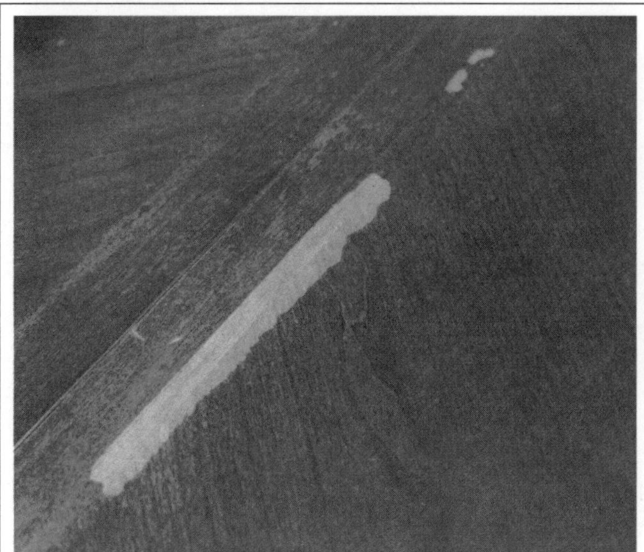

- An alternative to stripping is to carefully paint on new stain; the finish will be darker, but the job is easier.
- Lightly sand the damaged and surrounding areas with 120 and 150 sandpapers, and wipe away the dust.
- Brush on just enough matching oil stain to evenly cover the sanded area.
- Run the brush tips across the recoated area very lightly to even it out and allow it to cure for three days, then coat with varnish or polyurethane.

Clear Coat

- When recoating woodwork with a clear coating, try to match the type of material used on the surrounding woodwork and its sheen; on a furniture top, apply whatever coating will stand up best depending on how the furniture is used.
- Multiple coats of a modified oil finish are the easiest to apply and touch up.
- Apply at least three coats of varnish or polyurethane over bare wood.
- Fast-drying lacquer is available in spray cans.

WOOD FLOOR SCRATCHES

Touch up your wood floors and skip a complete refinishing with these simple tips

Wood floors look beautiful when they're new and freshly finished, but beauty can be fleeting as family life takes over. Wood floors get scratched by the usual culprits: grit on shoe soles, pet claws, dragging chairs and kids' toys. In the course of day-to-day family life, scratches tend to be unavoidable.

Small scratches can be repaired the same as furniture scratches. The depth of the scratch, in part, determines the repair. Deeper single scratches might need sanding out.

The key is not to overdo the amount of sanding but also to sand out enough – sometimes the complete length of a floorboard – in order for the touched-up area to match the surrounding finish and not stand out. The problem with

Sanding

- Mask off the edge of the entire length of the affected floorboard(s) with masking tape.
- Hand-sand (or machine-sand if dust isn't a problem) the scratch out with 80- and 100-grit sandpapers, being careful to stay inside the tape boundary, finishing with 120-grit paper.
- Sand the finish off the rest of the board(s), and vacuum and wipe off all the dust.
- Apply appropriate floor finish coats with foam brushes.

Sanding a Larger Area

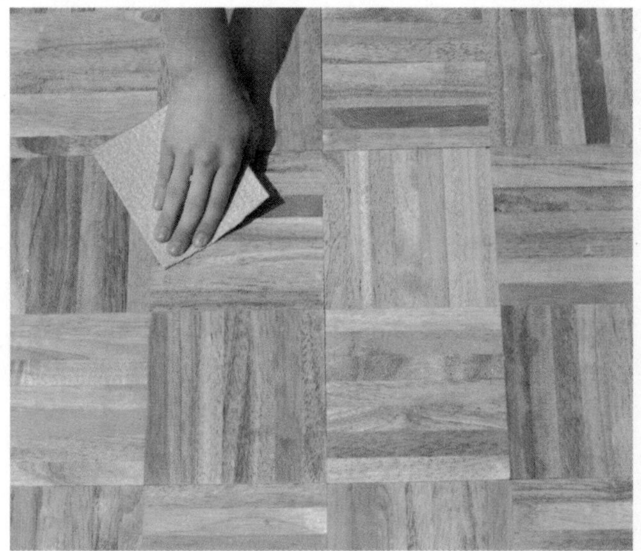

- A floor can have multiple scratches in the top coat over a large area that looks unappealing but doesn't justify a complete refinishing. The area can be recoated for an acceptable appearance and added protection.
- Sand the scratched area with 120-grit and 150-grit sandpapers, and vacuum and wipe away all dust.
- An existing oil-based finish can be softened with lacquer thinner.
- Recoat with the same finish – don't mix oil-based with water-based – following the grain of the wood.

attempting to clear-coat a repaired area in the centre of a board, for instance, is that the gloss never quite matches the surrounding finish.

If a large area of the floor has multiple but superficial scratches, it's appropriate to recoat a large area after lightly sanding and preparing the scratched area to receive an additional coat of finish.

Of course, the easiest repair is placing a rug over the damaged area until the entire floor gets refinished.

YELLOW LIGHT

Be sure the new finish used to touch up a scratched area is compatible with the existing finish. Water-based should go on water-based, oil-based on oil-based, etc. Applying wax can cause refinishing problems later if it seeps into the wood pores and can't be completely removed.

Clear Coat

- While wearing a respirator, apply an oil finish with a good-quality bristle brush or a pad applicator; the brush gives you a bit more control.
- With either an oil- or water-based finish, spread evenly along the entire length of two or three boards.
- Work quickly to maintain a wet edge as you apply from one section to the next.
- Follow the manufacturer's drying instructions, noting how long to wait before you can use the floor again.

Floor Refinisher

- Wood floor restoration products contain some solvent and wax or polymer-type finish and are used to clean and revive scratched and worn floors, but it's not the same as refinishing.
- This is a maintenance approach until a floor needs a complete refinishing.
- Used regularly, floor restorer/reviver products can be a good alternative to refinishing.
- Various specialist products for restoring hardwood floors are available from tool hire shops and online.

SCRATCHED WORKTOPS

Learn to buff out and repair scratches in even your toughest laminate worktops

Laminate worktops are made from layers of plastic-coated paper pressed together at high temperatures and under extreme pressure. They're mostly waterproof and moderately resistant to scratches. Plastic laminate has its roots in electrical insulators created in the early 20th century. This material is available in a multitude of colours, patterns, and glosses and is a practical and economical worktop material for kitchens and bathrooms.

Laminates vary in their composition. Some are coloured all the way through and others only on the surface. Scratches on the latter are more noticeable. Depending on the depth of the scratch or burn, you might be able to buff them out.

Caring for Laminate

- Sharp edges will damage plastic laminate, as will heavy metal objects moved across or dropped on it.
- Hot pans and abrasive cleaners also damage plastic laminate.
- Never use abrasive cleaners or scouring pads to clean the worktop. Stubborn stains can be removed with a non-abrasive cream cleaner. Use a nylon nail-brush and mild detergent to remove dirt ingrained in textured laminate.
- Dark colours fade and show damage more readily than textured or lighter colours.

Felt Pen

- Use a felt tip marker as close to the laminate colour as possible.
- Draw the tip over the scratch – if it's not a good match, erase it with a bit of lacquer thinner on a rag.
- Let a good match dry, and wipe away any excess ink around the scratch with lacquer thinner.
- Rub a little car wax into the scratch to restore the surface.

Some commercial products clean plastic laminate and fill the scratches with a liquid polymer that can be renewed from time to time. These products do not eliminate the scratches but make them less noticeable.

With professional help, plastic laminate can also be covered with new laminate, or worktops can be completely replaced with new material. For large burns that can't be buffed out or glossed over, cover and conceal them with another material until the entire worktop is renewed.

MAKE IT EASY

After it's been coloured with an appropriate marker, a small scratch can also be filled with carefully applied clear nail polish, wiping away the excess with lacquer thinner or nail polish remover. Wax polish can also be used, but nail polish or a similar clear varnish will last longer.

Butcher Block

- You might be able to buff some faint burns out of laminate with a cream cleaner, but more prominent burns cannot be cleaned out, although they can be covered up.
- Clean grease from area and sand it with 120-grit paper.
- Glue a piece of marble, a butcher's block or some heat-proof tiles over the burned area.
- Use just enough waterproof glue or adhesive to hold the material in place.

Install New Laminate

- Installing laminate takes experience, specific tools, and know-how. Measurements can't be changed once the new laminate is glued into place. For many, it might be best to call an expert.
- Remove the sink and measure the existing worktop. Then sand and wipe it free of dust.
- Cut the laminate to fit and glue it down with contact adhesive.
- After the adhesive dries, trim the laminate and cut a hole for the sink.

REPAIRING & REPLACING TILES

Repair chipped tiles quickly and easily without the help of a professional

Tiles create a tough surface for worktops, floors and shower enclosures, and can last for generations. Ceramic and porcelain tiles are made from different types of baked clay, with porcelain tile being the stronger of the two. Glazed finishes, essentially liquid glass, protect the tile from water and stains. As water resistant as tiling may be, its weak point is the grout, a cement-like material that seals the joints between tiles.

Tiles are installed in wet areas – bathrooms, kitchens and utility rooms – and in dry areas such as fireplaces. A chipped tile in either environment can be repaired, but wet areas require more diligence. Chipped and cracked tiles can be replaced with identical tiles if spares are available, but repairs can also

Using Epoxy Filler

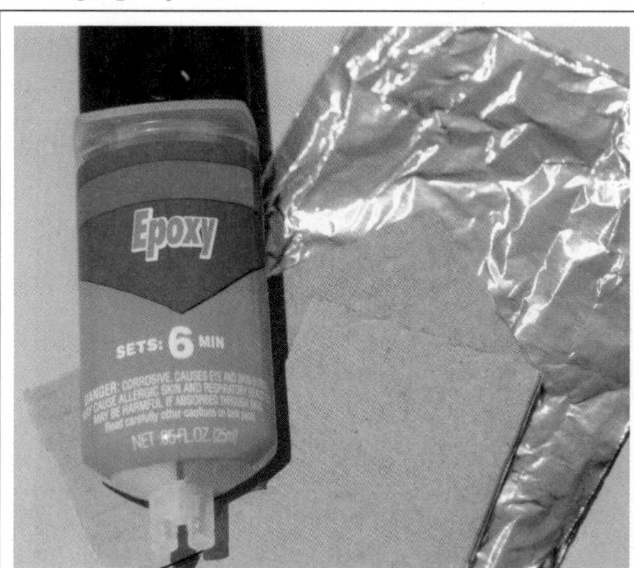

- Clean out the chipped area completely, digging out loose material with an old screwdriver.
- Prepare a small amount of paintable, waterproof epoxy filler.
- Use small pieces of cardboard covered with aluminium foil to keep the epoxy within the damaged area (some epoxies will self-level, and others require smoothing out with a putty knife).
- When the filler is dry, touch up with an oil-based paint to match the colour and finish of the tile.

Removing a Tile

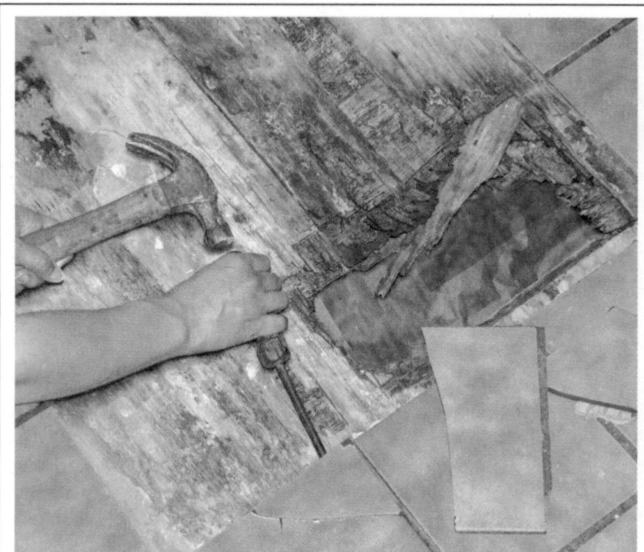

- To remove a tile, first carefully remove the old grout (wear safety glasses).
- Cut through the grout using a grout saw, available from hardware and DIY stores, or a utility knife, or by drilling a series of small adjoining holes. Scrape out any remaining grout with a stiff putty knife or old screwdriver.
- To ease removal, drill a series of short holes through the broken tile using a tile or ceramic cutting bit.
- Chip out the tile with a cold chisel.

be done with waterproof epoxy and oil-based paint in a colour matching the surrounding tile.

As strong as tiling is, damaged sections must be carefully removed to avoid damaging adjoining tiles: it's frustrating when you find yourself replacing an additional tile or two beyond your original repair.

Don't expect to find exact matches for tiles in old patterns or colours. If you don't have any spares, consider an artistic alternative with something in a contrasting or toning colour.

MAKE IT EASY

A chipped fireplace tile can be repaired with automotive body filler if epoxy isn't handy. Shape and sand the filler to match the missing area and paint when dry. Coat the paint with a bit of polyurethane to match the sheen on the surrounding tile.

Installing a Tile

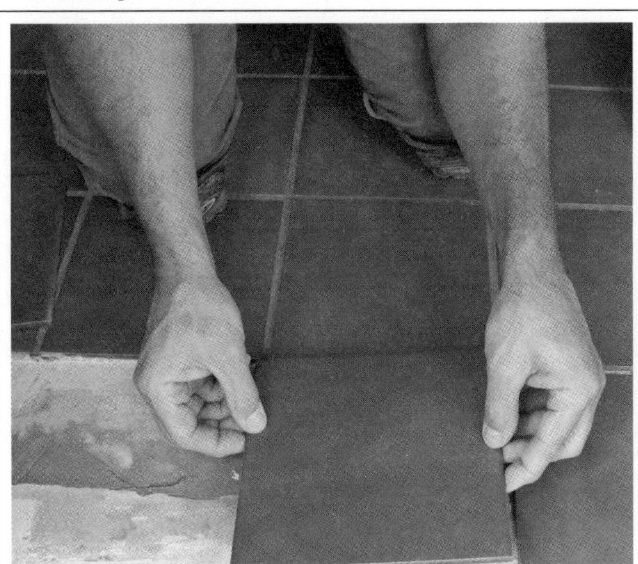

- With the broken tile removed, scrape away any old adhesive and wipe with a moist rag.
- Check the new tile for fit and match and spread tile adhesive on the back of the new tile to within 5 mm or so of the edges.
- Line the tile up with the surrounding tiles and press and hold in place.
- Secure the tile with masking tape and leave to dry according to the adhesive manufacturer's instructions.

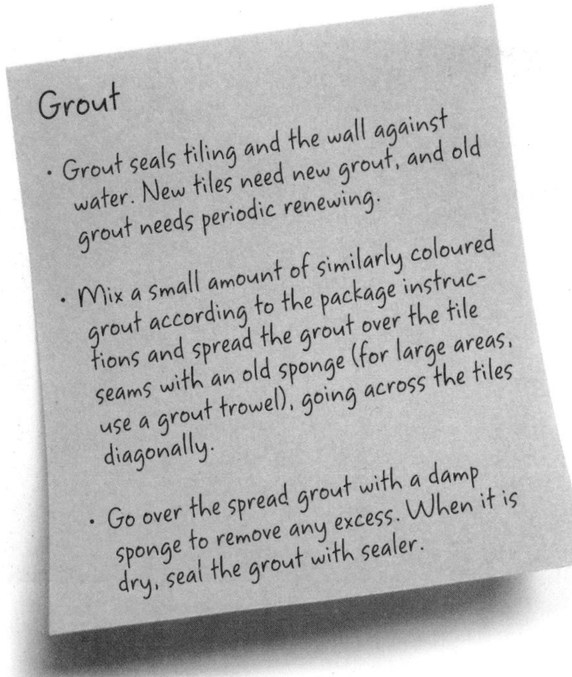

Grout
· Grout seals tiling and the wall against water. New tiles need new grout, and old grout needs periodic renewing.
· Mix a small amount of similarly coloured grout according to the package instructions and spread the grout over the tile seams with an old sponge (for large areas, use a grout trowel), going across the tiles diagonally.
· Go over the spread grout with a damp sponge to remove any excess. When it is dry, seal the grout with sealer.

REPAIRING A CHIPPED FINISH

You can't reproduce a factory finish, but you can still do a repair

Appliances are coated with some of the toughest paint around. Special touch-up paints are available with brushes attached to the bottle tops, but they will never match the durability or finished appearance of a factory coating. That said, no one wants to look at a paint chip, so even a less-than-perfect repair is better than none at all.

Metal sinks and baths have baked porcelain and ceramic finishes. These can chip if something heavy falls on them in just the right way and at just the right spot. Very old cast iron and steel baths often show stains and worn finishes that can be renewed by any number of bath refinishing processes, although none that uses sprayed-on epoxy and other exotic

Applying Epoxy Paint

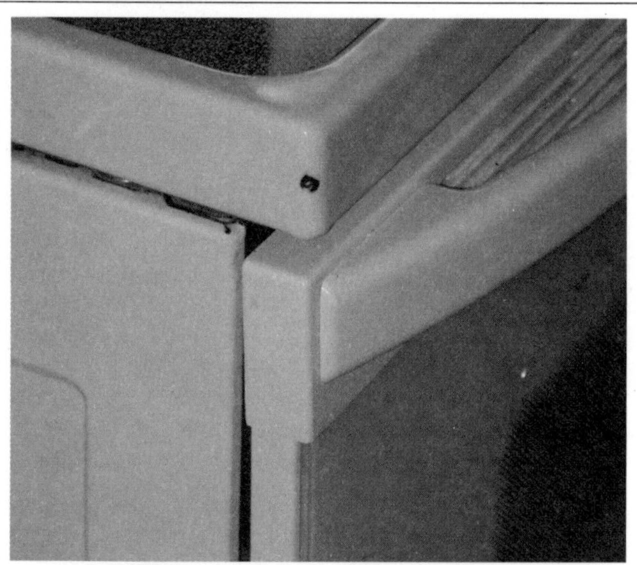

- Scuff the chipped area with 120-grit sandpaper, feathering the rough paint edges, and then wipe away all the dust.
- Apply two thin coats of appliance touch-up paint, available from appliance dealers, following the manufacturer's instructions.
- Depending on the manufacturer, this paint can sometimes be used on plumbing fixtures.
- Appliance touch-up paint is not long-lasting around water or high heat and will need recoating from time to time.

Porcelain Repair Kit 1

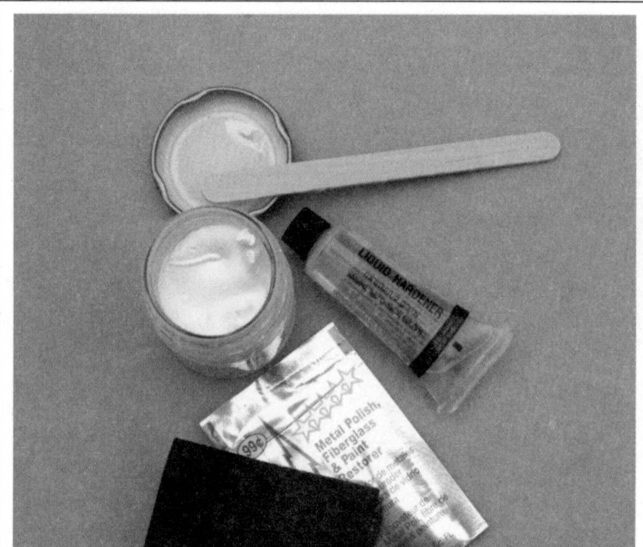

- Clean and lightly sand the chipped area, feathering the rough edges.
- Follow the instructions and mix just enough epoxy solution to fill the damaged area.
- Working quickly, as the material stiffens quickly, carefully brush in one thin coat and allow the epoxy to self-level, following with a second coat if needed.
- This repair will never be as strong as the original finish but will do an adequate job of covering a chipped area.

paints will equal the original baked-on porcelain. Some processes are better than others, and any that you consider using should be thoroughly researched first.

For in-home repairs of small chips, two-part epoxy solutions are more durable than pre-mixed epoxy paint. They do not require any follow-up sealant and should be monitored for potential recoating. Some of these epoxy solutions are sold in small kits for touching up chips and are available in popular appliance colours.

MAKE IT EASY

The key to retouching fixtures and appliances is to completely clean the area being repaired according to the paint or filler instructions. It must be kept dry and undisturbed while the coating cures. If the chip is deep, a second coat might be needed to match the surrounding surface.

Porcelain Repair Kit 2

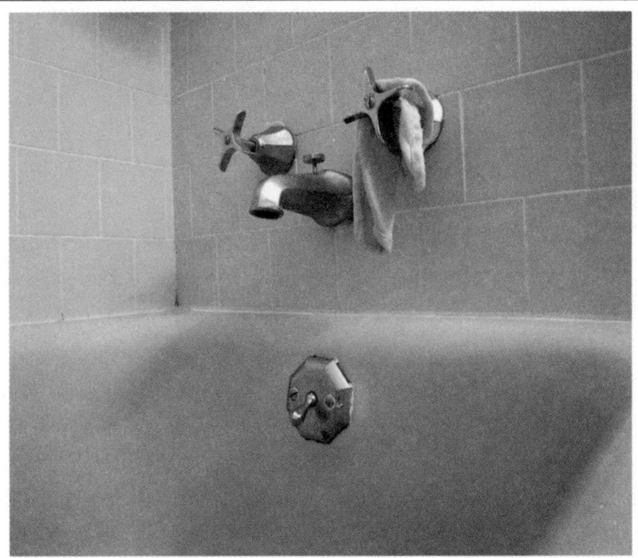

- Porc-a-Fix, available from some online suppliers, is pre-mixed in multiple shades, including older colours no longer available, to match coloured bathroom suites.
- Pre-mix assures proper adhesion and longer-lasting repair.
- Colour matching means the repair is less likely to stand out, but there will still be some difference in its appearance.
- Prepare the damaged area according to product instructions and apply, observing all drying times.

Chipped and Worn Taps

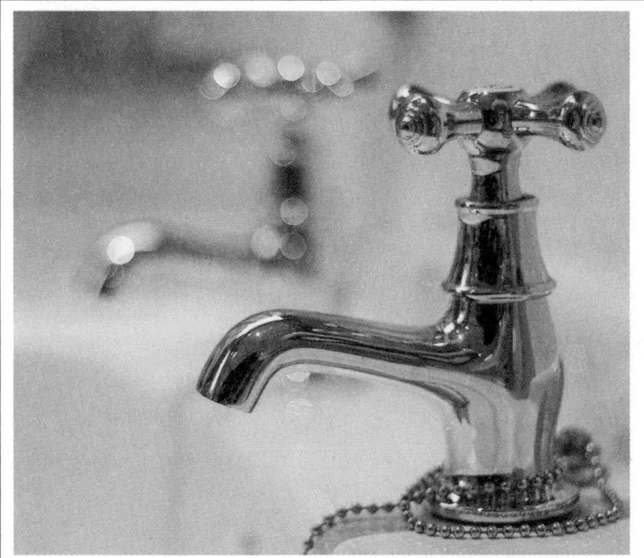

- There are expensive vintage replacements for worn bathroom taps, but you can do passable repairs with some solder, a metal alloy that, when melted, joins other metals together.
- Clean the corroded area with some fine sandpaper and wipe away the dust.
- Using a soldering iron and soldering wire (solder in wire form), gradually fill the area with a small amount of melted solder, allowing it to level out.
- When the area is full, polish the solder down with 000-grade steel wool.

TAPS

Stop taps dripping and save both water and your sanity with these simple steps

Dripping water – slow, random dripping water – shows up in movies from time to time as a way of driving one of the characters crazy. And it also drives homeowners crazy. Stay sane by stopping these drips quickly and easily.

Without taps, water would shoot through the open ends of pipes. A tap allows you to control how much water comes out at any given time. Inside the tap is a rubber or plastic washer or its equivalent. This washer compresses when the tap handle is in the off position and eventually it becomes worn and needs replacement. It lets you know by allowing a small amount of water to drip through the tap even though it's shut off.

Dismantling a Mixer Tap

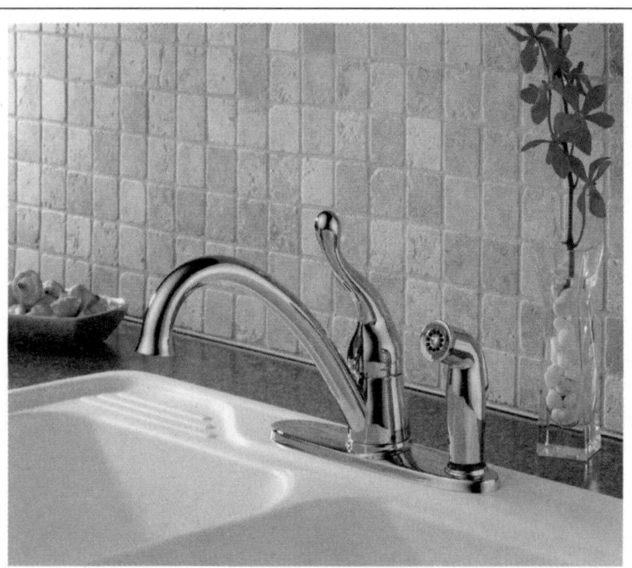

- Mixer taps are common in modern kitchens; each manufacturer uses a different cartridge or adjuster.
- Before replacing either a cartridge or ball assembly (don't bother with individual parts, just buy the whole assembly), shut the water off using the stopcock under the sink.
- Push the handle back and with an Allen key remove the hex screw that secures the handle.
- Remove the handle and spout.

Removing Washers

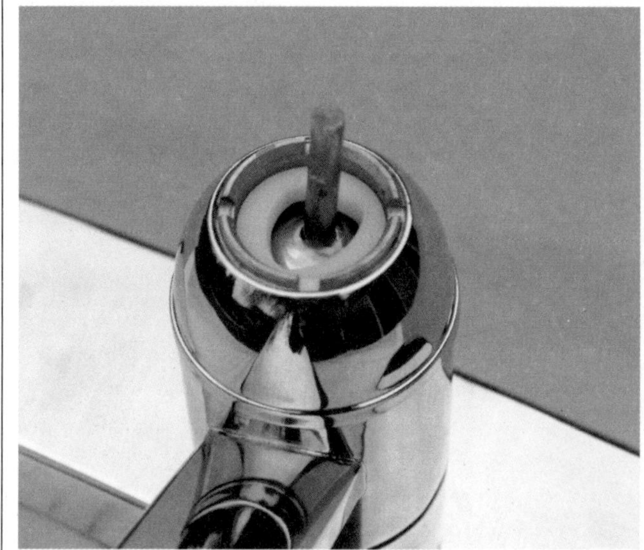

- With the handle and spout removed, the parts controlling the water mix will be visible.
- Each brand of tap is different; some will lift out while others require screws or retainer clips to be removed.
- Since there isn't one type of mixer tap, an online search by brand will show specific installation instructions.
- Take the part(s) to a hardware store or plumber's merchant for the correct replacement.

Replacing a washer isn't especially complicated, but knowing which washer or tap repair kit to get can be. No two are the same, and not every supplier carries the one you need. A phone call ahead of time with the tap brand can save you a trip. In the meantime, if the drip is really bad, shut the water off under the sink using the stopcock.

MAKE IT EASY

Stopcocks are installed at every toilet and sink or basin in a modern home for convenience and safety. They allow you to shut water off for repairs and in the event of a leak without shutting all the water off in the house. If you don't have them, consider having a plumber install them.

Reinstalling the Tap

- Wipe the tap body clean and dry before installing the new parts.
- Insert the new parts according to their installation instructions – the packet normally includes a special key if it is needed for the installation.
- It's easy to overtighten plumbing parts and cause new leaks, so carefully hand-tighten any parts requiring tightening.
- Replace the spout and tighten the hex screw that secures it to the tap, turn the water back on and check for leaks.

Fixing the Sprayer

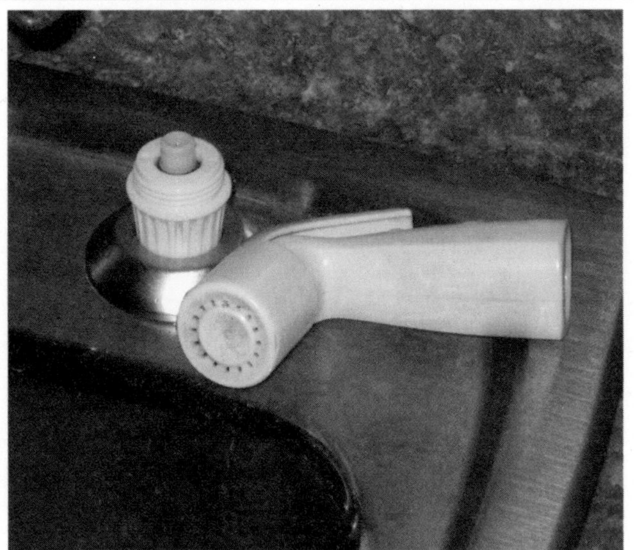

- For a broken sprayer head, shut the water off, unscrew the head, and install a universal replacement head.
- To replace the entire unit, shut the water off, unscrew the hose from the base of the tap, drain the hose into a small bucket, unscrew the mounting nut that secures the sprayer to the sink, and pull the hose out.
- Install the new sprayer according to the manufacturer's instructions.

TOILETS

A leaking toilet can stem from several problems and should be addressed quickly

A leaking toilet isn't fun. Floors can rot from ongoing leaks where the toilet sits on the floor. Water looks for the path of least resistance, and if that's a loose rubber seal, a worn seal or a valve in need of adjustment, that's where it will leak.

Some leaks aren't leaks at all. In very humid climates, a toilet cistern can 'sweat' due to condensation on the cold exterior, dripping water on to the floor. If the dripping is excessive, though, it's more likely to be an actual leak. Insulation kits for the inside of the cistern and special jackets for the outside should resolve the problem of condensation. Easier yet, place some plants on the floor under the cistern and let them benefit from the dripping.

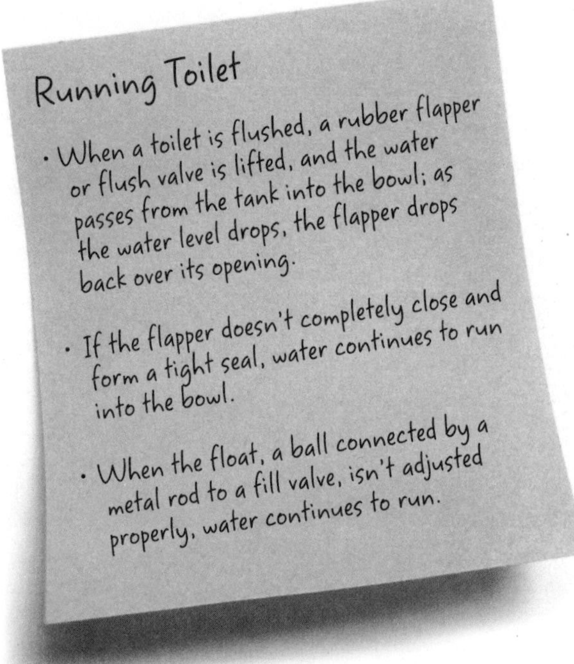

Running Toilet
• When a toilet is flushed, a rubber flapper or flush valve is lifted, and the water passes from the tank into the bowl; as the water level drops, the flapper drops back over its opening.
• If the flapper doesn't completely close and form a tight seal, water continues to run into the bowl.
• When the float, a ball connected by a metal rod to a fill valve, isn't adjusted properly, water continues to run.

Toilet Leaks

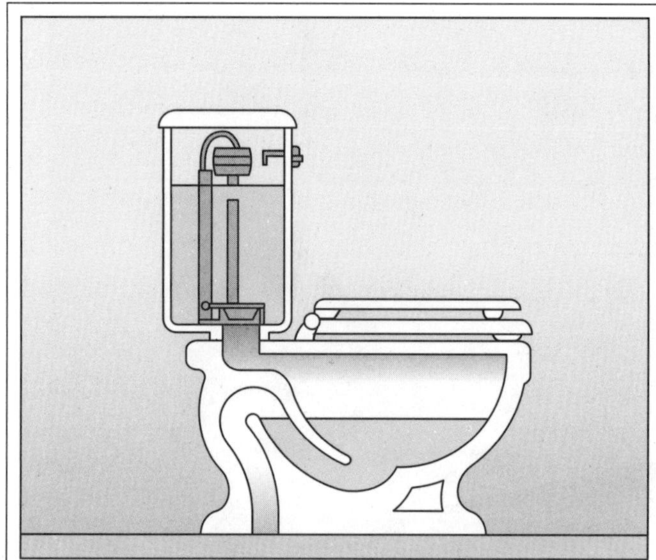

- The most visible toilet leak is at the base of the bowl on the floor and should be addressed immediately before the flooring is damaged.
- A leak between the cistern and the bowl indicates a leak in the seal between these two components or at the bolts that connect the cistern to the bowl.
- Continuously flowing water is due to a bad flapper valve.
- If water drips under the inlet valve supplying water to the toilet, it needs to be tightened or replaced.

Leaks from inside the cistern or the cold water supply line can be addressed by shutting off the water to the toilet, draining the cistern, and repairing the specific components. Leaks at the base of the toilet call for removing the toilet and examining the floor for soft or even rotted wood, which would need to be repaired before reinstalling. With close examination, you can determine the problem and the solution.

YELLOW LIGHT

Never stand on a toilet to get at something overhead. Use a small stepladder or utility stool. Toilets are made of vitreous china and are bolted to the floor as tightly as china can safely be secured. Standing on a toilet is inherently unstable and can jar it loose and cause a leak.

The Float

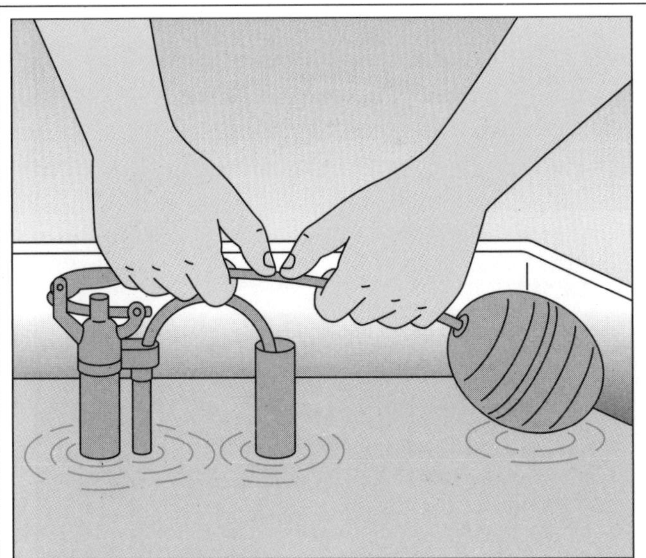

- The float falls towards the bottom of the cistern after each flush.
- As the cistern refills, the float rises and should stop when the tank is full again.
- If the water continues to run, pull up on the float until the water stops and then adjust the float to this level using the adjusting screw(s) at the top of the valve.
- Modern-style floats don't use a metal arm, but rather travel up and down the fill valve.

The Flush Valve

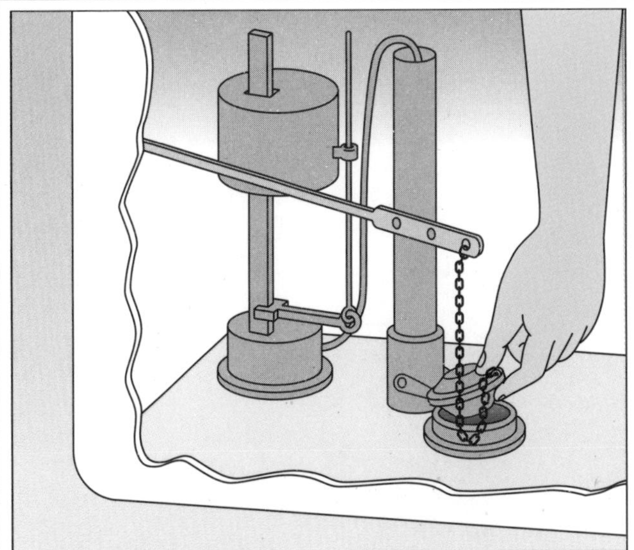

- Check that the flapper chain isn't jammed or the wrong length and caught under the flapper or not allowing it to close completely.
- To replace, shut off the water to the toilet, flush, remove the flapper, and take it to a hardware store for the correct replacement.
- Flappers do not require tools for removal or installation; they just slip over the overflow pipe or are attached with plastic hooks.
- Refill the cistern, test the flapper, and adjust as needed.

WASHING MACHINES

Repair washing machine leaks early to avoid big and expensive messes later

We don't give washing machines a lot of thought, but they can be a source of major leaks. Generally, they're dependable and keep running for years, but a washing machine can leak when one of the water supply hoses is damaged or when the machine itself is running. The latter isn't as critical since the amount of water leaked is often somewhat limited. When a hose leaks, though, especially if it bursts, it's a very big deal. Up to 2,000 litres of water an hour can pass through a burst washing machine hose.

Leaks while the washing machine is running can result from too much soap, which causes an overflow of suds. A bad drum seal or basket gasket will allow water to leak out as

Shutting Off the Water

- Washing machine inlet valves are available in various styles, such as a those you would have outside your house for a garden hose.
- Some older valves that haven't been turned in years can be stiff and difficult to move.
- Newer homes may have valves fitted in the wall behind the washing machine for convenience and a finished appearance.
- Various automatic valves are available, which electronically sense water leakage – especially important if a hose bursts – and shut the water down to minimize damage.

Washing Machine Hoses

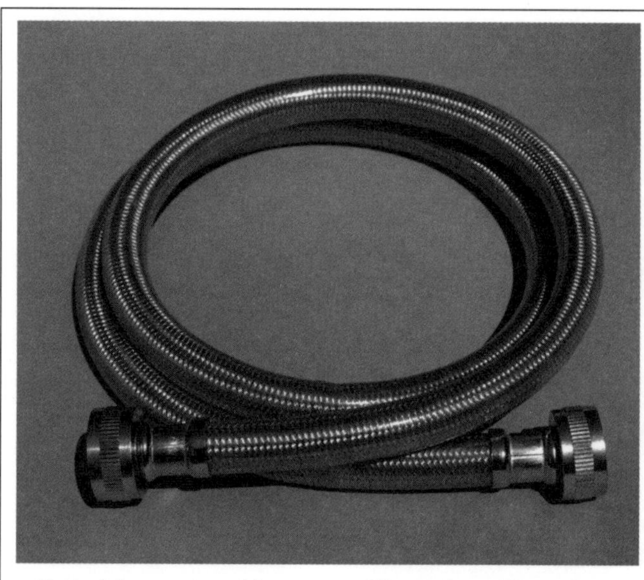

- Typical, low-cost washing-machine hoses are made from unreinforced rubber, although tougher reinforced rubber is available.
- Stainless steel braided hoses are burst-resistant, but no hose is burst-proof; insurance companies recommend replacing any hose every three to five years.
- Allow at least 10 cm of space between the back of the washing machine and the tap connection to avoid kinking the hose (hoses with right-angle connectors are available if this space is tight).
- Any leaking hose should be immediately replaced.

well. A machine might also leak slightly during one cycle of laundry and then not again. If the leak is minor, wash another load to compare and look for additional leaks. Continuing small leaks should be repaired before they become big leaks. However, if the machine is old and has seen better days, it might be better to buy a new one altogether.

MAKE IT EASY

To avoid damage from leaks, run washing machines (and dishwashers) only when you're home and can shut the water off if needed. Going on holiday? Turn the water off at the inlet valves or even at the main stopcock if the house is going to be empty, particularly during cold weather.

Installing New Hoses

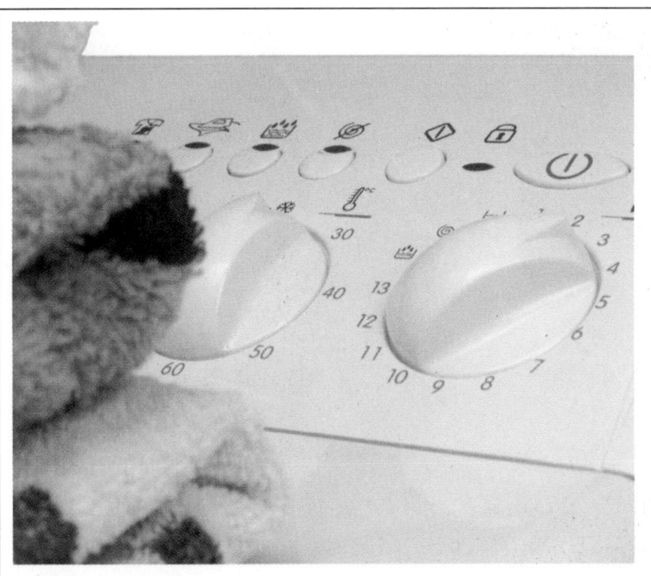

- With the water shut off, turn on the washing machine to expel any remaining water in the hoses.
- Place a bucket on the floor and loosen the old hoses with a vice grip or slip-joint pliers while holding on to the tap.
- Drain any remaining water in the hoses into the bucket.
- Install the new hoses by twisting the brass connectors, not the hoses themselves; turn the water on, and check for leaks.

Do You Repair or Replace the Machine?

- Some washing machine problems are easily avoidable, by making sure the machine is level and not overloading it.
- When a machine suddenly stops, check the power supply first.
- There can be numerous sources of problems: switches, a water pump, motor, bearings, hoses and electronics.
- You can buy a basic washing machine for under £200 – consider this when major repairs are needed on your machine.

UNBLOCKING SINKS & BASINS

Unblocking a clogged sink waste is usually easier than it looks

Why do sinks block? In the kitchen, any fat, oil or even soap can stick to the sides of pipes and accumulate over time, grabbing other gunk as it flows by. More often, it's too many food scraps, even when you have a waste disposal unit (not all units are created equal). The trap under the sink, a U-shaped section of the drain pipe designed to hold water so drains gas doesn't seep into the room, is an ideal place for food waste to accumulate if it isn't flushed out properly. Empty a sink full of hot water into the drains once a week to help prevent this build-up. Avoid washing food scraps and fat down the drain as well. Instead, pour any unwanted cooking fat into a bowl and leave it to solidify before throwing it away.

Keeping drains clear

- Unless a blockage is severe and has been accumulating for a long time, it will be inside the trap and easily removed.
- Chemical drain cleaners are available, but don't always work as effectively as a plunger and can be hazardous if used incorrectly.
- Kitchen drains are generally flushed out more than bathroom basins with high volumes of hot water from dishwashing, which helps keep them clear.
- Keeping fat out of kitchen drains goes a long way towards avoiding blockages.

Using a Plunger

- Add enough water to the sink to submerge the plunger cup and keep air out of it.
- Cover up the sink overflow with a towel; do the same to the other outlet in a double sink if only one drain is blocked.
- Sealing the overflow prevents the plunger from forcing water through it and losing its effectiveness.
- Push down on the plunger for 15 seconds or until the blockage is cleared. After running some water in the sink, plunge it again.

In bathrooms, it's soap and hair that combine as the number one clogging culprit. To solve the problem, a simple hair strainer in both the shower tray and the bath will reduce the chance of blocking the drains.

MAKE IT EASY

To keep drains clear, pour a couple of spoonfuls of bicarbonate of soda down them once a month, followed by a cup of white vinegar. The foaming action helps keep drains clean. Follow up by filling each sink with plain, very hot water and then emptying it down the drain.

To avoid mess, place a bucket under the trap to catch water as you remove it.

Removing the Trap

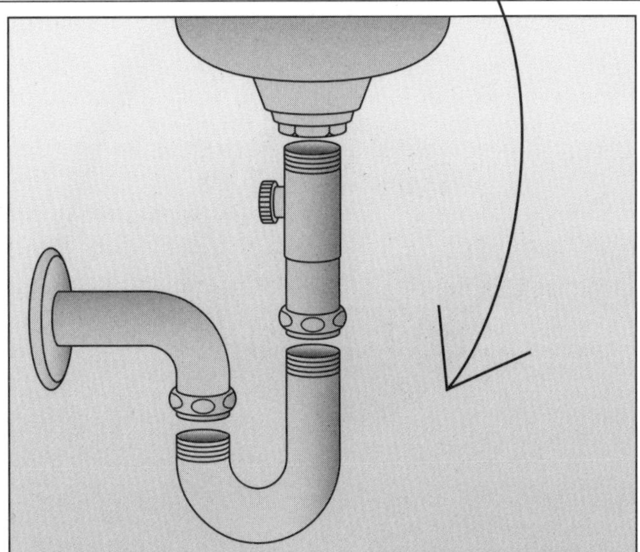

- Every sink has a trap, but there are several different styles and materials.
- Most new installations use PVC pipework, which can be disassembled without tools, while older chromed metal requires slip-joint pliers.
- Place a bucket under the trap to catch the water in it and undo the nuts that secure it to the wall pipe and the sink waste.
- Clean out the gunk, wash the trap in soap and water, reinstall, and run some water to test for leaks.

Using a Flexible Drain Cleaner

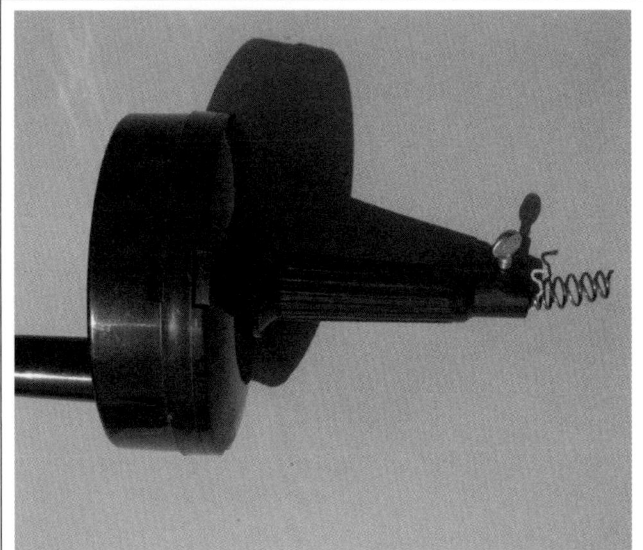

- Flexible drain cleaners, or augers, come in all sizes, from very small hand-operated models to motorized commercial models used for cleaning out sewers.
- Although you can auger down through the sink waste and round the U-bend, it's better to remove the trap first and auger beyond that if the trap isn't the problem.
- Slowly feed the coil into the pipe beyond the trap until you hit the blockage.
- Turn the crank to rotate the auger bit and break up the blockage.

UNBLOCKING TOILETS

Fix your blocked toilet problems, no matter what the source

We stop taking a toilet for granted when it blocks. We want to take care of it fast, get rid of the mess, and return to our daily routines, which, of course, include working toilets.

One source of a toilet blockage is obvious to all of us: too much bathroom tissue. Another is trying to flush away over-sized sanitary or personal items that should go in the bin. Items such as small bottles or tubes stored on top of the cistern, which sometimes drop into the toilet in mid-flush, are another terrific way to block it up.

Young children, alas, find toilets very intriguing. Potty training teaches them to flush, and they begin to wonder what else can disappear down this miniature watery vortex.

Fixing and Preventing Blocked Toilets

- Toilets are designed to move a certain volume of waste and water – anything beyond that and they can block.
- Tree roots penetrating the drainpipe running out to the sewer can also cause a toilet to back up.
- Never flush a blocked toilet expecting to clear the blockage – you'll only fill the bowl to the top or perhaps overflow it.
- As a precaution, shut the water off to the toilet.

Using a Plunger

- A heavier duty plunger with a cone-shaped section that unfolds from the cup is designed for toilets and better than a standard suction cup style.
- Place the plunger firmly at the bottom of the toilet and plunge vigorously 3–4 times without pulling the cup away from the toilet.
- After the last push, pull the plunger away to allow suction to help break up the blockage.
- Repeat if necessary and once the blockage is cleared, flush the toilet again.

In goes a stuffed animal, which indeed disappears, but it doesn't get very far. What you thought was a plunger job may now require the drain to be cleared using a flexible toilet auger. Even if your kids caused the problem unintentionally, having them help to fix it can be a valuable lesson for them.

MAKE IT EASY

Leave a plunger in every bathroom. It makes it more convenient when needed and less embarrassing for people who discover they need it, especially a guest who hardly wants to request a plunger from a host to unblock a toilet after using it. Decorative holders are available for storing plungers.

Using a Toilet Auger

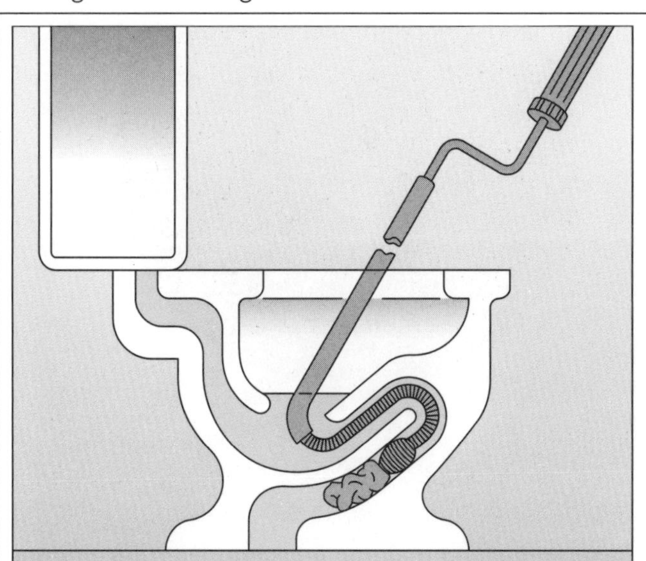

- When plunging doesn't clear the blockage, try a drain or toilet auger.
- A toilet auger has a fixed length of coiled steel attached to a curved, rigid pipe for accessing the inside of a toilet trap.
- Once the coiled end is fed inside the toilet, turn the handle on the other end and move the auger until it hits the blockage.
- Draw the auger back to pull the material into the bowl instead of pushing it farther into the drain.

Extreme Blockages

- When augering the toilet fails to clear a local blockage, the toilet will have to be removed. You might want to call a plumber.
- Use an auger large enough to clear the drain effectively – try a tool hire company.
- If you believe you've cleared the blockage, carefully pour some water down the drain and when you're satisfied it's getting through, reinstall the toilet.
- Flush the toilet to test the drain.

BATH & SHOWER WASTES

A little prevention against build-up keeps drains free flowing longer

The waste pipes from showers and baths often get clogged up. Each of us loses up to 100 hairs a day, and some of them are bound to end up in the bath or shower waste. Combined with soap and shampoo suds, this can add up to an eventual blockage. How will you know? The bath will drain progressively more slowly, even when you are showering. You'll find yourself standing in 5 cm of water that shouldn't be there.

Sometimes all it takes to clean out a shower drain is to remove the cover from the waste pipe and pull out the matted hair that's slowing the water. Other times, for more stubborn clogs, it takes a plunger or a plumber's auger, both of

Keeping Waste Pipes Clear

- Keeping hair out of a bath's waste pipe is easier than cleaning it out later.
- A simple plastic or metal strainer fitted over the waste opening is great preventative maintenance at almost no cost.
- Pour a kettle of boiling water down waste pipes once a week to help keep them clear.
- As soon as water starts to drain slowly, you have a blockage and should attend to it before it gets even messier to clean out.

Plunging a Shower Waste Pipe

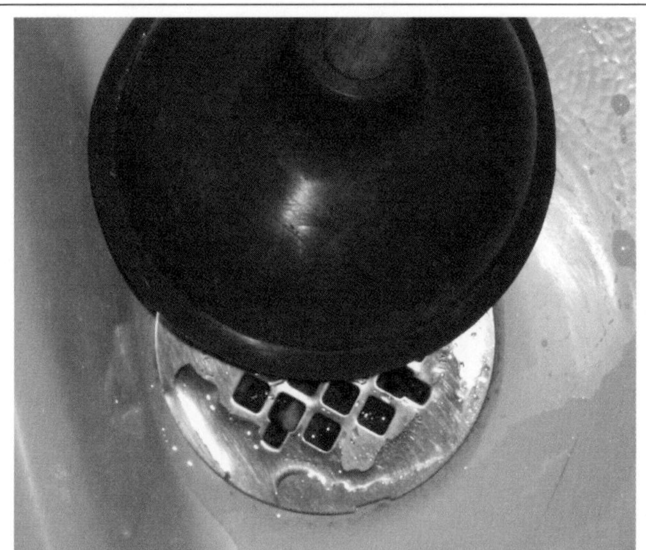

- Shower drains are easier to access than bath drains; to clean a shower drain, simply lift off the metal cover over the waste pipe and pull out any hair with a stiff, bent wire or metal skewer.
- Cover the open drain with a plunger and push and pull a few times to force any remaining obstructions down the waste pipe.
- For stubborn blockages, use a small plumber's auger to remove them.
- When finished, pour boiling water down the drain.

which are relatively easy to use. Bath wastes are a little more involved. There is some disassembly required, some cleaning, plunging, and perhaps some augering. A little prevention goes a long way to avoiding this messy job in future.

GREEN LIGHT

It is a good idea to make a habit of cleaning out any shed hair every time you take a shower or bath.

Use sharp-nosed pliers to clean out an obstruction in a bath waste.

Cleaning Out a Bath Waste Pipe

- Bath wastes that take a conventional plug have covers that screw directly to the drain pipe.
- To remove, turn the cover counterclockwise until it's loose and pull it from the drain.
- Clean out all obstructions – sharp-nosed pliers are useful for this job – and clean the drain opening and cover with disinfectant cleaner before reinstalling.
- Use a plunger or auger for stubborn blockages and pour boiling water down the drain.

Pop-up Wastes

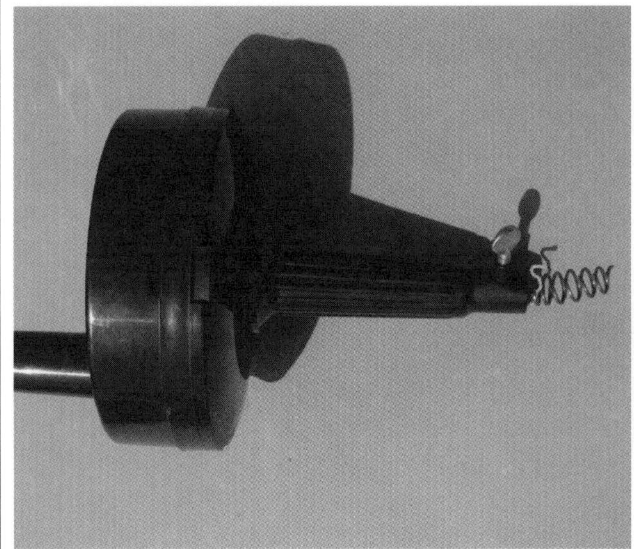

- Pop-up wastes can be trickier to disassemble and clean.
- A lever is connected to a lifting rod, which moves a plunger or drain cover that opens and closes the drain.
- Loosen the screws on either side of the lever and pull the mechanism up and out.
- Remove the waste pipe cover or stopper, depending on which type you have, and clean the drain out.

ROOFS

Fixes for patching a leaking roof and knowing when to call in a professional

Roofs leak at the most inconvenient times, such as when there's a storm raging outside, when we would prefer the rain also stay outside. Diligence and yearly inspections will head off some leaks but not all. Check for ageing roof tiles and deteriorating flashing, which, when combined with bad weather, can cause leaks. On older roofs there may be tell-tale signs, such as areas coated with black roofing tar, that may indicate previously patched leaks. Patched areas are more vulnerable to future leaks.

One problem is finding the actual source of a leak. Water leaking through a roof then follows the easiest pathway along rafters and down walls, which can be some distance

Leaks in the Loft

- An unfinished loft gives you a better chance of finding the source of a roof leak before it does any damage: in a converted loft you won't have access to the underside of the roof.
- When it's raining, find the drip and follow it back to the roof.
- If it's a direct overhead drip, consider yourself fortunate; your job is easier.
- When the water runs along rafters and supports, follow it carefully with a torch, checking that you've found the right spot.

Using a Nail as a Marker

- Once you're sure you've found the source of the leak, you may be able to drive a long nail up through the roof from inside.
- Note approximately where the leak is located so you'll know where to find it on the outside of the roof.
- The nail won't make the leak any worse but allows you to locate it when you're outside.
- On the roof, pound the nail back in then replace any missing tiles or worn roofing materials.

from the leak's point of origin. Even experienced roofers can be puzzled at the precise source of a leak. This is one reason why some of those patches have been applied more than once and the leak still hasn't stopped – even if the patch appears to be in the right place. Until the leak can be identified and sealed, a bucket in the loft will be your best stop-gap measure.

YELLOW LIGHT

Wear nonslip shoes and take your time when walking on your roof. Secure your ladder by pounding stakes in front of its feet if the ladder is on soft ground or by tying off the bottom rung to a secure point on the house if the ladder is on concrete.

Containing the Water

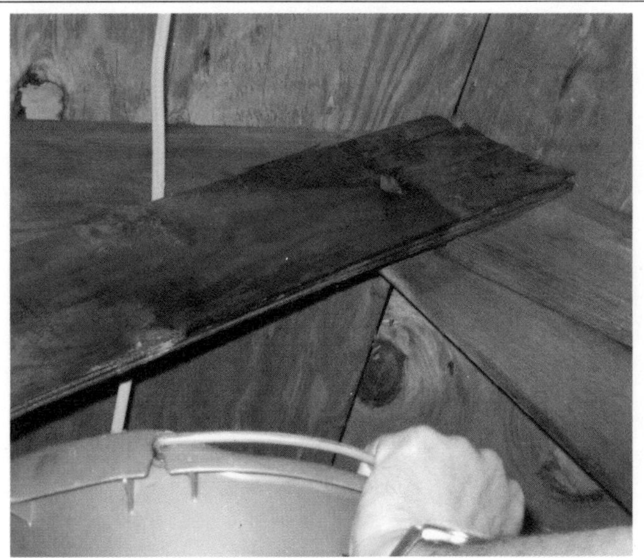

- Place a bucket under the leak and observe how fast it fills up.
- Chances are, the leak will be slow and can even be ignored for the moment as long as it isn't soaking insulation or dripping near wiring.
- If the bucket fills slowly, the water will evaporate during dry days.
- After the leak is repaired, keep the bucket in place for a season and check it for water after rainy days, especially rainy days of high wind.

Temporary Repairs

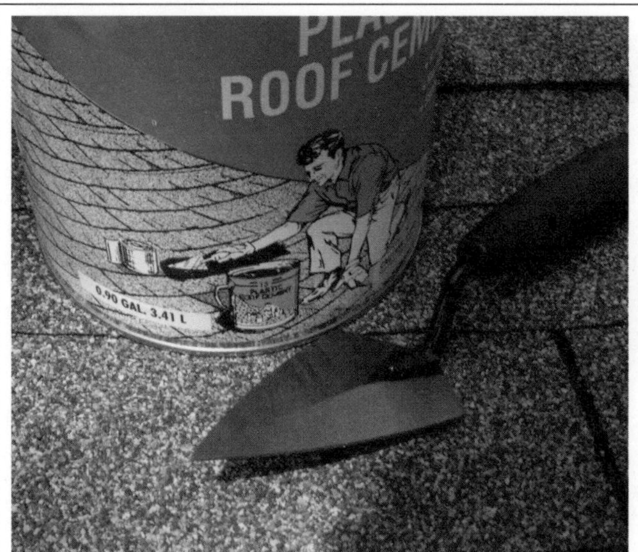

- Roofing sealants can be a quick fix for leaky roofs but don't offer a permanent repair.
- Many leaks occur around the metal flashing that acts as a transition from roof tiles to chimneys, walls, dormers and other protrusions through the roof.
- Use sections of flashing to patch holes in the existing flashing or to replace missing tiles when no spares are available.
- Slide a flashing patch up and under the tile(s) above its installation point.

GUTTERS & DOWNPIPES

Stop leaking gutters and avoid bigger problems like wet foundations later

All houses have rain gutters. Their main purpose is to funnel and direct rain running off the roof away from the overhanging sections of the roof, and keep it clear of the walls and the foundations of the building. Most gutter systems empty into storm drains through the downpipes at several points around the building.

Gutters were once made from wood lined with lead; from the late 18th-century cast iron was substituted. Metal gutters still remain on older homes, and maintaining and replacing them can be expensive. Modern guttering systems are mostly of extruded aluminium or uPVC. Each material has its advantages and drawbacks, and all types, with maintenance

Gutter Leak

- When gutters are installed with the proper slope to avoid standing water, they have a better chance of avoiding holes and leaks.
- Cast iron gutters require regular painting to prevent rust, but are long-lasting if well maintained.
- Water also accumulates when gutters are not cleaned out regularly.
- Wherever two gutter sections are joined or a downpipe is installed there's a potential for leaks.

Gutter Seams

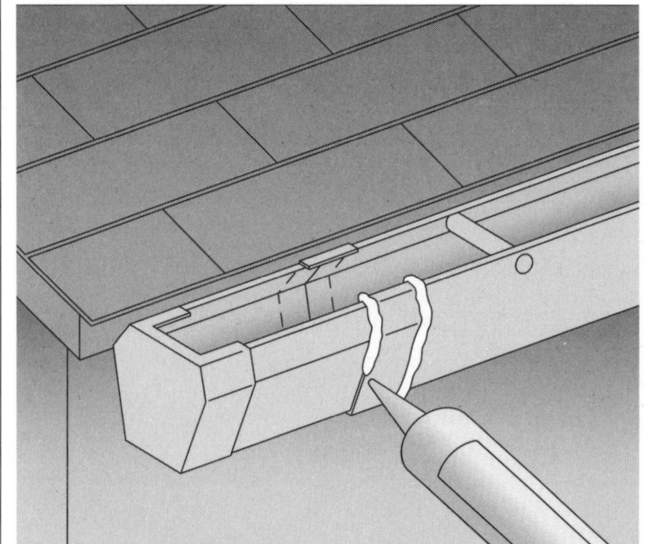

- Aluminium gutters are sized and cut to fit, but individual sections are joined at corners, forming seams.
- The seams are sealed with gutter and flashing sealant, which is specially formulated for this application although silicone sealant will work if necessary.
- Some leaks show up in wind-driven rain only, and the resulting damage takes years to show up.
- Reapplying a generous amount of sealant to any suspect seam should stop any leaks.

and care, will give long-lasting service. Leaking gutters, like any source of leaks, should be repaired before they cause greater damage elsewhere. Water goes looking for trouble whenever it gets the opportunity. Plug the hole, seal the gap, and keep water flowing where you want it to.

ZOOM

Roof-mounted rainwater collection systems and troughs have existed for thousands of years. The dissolution of the monasteries in 1539 made large quantities of recycled lead available for elaborate gutter installations. Colonial-era gutters in America were initially made from wood and later lead and eventually other metals, including copper and tinplate.

Epoxy Repair

- Repair a leaking wood gutter with waterproof epoxy. Clean out the rotted material from the dry gutter, brush it with a wood preservative, and when that cures, fill it with the epoxy according to the manufacturer's instructions.
- Repair rust spots in a metal gutter with a wire brush, spray it with rust preventative paint, use an automotive fibreglass kit with mesh screen to repair, and spray paint the patch.
- Any patch should be monitored and considered impermanent.

Testing with Water

- Once your repair has cured, fill the gutter with water and check for additional leaks.
- If the water is not draining properly towards the downpipe, the slope of the gutter needs adjustment.
- Check the gutter hangers for tight fasteners and bends from supporting too much weight.
- Adjusting the hangers, bending them, or even adding to them can readjust the slope so the water drains correctly.

WINDOWS

Seal window leaks before they seep into walls and cause more damage

Old windows can go for decades and never leak. New windows can leak during the first severe storm. How come? It has to do with the installation and the flashing. A properly installed window with the correct flashing and sealing should stay leak free indefinitely. A bad design or construction detail can cause even the most expensive window to leak. The leak most often occurs where it's attached to the wall or when water gets behind the flashing and then behind the window. Improperly flashed windows are a regular cause of water infiltration in homes.

Old windows can leak at the glass when the glazing compound or putty deteriorates and falls off, which generally

Windows

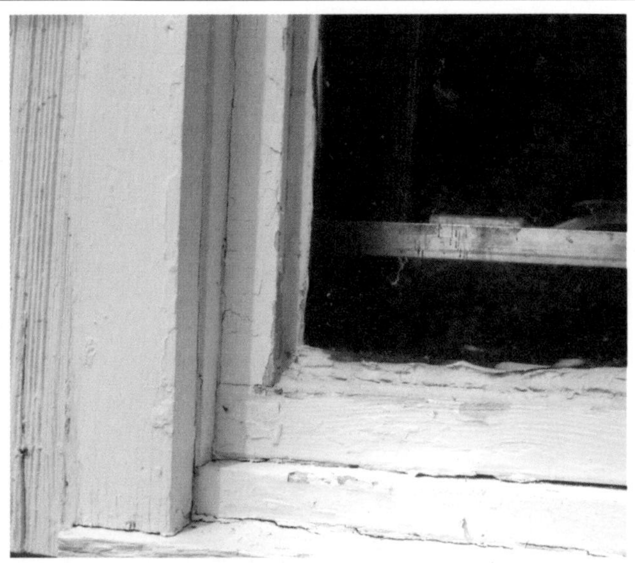

- Windows leak at the glass, the glass seals and the flashing.
- Older wood windows can leak where the glass butts up against the wood frame if the exterior putty is missing or badly cracked.
- Sealant should not be used to take the place of proper flashing but can supplement it.
- Rare leaks from unusually hard driven rain should be monitored but are probably unimportant.

Cover Window with Plastic

- Whenever a window leak is elusive, or if excess water comes in, cover the outside of the window with plastic to prevent further damage.
- If water still comes in, the leak could be coming from higher up in the wall and dripping down through the window.
- Wood windows are particularly susceptible to water damage, which can lead to rot.
- Tack the plastic up using wood strips and small nails or exterior-grade duct tape.

happens if the putty goes unpainted and unsealed. They can also leak during periods of wind-driven rain blowing in from the windowsill. Regardless of whether they are old or new, the main problem with leaking windows is water seeping into the walls and causing damage. Although it sounds like a broken record by now, seal those leaks before they cause you bigger headaches.

Interior Moisture on Single-Pane Windows

- Older wood and metal windows are single pane, compared with new double- or triple-glazed windows with two or three panes sandwiched together.
- In cold winter climates, interior moisture condenses on these panes and can give the appearance of leaks.
- Excess condensation will corrode steel windows and deteriorate wood windows, so check them routinely.

MAKE IT EASY

Not sure where a window is leaking? Wait until the weather clears and then examine it thoroughly on the outside for cracks, loose putty or flashing. It's important you stop the damage before continued exposure to the weather makes it worse.

Sealants

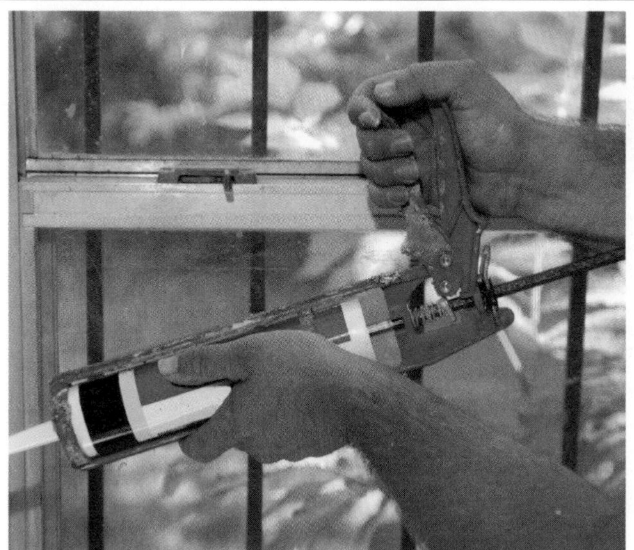

- Sealant is used to prevent water from washing through seams in the exterior window surround or where the surround and sill meet the wall of the house.
- It isn't a miracle cure, and overly thick applications can fail.
- Old, worn sealant can be removed with a utility knife before being replaced.
- Be sure to apply sealant during dry conditions only.

CLEARING GUTTERS

Tackle this problem to avoid damage to house paint and walls

Gutters are intended to collect water running off your roof, but they also catch leaves, twigs and tennis balls tossed on the roof. Some of this debris will wash down (and possibly clog the downpipe), but once enough of it accumulates, it will slow down the flow of water to the point that the gutter starts to overflow. An overflowing gutter means trouble because sheets of water flowing down the house walls can cause them to deteriorate and eventually lead to damp inside your house.

There are plenty of gutter cover designs that claim you'll never have to clean your gutters again. Some do a decent job of keeping large leaves and twigs out but not smaller

Clogged Gutter

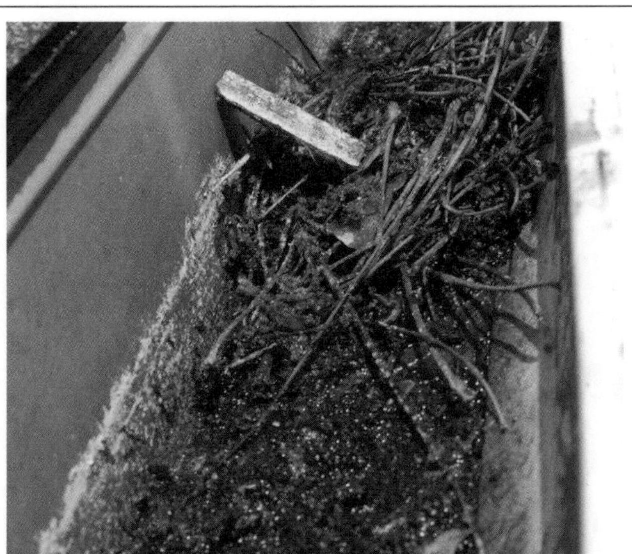

- Gutters get clogged with anything that can fall from a tree or blow up on a roof.
- As clutter accumulates, it holds water, which adds to the gutters' weight.
- Heavier gutters can pull away from their fixings, both loosening them and affecting their slope, adding to the drainage problem caused by the debris.
- There is no recommended number of cleanings throughout the year, but do a minimum routine cleaning in spring and autumn.

A Note on Safety

- To clean gutters, you need a ladder, and that requires precautions and personal comfort with heights.
- Be sure that your ladder is level and straight and that you don't overreach instead of moving the ladder closer to the area you need to clean.
- Wear rubber gloves when cleaning out gutters.
- To avoid too much mess on the ground, carry a bucket with you to collect the debris as you scoop it out.

seeds, pods and dirt. There will probably never be a gutter that doesn't need some cleaning, and unless a gutter cover is easy to remove, it might actually make gutter cleaning tougher to do.

Regular cleaning prevents clogging and provides an opportunity to do some roof inspection while scooping out dead vegetation. How often you clean gutters depends on how full they get. Seasonal checks will let you know.

YELLOW LIGHT

If you use an extension ladder, secure the legs to prevent slippage. A stepladder should be level and opened in a fully extended and locked position. You can't grab on to a gutter and depend on it to support you. Your ladder should be sturdy enough to allow you to do the job safely.

Gutter Scoop

- There are tools that purport to let you clean lower-level gutters from ground level, including tongs, water blast systems, and scrapers.
- Unfortunately, cleaning gutters requires you to see what you're doing up close, with a lot of hand scooping if the debris is wet.
- If the debris is dry, much of it can be removed with a blower.
- A plastic bottle can be cut into a scoop shape to make an inexpensive gutter-cleaning tool.

Hosing the Gutters

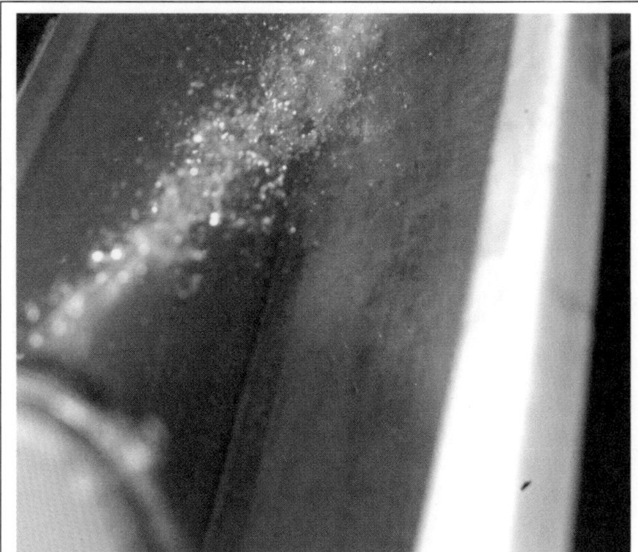

- Don't try to wash a large volume of gutter debris out with a garden hose, as it will push too much of it into the downpipe, where it can cause more blockages and fill the gutter with water.
- After scooping out the gutters, hose them down.
- To avoid clogging the downpipes while you are flushing the gutters, loosen and remove their bottom ends to keep any debris out of the drains.

UNBLOCKING DOWNPIPES

Clean out downpipes at the same time as your gutters to avoid water damage to the house

A blockage in a downpipe is not as easy to spot as debris in a gutter. The blockage could be at the top, in the elbow, or near the bottom of the downpipe. Sometimes a thorough hosing will clear it out, but at other times this just forces the clogged material further into the downpipe or drainage system.

Older downpipes are made of iron, and the elbows (the curved sections that often connect the gutters and the downpipes) can rust if they get too full of debris. The debris clogs the elbow, which causes water to build up here instead of passing through and allowing the elbow to dry out.

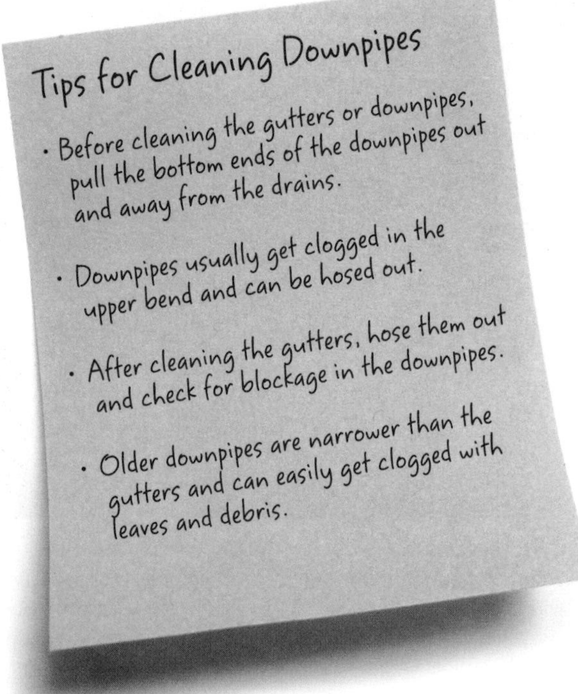

Tips for Cleaning Downpipes
· Before cleaning the gutters or downpipes, pull the bottom ends of the downpipes out and away from the drains.
· Downpipes usually get clogged in the upper bend and can be hosed out.
· After cleaning the gutters, hose them out and check for blockage in the downpipes.
· Older downpipes are narrower than the gutters and can easily get clogged with leaves and debris.

Hosing Out the Downpipe

- Pull out the clogged material from the bend with a piece of bent wire with a hook on the end before cleaning the bend with an auger.
- In metal downpipes the bend can be corroded inside by years of standing water, so be careful with the wire.
- Insert the hose nozzle at the top of the downpipe, wrapping a rag around it for a tight seal.
- Open the tap full force until the water shoots out at the bottom of the downpipe.

To fix this, you may have to dismantle the downpipe. Some downpipes are easier to loosen and remove than others should this be necessary to clean them out.

To prevent this mess, downpipe screens are available to keep leaves and large debris out. Be sure to routinely clean the area around the screens to avoid blockages at the top of the downpipe.

GREEN LIGHT

Keeping your gutters and downpipes clear will help prevent future problems. See the maintenance timeline at the end of the book for friendly reminders on when to do things throughout the year.

Augering the Downpipe

- If an auger is necessary, use a manual one and turn it slowly, pulling and pushing in and out until the blockage is broken up.
- Run the hose into the downpipe to check that it's clear.
- Run the hose into the drain as well to confirm it's clear.
- Reconnect the downpipe to the drain and check that it's secure at the gutter as well.

Preventing Downpipe Build-Up

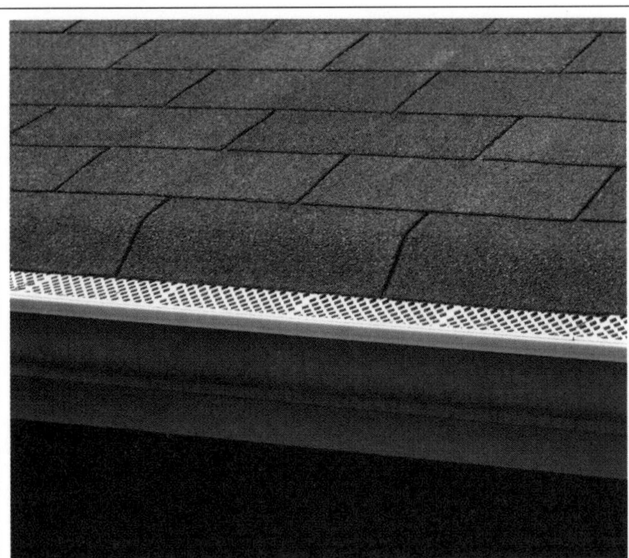

- Keep leaves and twigs out of downpipes by installing a leaf guard over the top of each one.
- Remove accumulated leaves before they cause water to back up.
- Avoid leaf guard systems and screens for entire gutters, as they often do not prevent smaller debris from accumulating in the gutters and can make cleaning difficult.
- If your downpipes empty on to splash blocks instead of into drains, add extensions to ensure that water empties away from the house foundation.

UNBLOCKING OUTSIDE DRAINS

Fixing outside drains prevents floods and allows them to do their job properly

Some outside drains are connected to local storm drains, and others empty into French drains on the property. A French drain, named after Henry French, is essentially a trench or pit filled with gravel or other small stones, constructed to absorb and re-route water. The top is usually covered with grass to hide it. The thickness of the pipe influences where it can be used and how susceptible it is to damage.

Older drains consist of sections of clay or concrete pipes butted together; they are often cracked or damaged by intrusive tree roots. In the event of a blockage, there is only a limited amount of cleaning you can do yourself, and some

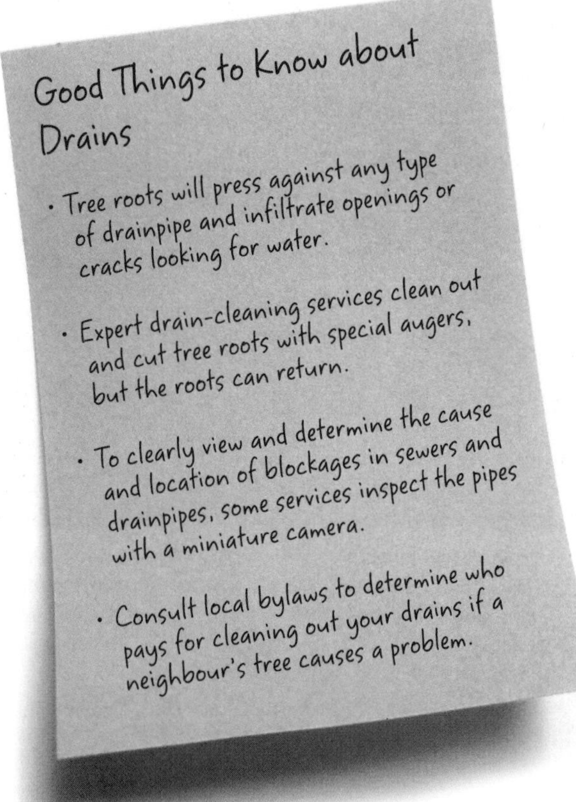

Good Things to Know about Drains

• Tree roots will press against any type of drainpipe and infiltrate openings or cracks looking for water.

• Expert drain-cleaning services clean out and cut tree roots with special augers, but the roots can return.

• To clearly view and determine the cause and location of blockages in sewers and drainpipes, some services inspect the pipes with a miniature camera.

• Consult local bylaws to determine who pays for cleaning out your drains if a neighbour's tree causes a problem.

Outside Drain

- Outside drains typically empty into local storm sewers.
- They remove excess rainwater and snow melt, preventing overly soggy garden areas that could lead to problem soil conditions.
- For gardens lacking drains but needing to control run-off or stop water accumulation, French drains – trenches full of gravel or perforated drainpipe – are an option.
- Adding drainage can affect a neighbour's property and may require permission from the local council.

drains need to be replaced altogether.

How do you know if a drain needs to be replaced? Drain cleaning companies and plumbers send special cameras down through the pipe to determine exactly what's causing the blockage. This is the only way, other than digging, that you'll know whether your drains are salvageable. A camera probe is much cheaper than replacement, so enlist the aid of a professional before you decide on replacement.

YELLOW LIGHT

Be careful using drain cleaners when cleaning out plastic drainpipes. The force of spinning blades can destroy perforated, thin-walled drainpipes, which can be cleaned by hand-driven augers or high-speed water jets. If you're unsure what your drainpipes are constructed from, use a conservative approach when cleaning them.

OUTSIDE LEAKS/CLOGS

Hosing Drainpipes

- Outside drains receive a lot of dirt and silt, which gradually accumulate in the drainpipe.
- Check your drains every few months and scoop out the dirt before it becomes a problem.
- After removing the dirt, run a hose down the drainpipe at full force to confirm there is no blockage.
- Keep drain covers clear of leaves and grass clippings whenever you're gardening.

Augering Drainpipes

- Drains on your property can get clogged and require cleaning to avoid overflowing.
- Only hard materials – rigid plastic, clay and concrete pipes – can withstand cleaning and clearing with a powered plumber's auger.
- Corrugated drainpipes (made of thin-walled plastic) are inexpensive but not built to withstand mechanical cleaning.
- Short of digging up corrugated pipes, run a hose in with a high-pressure nozzle to eliminate blockages.

FLOORS: WHAT TO TRY FIRST

Squeaky floors are annoying – here are the initial steps to eliminating them

Traditional wooden floors in older properties are composed of floorboards laid over joists and nailed in place. In newer buildings a subfloor of plywood or chipboard may be covered by carpet or a finished wood floor.

Over time, wooden floors can develop squeaks as nails loosen and boards shift. Changes in moisture levels add to the squeaking problem. During seasonal changes, unfinished wood can absorb and later lose moisture. As the wood expands and shrinks, the result is the squeaking noises you hear as you walk around.

You can take on some of the simple solutions below to eliminate or diminish squeaky floors, especially floors whose

Under the Floor

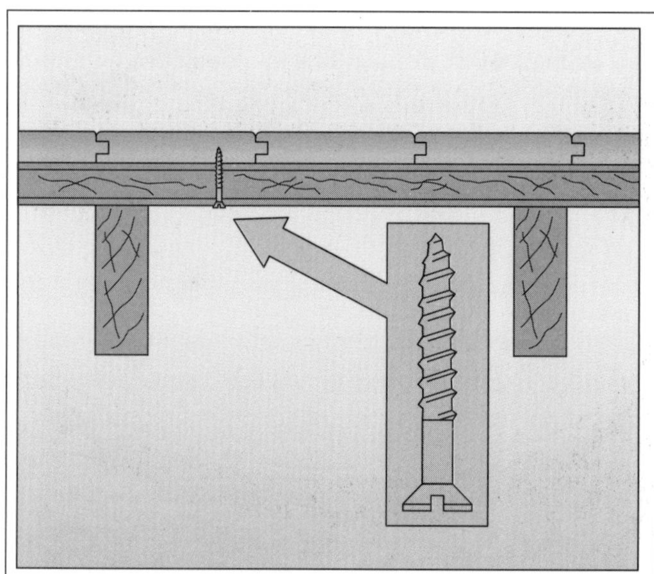

- If they are closely laid, floorboards can rub together, causing squeaks.
- Filling the joints between these boards with powdered graphite or talcum powder, or spraying with silicone, can temporarily stop squeaking.
- Longer-term solutions call for some combination of shims, cross supports, bracing or fasteners,.
- If space under the floor is accessible and you can get to the joists and subfloor, you can reinforce and 'beef up' the area around the squeak.

Installing a Shim

- While someone walks around the squeaky area, go below to the exposed joists until you locate the noise.
- Spread glue on a shim and hammer it between the joists and the subfloor until it's just tight.
- Have your helper walk around again to confirm that the squeak is gone or show that you need more shims.

underside – the joists and the subfloor – is exposed and accessible. It can take some time to locate and correct the problem, but it's better than listening to squeaking every time you walk across a room.

MAKE IT EASY

If your floor squeaks according to the season, consider sealing the exposed wood – with paint, varnish or any finish readily available – as part of your solution. Instead of buying specialized hardware, simple angle irons, which are more readily available, can be screwed into joists and subflooring to eliminate or reduce squeaks.

Adding Support

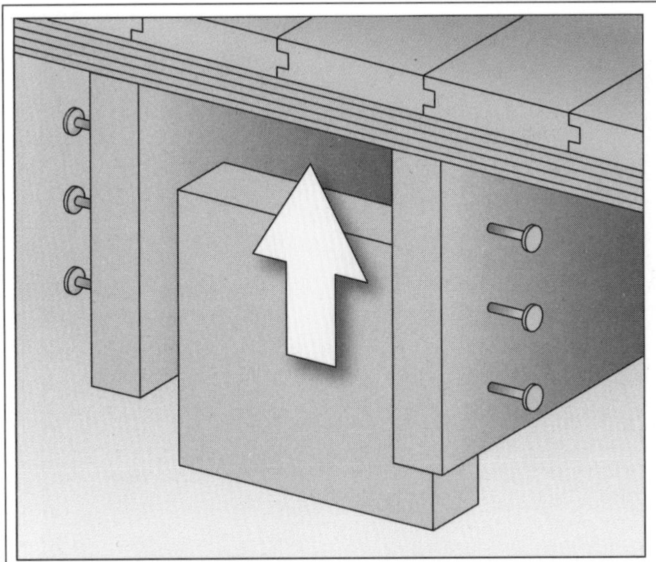

- For larger areas, screw and glue a block of timber into the joist and into the subfloor itself.
- Be sure your screws don't go all the way through the subfloor.
- Screw and glue a section of 20-mm plywood – wide enough to reach each joist – into any two adjoining sections of subflooring under a squeak.

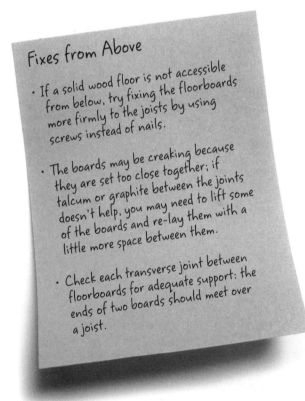

Fixes from Above

- If a solid wood floor is not accessible from below, try fixing the floorboards more firmly to the joists by using screws instead of nails.
- The boards may be creaking because they are set too close together; if talcum or graphite between the joints doesn't help, you may need to lift some of the boards and re-lay them with a little more space between them.
- Check each transverse joint between floorboards for adequate support: the ends of two boards should meet over a joist.

FLOORS: WHAT TO TRY NEXT

With no access underneath the floor, you need a different strategy to fix those squeaks

Squeaky ground-level floors with open basement ceilings are easy to get at and fix, but what do you do with a squeaky second or third floor? You need to approach the repair directly through the top of the floor itself, and this can be intimidating. These repairs are a minor challenge, and you may want to call in the help of an expert for this process. But with care and attention, you can do them without much trouble. The first and main hurdle is to locate the floor joists.

Like floors, stair treads can also squeak since they're used so heavily. The same repair issues and techniques apply. All of these repairs call for the least amount of intrusion, so

Finding the Joists

- The joists, the timbers supporting the floor, are regularly spaced and normally run in the direction of a building's narrowest dimension.
- Tap (or use a stud finder) on the ceiling below the joists until you hear a dull thud – this is a joist. Find another to establish the spacing.
- Starting at an outside wall, tap on the floor with the handle of a hammer to find a joist.
- Carpet over plywood or chipboard can be loosened and rolled back to find joists.

Drilling into a Wood Floor

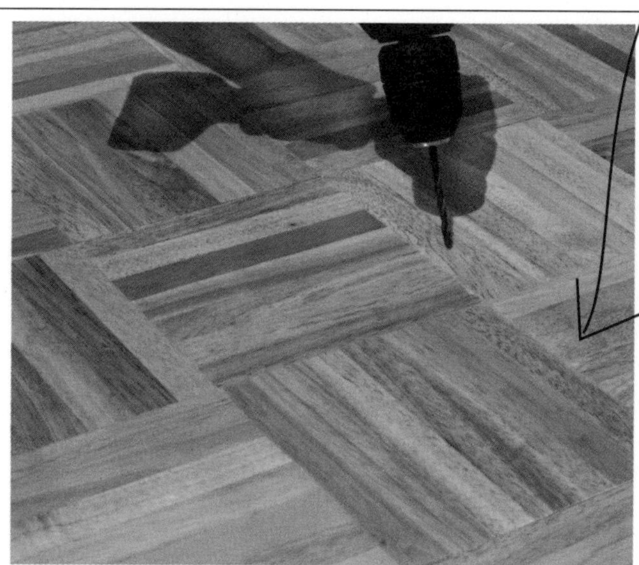

- Determine or make your best guess where the joist is located and follow it to an exterior wall.
- Near the skirting board, use a long, narrow drill bit to drill down through the subfloor and into the joist.
- It might take several test holes to find a joist.
- Once the joist is found, follow its course across the floor to the area of the squeak.

use only as many screws or nails as necessary to eliminate the squeak.

Have patience. It might take a few tries to find the joist.

Installing a Fastener

- Drill one pilot hole per nail or screw into the joist near the squeak.
- Nail in a long lost-head nail, and punch it below the level of the wood floor or carpet.
- Insert a 75mm screw using a drill and Phillips screw bit – if going through carpet, tape the screw threads to prevent them from grabbing and pulling at carpet threads.
- Drive the screw head until it's flush with the subflooring; fill in any holes in a wood floor with wood filler.

Stair Treads

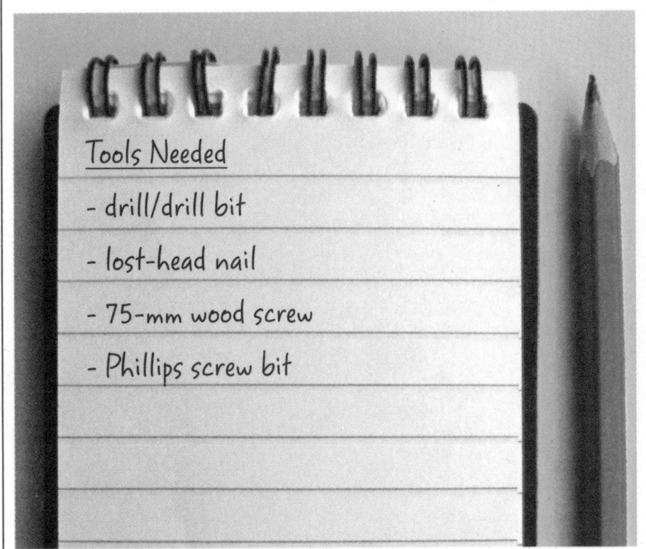

Tools Needed
- drill/drill bit
- lost-head nail
- 75-mm wood screw
- Phillips screw bit

- Stairs often squeak when the tread (the part you walk on) loosens and begins rubbing. The repairs depend on whether the underside of the stairs is exposed or not.
- From an exposed underside, glue and nail a strip of wood 30 cm long into the riser and the squeaky tread.
- From above, pre-drill a pilot hole through the nose of the tread into the riser below and secure with nails or screws.
- Nail the tread at an angle into the stringers for further tightening.

STICKING DOORS

A sticking door can pull paint off the jamb – fix it and avoid this

Doors can function for years and then start to stick. A slight shifting in the door frame is one possibility, as is the gradual absorption of just enough moisture for the door to expand and finally no longer fit the frame as it once did.

Any door can expand: the problem is not restricted to exterior doors. Once the door no longer fits and clears the jamb it will stick and bind. Some select and limited trimming of the sticking surfaces generally resolves the problem, but the key is to trim only as much wood as necessary and not to be too aggressive about it. If you remove too much, you will end up with a gap around the door that lets warm air out and cold draughts in in the winter.

Slightly Open Door

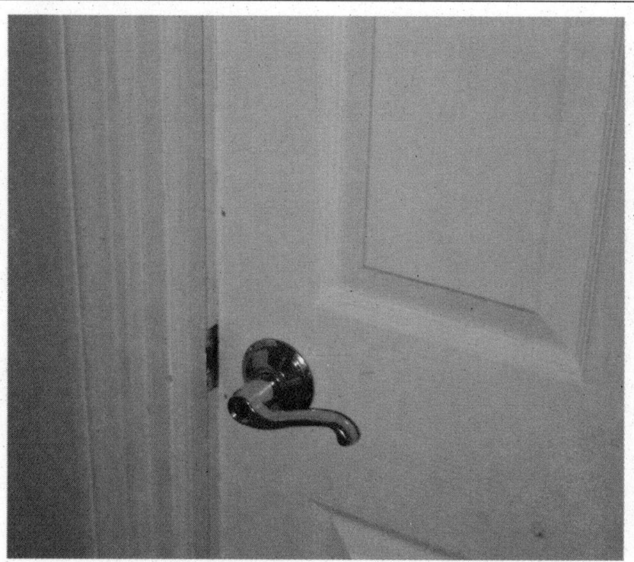

- First, examine the door and determine exactly where it's sticking.
- Unless all four edges of a door are sealed, the wood can absorb moisture, expand or warp and stick.
- Shifting in the door jamb or the adjacent wall can cause a door to rub, but this is very seldom the problem.
- Loose hinges or a loose catch can cause opening and closing problems, as can an excessive build-up of paint on the edges of the door and on the jamb.

A Quick Fix

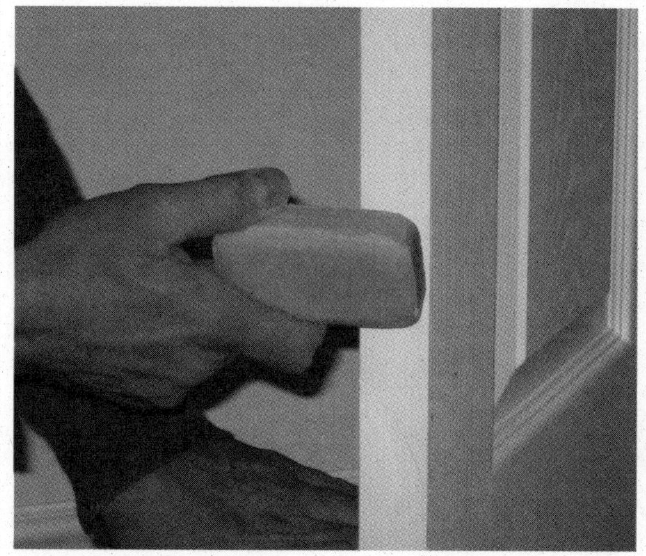

- Some sticking is seasonal, and a little paraffin or candle wax can get you by until the weather turns drier.
- Determine where the door is sticking, check that the hinges are tight and the catch isn't sticking, and rub the edge of the door with paraffin wax or soap.
- After testing the door, wipe off any excess soap or wax with a clean rag.

Doors typically have a gap of about 3 mm between their edges and the frame for clearance, ease of opening and closing, and to accommodate draught-proofing strips around exterior doors. Yours might not be this exact, but you don't want it to be any bigger as a result of your repair.

YELLOW LIGHT

If you intend to paint the door, remove all soap or wax from any painted areas before recoating. If after the removal the door sticks again, it will need to be trimmed or planed down a little before painting. Otherwise, it can pull the new paint off the jamb or door edge.

Trimming the Door

- Mark off the sticking area on the jamb with a pencil.
- Use a very sharp paint scraper to shave all the paint off until exposed wood is visible.
- If the door still sticks, trim off the corresponding area on the door edge and sand any scraped areas with 100- and 120-grit papers until smooth.
- If the top or bottom of a door needs trimming, keep the door in place and use coarse sandpaper instead of a scraper.

Priming and Painting the Door

- New finishes stand out against existing ones, so minimize the amount of recoating while still sealing exposed wood.
- Always paint exposed top and bottom edges of a door – these easily absorb moisture and expand.
- Tape off the interior and exterior areas near the edge so the new paint stays only on the edge.
- Do the same on the door frame.

STICKING WINDOWS

Learn some simple solutions for sticking windows, even new uPVC ones

Windows stick when tracks wear down, paint gums things up, and draught proofing gets slightly bent. Old wooden window frames are generally the stickiest, and they should be – they've been around longer, have been moved more often, and have been painted over and over again to the point that some barely move at all. All windows need some attention from time to time, however, regardless of the material they're constructed from or their age.

Wood casement windows open and close like doors, and sticking ones can be repaired in the same way as sticking doors (see previous pages). Metal sliding windows normally don't have paint problems as they typically remain unpainted,

uPVC Windows

- Open the window completely and thoroughly clean the track with fine steel wool and liquid car polish/wax.
- Wipe away any residue and test the window.
- Rub the track with additional wax or spray with silicone. Reapply the silicone spray once a month.
- Clean the tracks again as needed (about once a year), but avoid getting any cleaners or spray lubricants on the brush-style draught proofing often found with uPVC windows.

Wooden Sash Windows

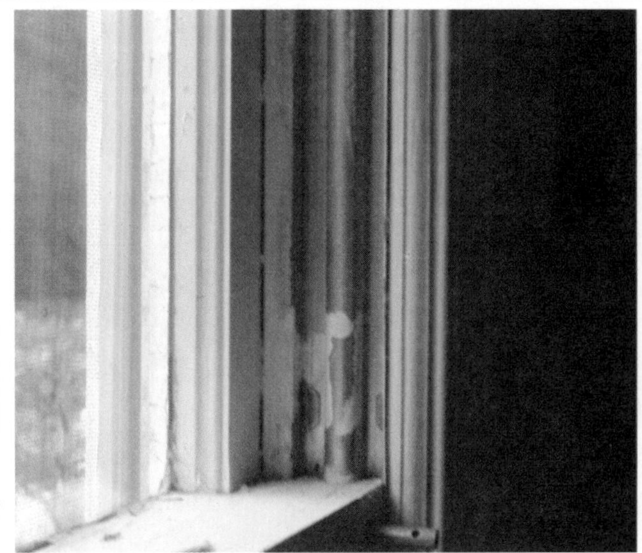

- Spray any area where the window sash moves with plenty of spray silicone or WD-40, moving the sash repeatedly until it slides smoothly.
- If the sash is especially stiff, take your time moving it – if movements are too abrupt, the sash cords can break.
- If excess paint is the problem, open the sash as far as possible, and scrape and sand any painted edge that the sash slides against.
- Touch up any scraped areas.

but metal-on-metal movement calls for lubrication that these windows can be sorely lacking. Like metal windows, sliding uPVC windows are also prone to sticking. This material, like wood, expands and contracts as the temperature changes – another factor in sticking.

Removing surface corrosion, dirt and grime goes a long way towards alleviating sticking windows. Stripping or sanding the paint off a window is another option for stopping sticky windows long-term. These are homeowner-friendly projects and don't require a professional contractor.

ZOOM

A severe build-up of paint on older wooden window frames can most effectively be removed by dismantlling the window completely, removing the sashes and stripping or sanding the paint off, then priming and repainting the frames. This is a more involved task but can be done by a homeowner.

Wood Casement Windows

- Determine where the window is sticking, mark it, and trim down that section of the jamb with a sharp paint scraper.
- If necessary, scrape down the edge of the window as well, but be careful around any integral draught proofing often found on newer casement windows.
- Test the window, and continue trimming if needed.
- Sand, prime, and paint all scraped areas.

Aluminium Windows

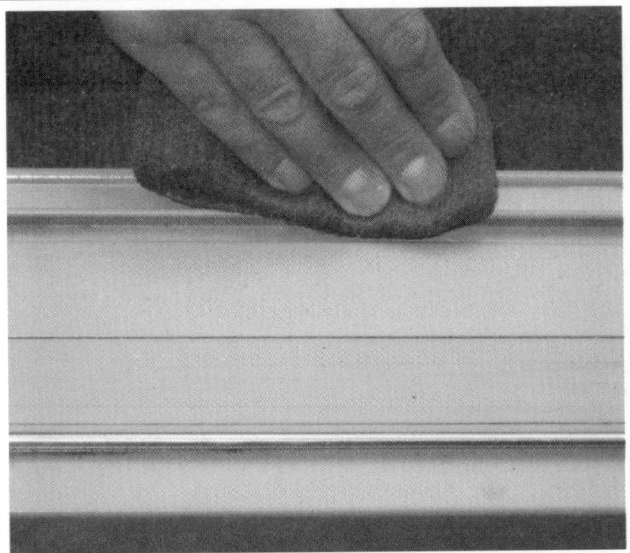

- Sliding aluminium windows last forever and won't warp, but they can bind after years of use.
- Clean the window track with fine steel wool and car polishing compound, either liquid or paste.
- Wipe off all cleaner residues, apply a coat of car wax, and lubricate all locks and fittings.

STICKING FURNITURE DRAWERS

Keep drawers from sticking and make opening them easier

Wooden drawers made before the era of drawer slides – those wonderful metal supports that run along the sides of drawers – can swell up and stick shut depending on weather conditions, loose corners, splits in the sides or a loose bottom.

Repairs are not complicated and do not require special tools. If you can't find the specific problem, just do a general overhaul. It won't take long to sand, seal and lubricate a single drawer and get it back in action. You'll get more noticeable results with smaller drawers than larger ones, but both will benefit from a tune-up.

Newer drawers with sliders or runners can also use some attention from time to time, as well as when the sliders

Wooden Drawer

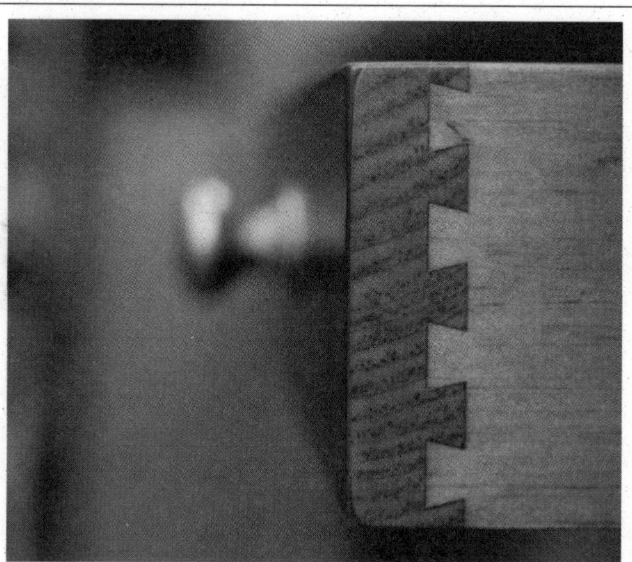

- Drawers stick when they become misaligned after repeated use or when they absorb moisture and expand.
- Older drawers slide wood on wood, which can bind.
- Newer drawers move on metal slides, whose screws can loosen over time – remove the drawer, tighten the screws, and apply paraffin or spray silicone to the slides.
- A broken drawer with loose corners or bottom will need repairing before you adjust it for movement.

Wooden Drawer Without Runners

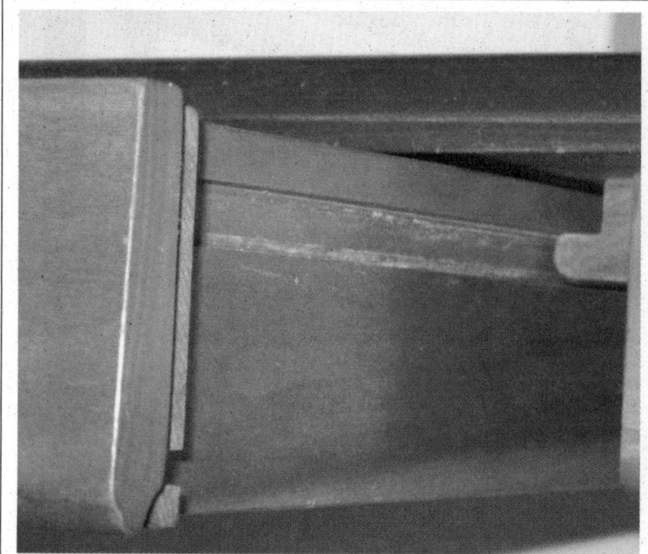

- Older wooden drawers slide within an opening using their own sides or small blocks as the guides; these wear down over time and need upkeep.
- Remove the drawer and rub the sides with paraffin or soap, or spray with silicone. Check the alignment.
- Lightly sand down tight drawers and then apply paraffin, soap or silicone spray.
- A worn wooden drawer might need a shim or guide added for smoother movement.

begin to loosen. Once you know how to repair these drawers, you won't have to yank on them when you want to get dressed in the morning.

Sealing the sanded areas with an oil or wax will help keep your drawers gliding smoothly.

YELLOW LIGHT

If you have a true antique, consult a dealer or restorer about how much sanding or alteration you can do to a drawer before you affect the value of the piece. Your treatment options might be limited in order to retain the furniture's originality and appearance.

Sanding a Drawer

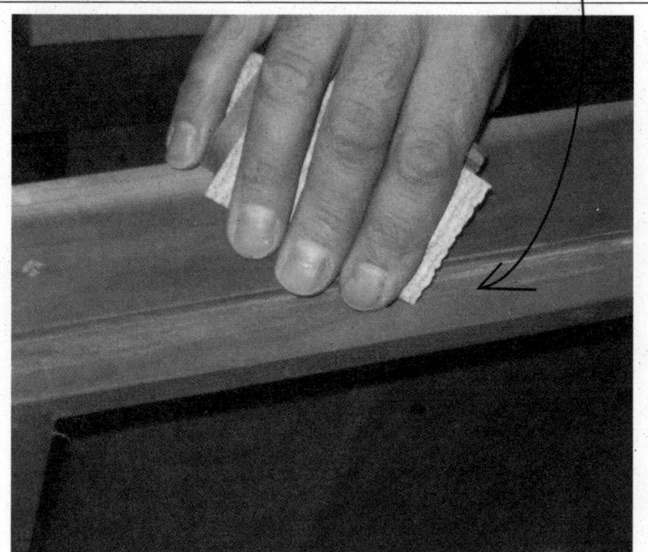

- An electric sander makes short work of some sticking drawers, especially the fronts if the edges are gummed up with paint.
- Remove the drawer and sand the sides and edges with a block sander and 80-grit paper, smoothing with 100-grit paper (while the drawer is out, sand off stains on the inside, too).
- Don't worry about taking too much wood off the sides; a block sander isn't that aggressive.
- Seal the sanded areas with a penetrating oil or wax.

Furniture Drawer with Sliders/Runners

- Purists won't install metal drawer runners on old furniture, but they do make life easier and can prevent wear and tear to drawers.
- Several styles of drawer runners are available with different mounting locations.
- The guides are aligned and screwed to the drawer and the cabinet or chest.
- No cutting or alterations are required, but start with a small drawer, if available, to get a feel for the installation.

STICKING DOOR LOCKS

Repair your jammed door lock before it puts you in a jam

Most front doors have two locks: you may have a cylinder lock or night latch, possibly fitted in the door knob, together with a mortise lock for additional security. Cylinder locks are typically a pin-and-tumbler design, featuring a series of small pins of different lengths. When a key is inserted, the key's notches are cut to match up with the pins and move them to either lock or unlock the door. Mortise locks generally use lever mechanisms. Moving metal lock parts, like moving wood parts, can wear down, stick, or even jam up after enough daily usage. Locks can also get stuck in the door strike, the metal section of the catch installed in the door jamb. The sliding bolt part of the lock slides into the strike, and if the strike is misaligned or not set correctly, the lock will stick and be difficult to operate.

Checking with Key

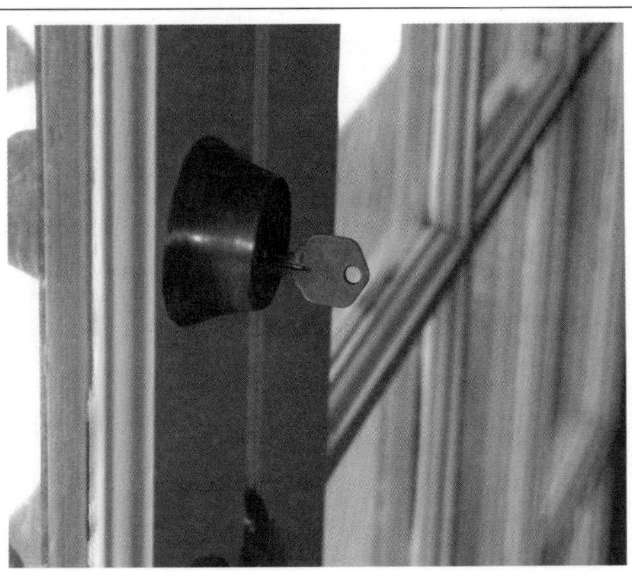

- Test a sticking door lock by opening the door and moving the lock with the key and the thumb turn.
- If the lock does not move freely, then it's sticking; if it does, the strike bolt isn't lining up with the strike in the door jamb.
- If the bolt and strike aren't lining up vertically, check that the door hinge screws are tight.
- If only the key side is sticking, try another key to confirm that one key isn't excessively worn down.

Powdered Graphite

- If the lock sticks with the door open, spray the inside with powdered graphite, available at hardware and car parts stores.
- Squeeze the powder into the lock through the keyhole and at the latch and strike the bolt a few times to distribute the graphite.
- Spray additional graphite on the key, and work it into the lock as well.
- If powdered graphite isn't available and the lock must be lubricated immediately, spray silicone into the keyhole and catch.

A little detective work, patience and the right lubricant will solve most of your lock problems. This is an easy project for a homeowner and doesn't require any additional professional help.

Sometimes a plastic liner inside the strike causes the door to stick.

YELLOW LIGHT

Don't mix lubricants (silicone and graphite). You'll get a sticky mess and make things worse. Out of graphite? Rub the key with some pencil graphite (the 'lead' in a lead pencil) and work it into the lock, or grind the pencil graphite into a powder and liberally coat the key with it.

Door Strike

- The door strike fits into the door jamb, and the latch and the slide bolt fit into the strike to secure the door.
- Check inside the strike for a plastic liner, which can sometimes cause sticking, and remove it.
- You might need to file down the strike until it matches up with the slide bolt.
- If filing isn't practical, move the strike slightly. Enlarge the hole in the jamb with a wood chisel and drill new screw holes.

Disassembling

- Standard cylinder locks come apart by removing screws that pass through the lock assembly, usually from the inside of the door.
- Older mortise locks have screws near the interior door knob and on the door edge where the strike bolt moves in and out.
- Remove any fasteners securing the lock and pull the lock from the door.
- Look for broken parts, clean out any dirt, and lubricate with graphite before reassembling.

HOLES IN PLASTER

Fixing plaster holes is not as difficult as it looks and doesn't need professional help

Plastered walls are typically made up of three coats of different types of plaster, making them very sturdy. As hard as plaster is, swinging door knobs, removing shelf brackets, and things that go bump in the night can all leave holes to be repaired. Fortunately, we don't have to repair with three coats of plaster any longer. Powder and ready-mixed fillers are readily available at DIY stores for one-part repairs that any novice can do.

Powder filler dries fast, so mix only as much as can be worked in about five minutes. It's intended to be mixed and used quickly and should be smoothed off with a knife to minimize sanding.

Removing Loose Plaster

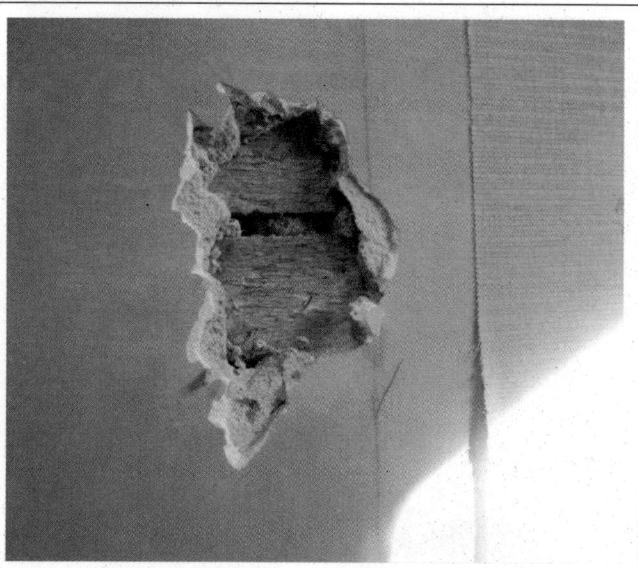

- Place a dust sheet on the floor, and clean out all loose plaster with a putty knife or old screwdriver.
- On a lath and plaster wall, dig back to the lath using an old screwdriver or the point of a putty knife.
- Break plaster away until solid plaster is found without crumbling – be cautious, it's easy to remove too much.

Clear Away Dust

- Brush the dust and loose bits off with an old paint-brush or vacuum out.
- Even small holes can have more loose plaster around them than you might suspect, so clean these thoroughly.
- Spray water on the exposed plaster, lath and surrounding edge of the old plaster.

Small repairs done with powder filler are indistinguishable in appearance and hardness from the surrounding plaster. For larger areas, depending on the size, traditional plaster may be called for. An option for a hole larger than 5 cm across is to cut a section of plasterboard and fasten it to where the plaster is missing or removed from the original wall. Then skim over the area with finishing plaster.

MAKE IT EASY

Mixing a small amount of vinegar – about 10 per cent of the required liquid – with dry plaster mix in lieu of water will slow down the drying and allow more time to smooth it out. Before mixing, be sure the area to be repaired is completely ready, with all loose plaster removed.

Smoothing It Out

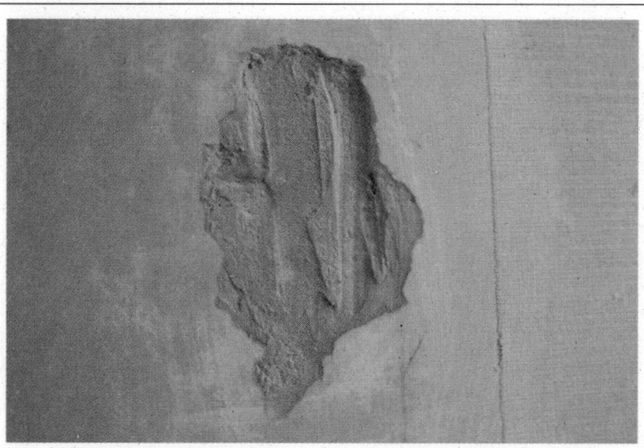

- As many as two or three layers of plaster or other fillers might be needed, depending on the size of the hole being repaired.
- Allow each layer to dry completely – most are fast drying, 20 minutes or less, depending on how thick a layer is applied.
- An experienced plasterer can obtain a smooth finish using only plaster, without sanding. If you're not a pro, apply a final layer of filler and smooth it with a filling knife, leaving it slightly proud of the surface.
- Wait for the filler to dry completely before sanding it level with the wall using a sanding block.
- Brush any dust away from the patch.

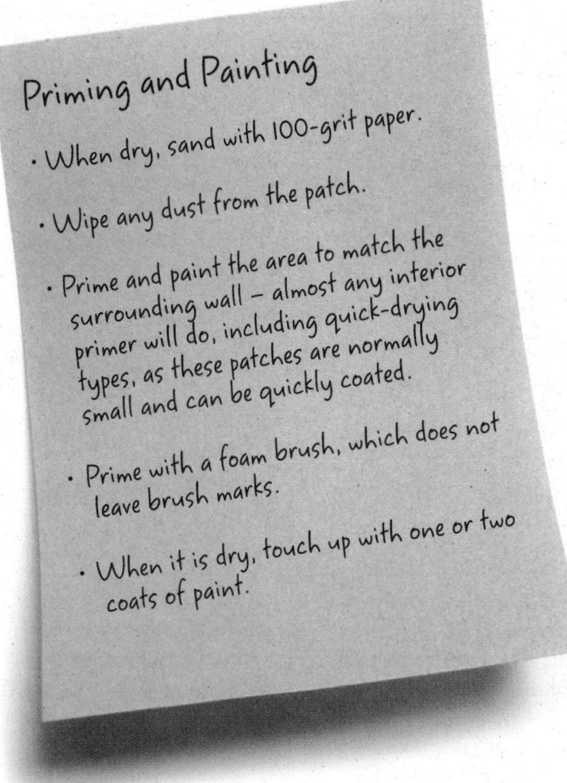

Priming and Painting
• When dry, sand with 100-grit paper.
• Wipe any dust from the patch.
• Prime and paint the area to match the surrounding wall – almost any interior primer will do, including quick-drying types, as these patches are normally small and can be quickly coated.
• Prime with a foam brush, which does not leave brush marks.
• When it is dry, touch up with one or two coats of paint.

REPAIRING CRACKS IN PLASTER

A bit of movement, and plaster can crack – here's how to fix it

Plaster is hard, but it can still crack. If there is settlement in a new building, or studwork in a partition wall moves or shifts a little due to expansion and contraction from unexpected moisture, the plaster moves with it. Whereas wood is flexible and has room to move, plaster does not, so cracks develop.

Plaster cracks often have a logic of their own. It all depends on has what moved underneath a section of a wall or ceiling. And these cracks can be long. Simply running some filler over them, a far too common approach, doesn't fix them, nor does the smear of filler look at all attractive.

A plaster crack should be opened up and made larger, preferably down to the underlying structure, and then filled. A proper repair will last. You might get new cracks over time, but the repaired cracks should mostly stay closed.

Widening the Crack

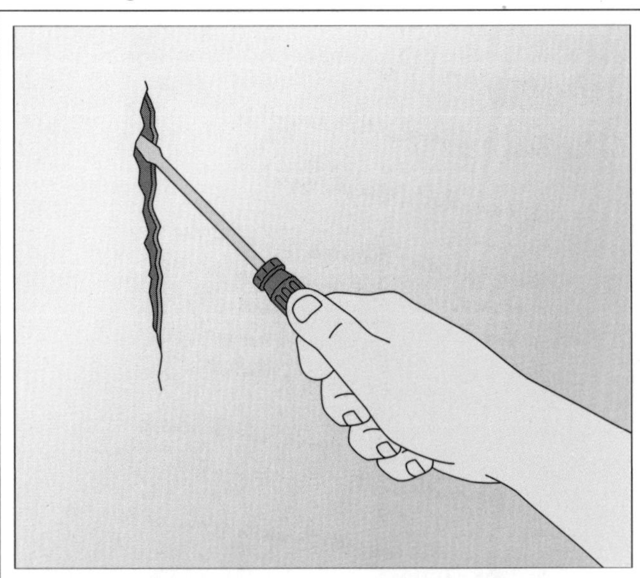

- Widen and dig out the crack using an old screwdriver or the point of a stiff putty knife.
- If you don't mind lots of dust, use a drill with a grinding wheel attachment to grind the crack back to the lath or brickwork.
- On partition walls, some people prefer to apply fibreglass tape over the crack and 'mud' it over with several layers of plasterboard compound.
- Filled cracks might return, but taped cracks require more finesse applying the plasterboard compound.

Applying Filler

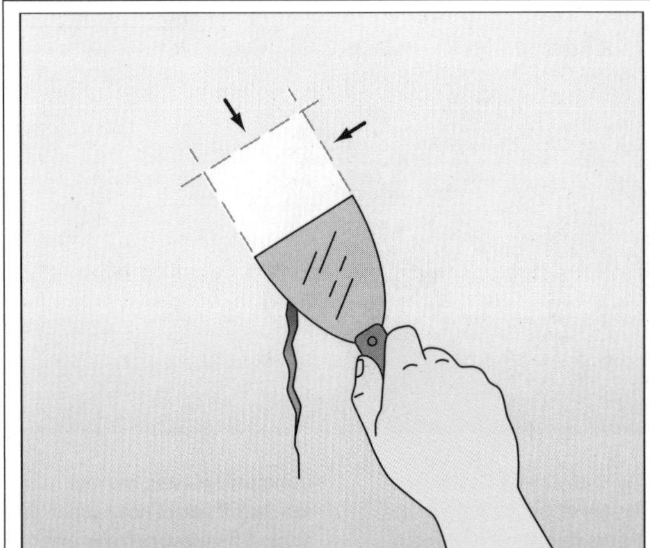

- After the crack has been cleaned out, wet it, pack it with filler, and smooth it with a putty knife.
- Narrow cracks can usually be filled with one application of filler, while wider cracks require two applications.
- Taped cracks call for two to three thin coats of plasterboard compound, spread thinly about 15 cm beyond each edge of the tape.
- Don't rush sanding the joint compound – sand it only when it's completely hard.

Some cracks are so fine you have to decide if they're worth repairing or simply painting over. If you paint them over, there is some risk they will enlarge later with future movement, so weigh your options – repair now or maybe repair later.

Applying the Final Coat

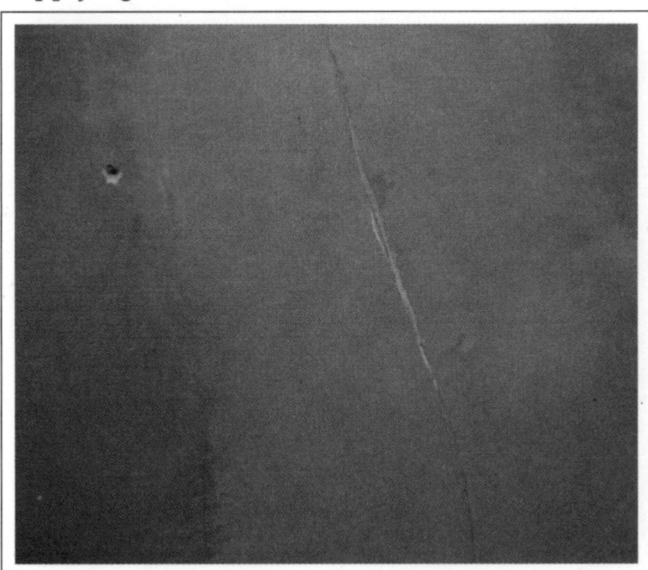

- Judge by its appearance whether you need to finish coat the crack.
- When dry, if the filled crack needs another coat, apply a thin coat of plasterboard compound, and sand when dry with 100-grit paper.
- After the last plasterboard compound layer is sanded over the taped repair, run your hand over the patch to check it is smooth – you don't want a lumpy repair to stick out.
- Be sure the compound completely covers any fibreglass tape, otherwise it will show through the paint.

Sanding and Painting

- Repaired cracks get primed and painted the same way as repaired holes.
- If a room has multiple cracks, reckon on repainting it entirely – otherwise the repainted areas will stand out too much.
- Prime the crack with a foam brush to avoid brush marks and then apply thin coats of paint until the repair is covered.
- Spread the last coat of paint out thinly away from the repair to blend in better.

HOLES IN PLASTERBOARD

Fixing imperfections in partition walls can be done without the help of a professional

Plasterboard has been around since World War I, but it took the labour and materials shortages of World War II and the demand for housing after the war for it to take over from traditional plaster. Unlike plaster, plasterboard is produced in ready-to-install sheets of gypsum sandwiched between sheets of durable paper, and is nailed directly to timber supports. Installing plasterboard was and is a lower skilled trade than plastering, although it still calls for strength and speed.

The joints between pieces of plasterboard are finished with several coats of joint compound and paper or fibreglass tape. After drying, each coat is sanded smooth before the next coat is applied. The joint compound comes in three types:

Dents and Holes

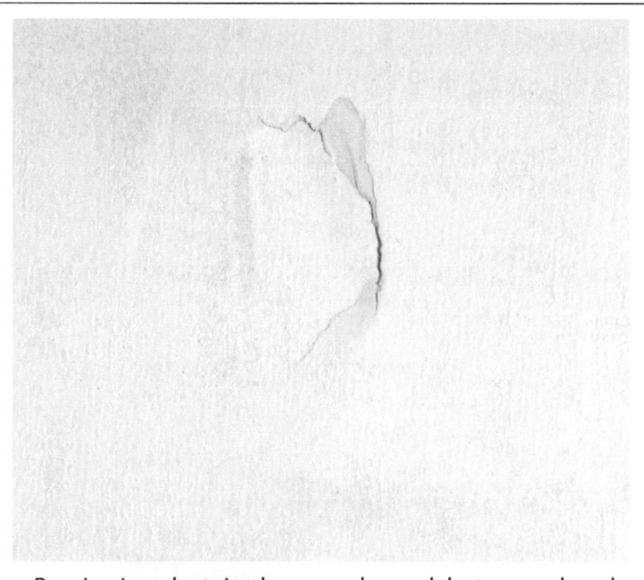

- Repair minor dents in plasterboard with ready-mixed or powder filler.
- Use a repair kit or fibreglass joint tape (single or double layer) to cover larger holes.
- Apply three layers of plasterboard compound, spreading about 15 cm beyond the tape, and sand each layer when dry.
- If the wall has a textured finish, texture the last coat while still wet with a sponge, roller or other appropriate tool to match the surrounding area.

Repair Kits

- A partition wall doesn't have anything behind it between the studs – there's nothing to hold any filler in place.
- Self-adhesive mesh and plasterboard repair kits are available for holes up to 15 cm square.
- Attach the mesh, spread some plasterboard compound, and allow to dry before sanding and painting.
- Holes larger than this will need to have some backing installed and a plasterboard patch attached.

all-purpose, topping and quick set. All-purpose joint compound is widely available, making it convenient for you to handle your own repairs. It comes ready-mixed in plastic tubs and will do just what its name suggests. It will work for any plasterboard taping or repair purpose. It shrinks a bit more than the other two and, when dry, takes longer to sand to a smooth finish, but it's ready to use and stores easily.

MAKE IT EASY

Plasterboard is sold in sheets that are far larger than you'll ever need for small repairs. It's worth saving a few offcuts if you have building work done at home, or grabbing them from a construction site when you see them, and storing them in a dry place for possible future use.

Cutting Out the Damaged Area

- With a pencil and straight edge, draw an square or rectangle 25 mm bigger in each direction around the damaged area.
- Cut this area out with a utility knife or keyhole saw.
- Place thin strips of wood – plywood scraps will do – inside the wall and behind the plasterboard and secure them by screwing through the plasterboard and into the strips.
- The plasterboard can also be carefully cut out with an electric jigsaw.

Installing the Patch

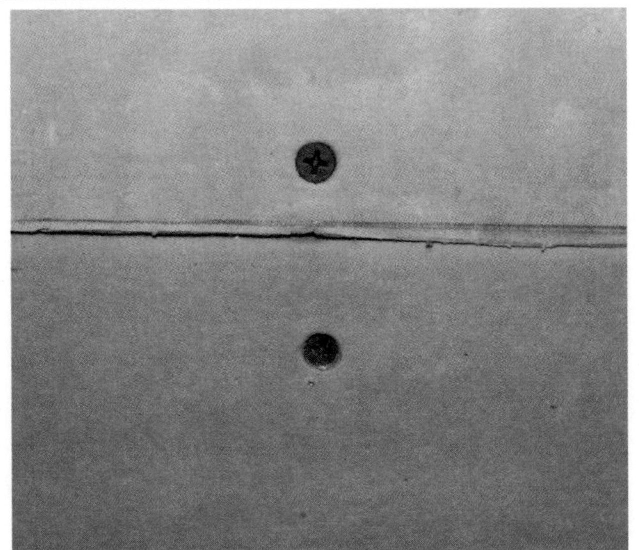

- With the backing in place, a piece of scrap plasterboard can be installed, taped and finished.
- Cut a section of plasterboard the same thickness as the existing board to size; glue and screw this patch to the backing supports.
- Tape the edges and apply three coats of plasterboard compound, extending out about 15 cm, sanding each smooth, and applying a textured finish if needed.
- Prime and paint the repaired section.

CRACKS IN PLASTERBOARD

Because plasterboard often cracks at the taped joints, the repairs necessary are different than for plaster

Plasterboard is a stiff material, but it does move along with the underlying studs it's attached to on walls and ceilings, especially as the wood battens lose some of their water content and dry out. As the wood moves, it can pull away from the nails or screws securing the plasterboard. Cracks show through in various ways. Sometimes all you'll notice is a nail or screw head 'popping' through the surface. In other instances, the boards move at the joints, and the tape and joint compound are torn and damaged.

To make a repair you need to remove all the loose tape and joint compound from the damaged area. At that point, you can retape and 'mud' the crack, but unless it's a very long

Cutting Away Torn Tape

- Cracks in plasterboard occur at taped seams where two sheets of board come together and the seam is covered with tape and joint compound.
- Cut away any loose tape and joint compound.
- Fill in the damaged area with plaster filler, forcing it into the joint and smoothing it with a putty knife.
- When the filler is dry, recoat with joint compound, texturing if necessary, followed by priming and painting to match the surrounding area.

Tape Repair

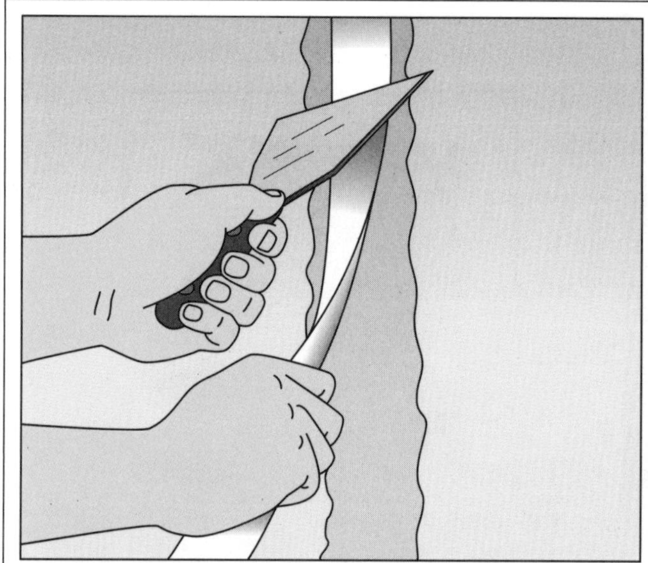

- Use paper or self-adhesive fibreglass tape to retape cracks and duplicate the original construction.
- Remove loose tape and joint compound, apply a thin coat of joint compound, and cut a piece of new paper tape the length of the crack.
- Press the paper tape into the compound with a putty knife and spread a thin layer of compound over the top of the tape until it's smooth, extending out about 15 cm from the tape edges.
- Fibreglass tape is self-adhesive and applies directly to the wall board; do not apply it to joint compound.

crack with a lot of tape damage, it's faster and simpler to use patching plaster or other filler. Patching plaster will fill and replace any smaller damaged taped areas without compromising the joint or appearance.

YELLOW LIGHT

If a crack in your plaster is wet, you have a water problem that must be dealt with before the crack is repaired. This will probably call for removing a larger area of the wall surface. A long crack in plaster that is not at a joint suggests major settling, and the cause should be investigated.

Applying More Coats/Texture

- It's easy to apply joint compound too thickly and end up with a lumpy repair – good taping and 'mudding' takes practice.
- All coats should be spread thin with a wide finish knife or putty knife.
- Always use a clean knife for spreading – all bits of dried joint compound should be wiped from the edge.
- Sand off any ridges, high spots, and rough edges with 100-grit sandpaper (the last coat should require little sanding).

Nails

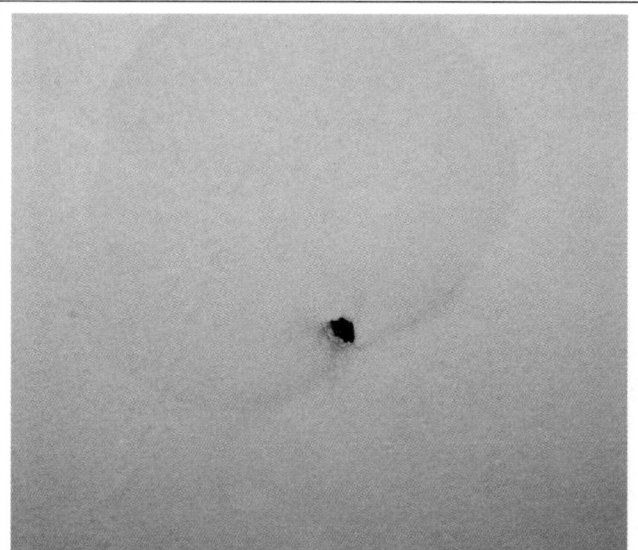

- If a plasterboard nail pops out, drive it back in with a hammer and nail punch.
- If a screw shows, lightly tap a Phillips screwdriver into the head and tighten it by hand.
- Screw the plasterboard to the stud about 75 mm above and below the loose screw/nail.
- Press a small amount of filler over all nail/screw heads with a putty knife, sand the filler when it dries, and prime and paint with an artist's brush for the least visible retouching.

CRACKS IN CONCRETE

Fill serious concrete cracks to keep the area safe and prevent water from seeping in

While it's one of the hardest materials used in construction, concrete is still susceptible to cracks. This isn't necessarily a sign of weakness, but it's in the nature of the material and its installation. Concrete shrinks a little as it cures and also swells and shrinks as it absorbs and loses moisture, although these changes won't always cause cracks.

Water not only turns dry concrete mix into pliable, usable material but also chemically reacts with the cement in the concrete mix, starting the hardening process. Without water, concrete wouldn't cure and harden properly. Curing can go on for years, which explains why cracks can show up any time. The way the concrete was mixed and poured, the weather

Filling Hairline Cracks

- Small hairline cracks and slightly larger ones can be filled with acrylic concrete filler with silicone. Filling cracks brings no guarantees, but when it works, it's a simple repair with good results.
- Vacuum the crack out to remove any loose particles, then fill following the directions on the cartridge.
- Press the filler into the crack and scrape it off the concrete surface with a putty knife, leaving only a thin film.
- Reapply if needed to fill the crack to its top.

Cleaning Out Larger Cracks

- Wear safety glasses when removing loose material with either a hammer and cold chisel or an old unwanted screwdriver, making the bottom of the crack wider than the top.
- If dust isn't a problem, use a grinding wheel attached to a drill as a fast way of clearing out a crack.
- Vacuum up all loose debris and dust.
- Apply a suitable concrete repair mix and press it down tightly into the crack to fill it completely.

conditions, the amount of water in the mix, and the ground preparation all affect the degree of cracking in a poured concrete slab. Even under the best of conditions, shifting soil under concrete can create conditions that cause cracks.

Cracks can be serious or merely cosmetic and nonstructural. Hairline cracks are good examples of cosmetic, leave-them-alone cracks. More noticeable cracks, however, should be filled to improve appearances, ensure safety (if the edge of the crack is a tripping hazard) and stop water seeping in and worsening the crack.

RED LIGHT

Cracks in a concrete floor are one thing, but deep cracks in concrete walls can be structural issues and should be reviewed by an engineer or contractor. Your home might not be endangered, but you don't want severe cracks to progress if simple repairs are possible.

Cleaning Out a Hole

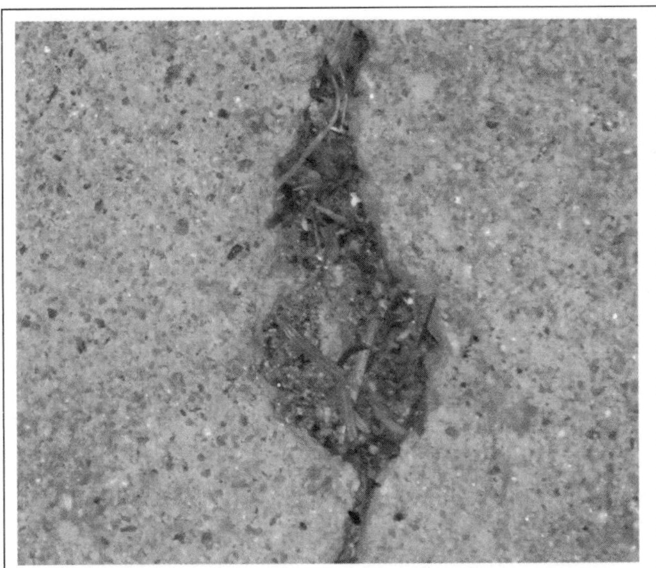

- Clean holes in concrete of all loose, damaged material using a hammer and old screwdriver or cold chisel.
- Clean all exposed sides of the hole with a wire brush, vacuum out the loose debris, wet the area, and fill it with two-part epoxy cement, following the manufacturer's instructions and pressing it in tightly.
- Slowly build up the material as you fill the hole.
- Smooth the final layer with a broad putty knife.

Large Holes

- Depending on the location of the hole and whether cars will drive over the repaired area, a large hole may call for different types of concrete mix.
- A concrete mix with gravel added rather than an all-sand mix will withstand the weight of a car for drive and garage floor repairs – ask your supplier for the appropriate mix.
- A large hole can require more aggressive cleaning out, including the use of a sledgehammer, so you might need an expert here.
- Mix the concrete thoroughly according to the package instructions, press it into the hole and follow the curing instructions.

CRACKED GLASS

You can't repair a cracked pane of glass, but you can replace it

Window glass is a mixture of sand, lime and soda, all heated together until liquefied and then poured on to molten tin to form flat sheets of 'float glass'. Transparent and weatherproof, it's the ideal material for windows and should remain crack-free for a lifetime if we don't traumatize it by kicking footballs through it, slamming windows closed, or running a high-temperature heat gun against it. But we do traumatize glass and occasionally need to replace it while avoiding future traumas.

Replacing single-pane glass is relatively simple. Glass is available from most hardware stores or local glass shops at a reasonable cost, and removing the broken pane doesn't require any special tools. It's also somewhat intuitive: you can tell by looking how it's secured in the window frame.

Aluminium Windows

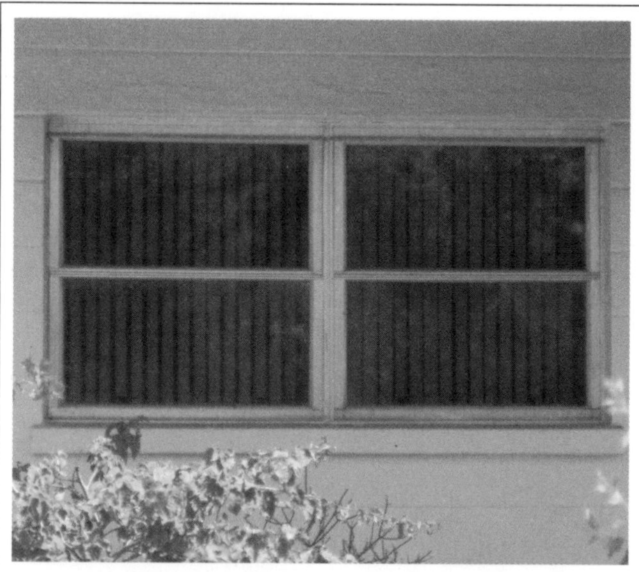

- Single-pane glass in steel or aluminium windows may be held in place with putty, a sealant, metal clips or by a metal frame screwed at the corners.
- Spring tension clips inserted into the frame, help to hold puttied glass in place.
- When measuring for replacement glass, buy a piece about 3 mm shorter in each direction than your measurements for easy fitting.
- Install the new glass using the same material (such as putty) that was used before.

Wood Windows

- In older wood-framed sash windows, glass is held in place with glazing sprigs – small sharp fasteners pressed into the frame against the glass – and putty, which creates a seal around the panes.
- Chipping the old putty out is the toughest and most time-consuming part of the job – it must all be cleaned out.
- Measure the new glass and subtract 3 mm from each dimension when ordering replacement glass.

Repairing a double-glazed unit isn't so intuitive, so sometimes the aid of a professional glazier may be needed. That said, modern glass is less likely to crack than old glass, in part because of its age (it's had less exposure to traumatizing incidents), but also because of improved manufacturing methods and thickness. Any cracked glass can be repaired, but unless the pane is in danger of falling out, repairs aren't critical.

YELLOW LIGHT

Unsure if the crack might get worse and the pane possibly fall out, but you can't repair it right away? Tape both sides of the crack with Scotch clear packaging tape, which stands out less than other tapes. The glass is less likely to fall out and injure anyone walking below it.

Sealants

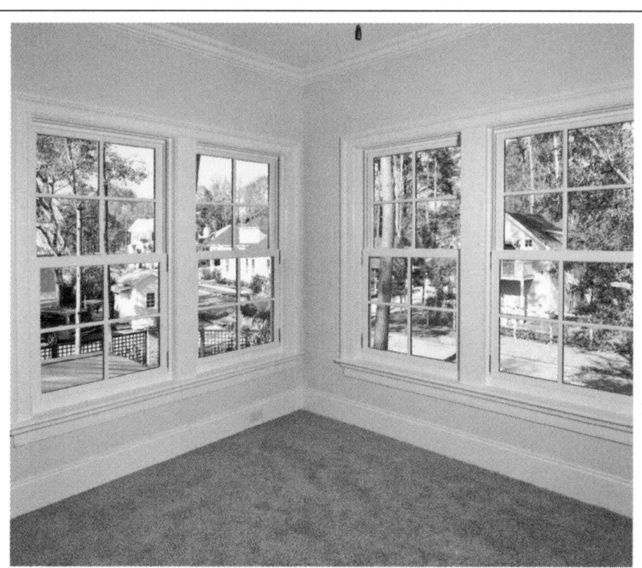

- Putty was the standard sealant for single-pane glass for years, and is still used today for repairs.
- Remove all the putty from the can and knead it like dough to soften it and redistribute the linseed oil, which may have separated out, before use.
- In metal frames, glass is sometimes secured with glazing tape and then sealed with silicone sealant.
- For paintable sealants such as putty, follow the manufacturer's instructions for curing times before painting.

Fixing Insulated and Single-Pane Glass

- Single-pane glass can be cut in any glass shop or hardware store, but a double-glazed unit has to be made to order unless your window manufacturer keeps the size you need in stock.
- Each window manufacturer has different assembly methods and fasteners.
- If there is no apparent way to remove a pane of broken glass, contact the window manufacturer for directions or call a glazier.
- In some cases, the entire window might need to be replaced if the glass cannot be removed.

HOW YOUR SYSTEM WORKS

Learn the ins and outs of your electrical system to prepare for maintenance and safety in the future

We don't see electricity, but we see the results: it runs appliances, turns on the lights and displays television shows. We pay attention to it only when it isn't working or when the bill comes. Modern electrical systems are very reliable and safe. The only changes that occur are updates to regulations concerning electrical installations and a never-ending supply of new devices to plug in and turn on. Older systems may still be safe, but problems can occur when changes are made that don't meet current regulations and safety requirements.

According to the British Fire and Rescue service, over 47,000 accidental fires in homes are reported annually, of which 17 per cent are due to electrical faults and a further 26 per cent

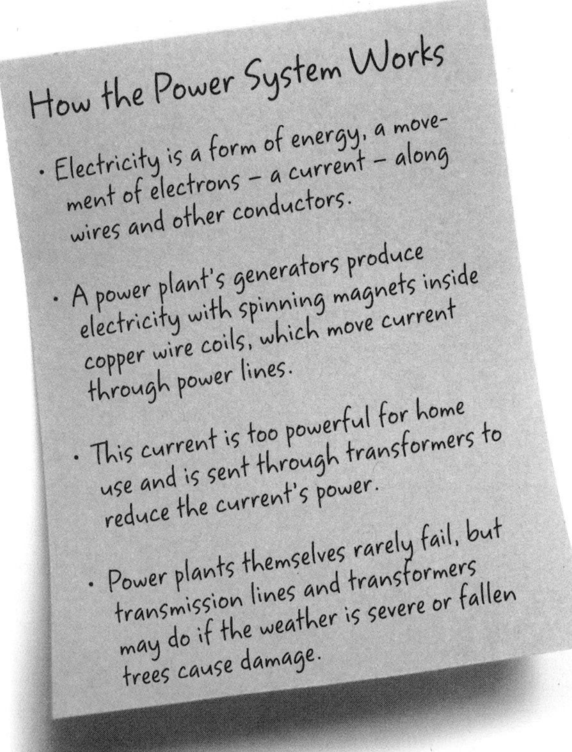

How the Power System Works
• Electricity is a form of energy, a movement of electrons – a current – along wires and other conductors.
• A power plant's generators produce electricity with spinning magnets inside copper wire coils, which move current through power lines.
• This current is too powerful for home use and is sent through transformers to reduce the current's power.
• Power plants themselves rarely fail, but transmission lines and transformers may do if the weather is severe or fallen trees cause damage.

The Consumer Unit

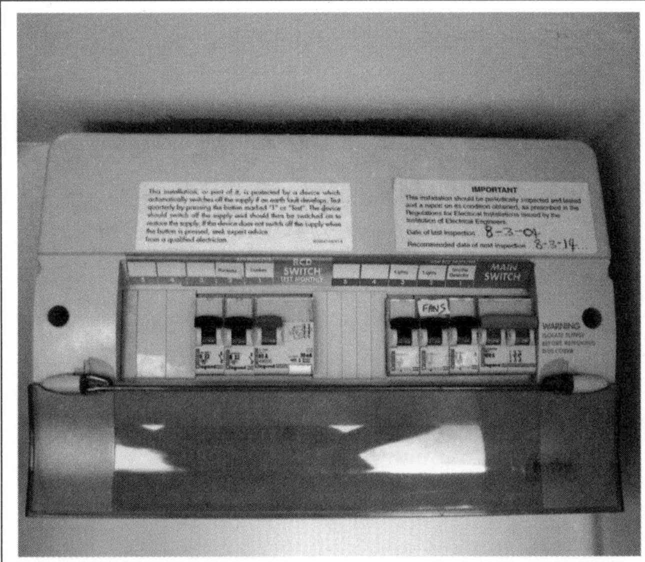

- A consumer unit or fuse box distributes electricity to lights, appliances and power sockets and protects the wiring. The more circuits there are the better, since too many loads, or loads demanding a lot of electricity on a single circuit, can cause problems.
- Fuses and circuit breakers stop electricity in overloaded circuits.
- Fuse boxes are no longer installed, and if you still have one in your home you need to get a qualified electrician to replace it with an up-to-date consumer unit.

to misuse of electrical appliances. Almost 12,000 fires a year are caused by misuse of cooking appliances, including microwave ovens, so special care is needed in the kitchen.

Understanding the limits of your system will keep you safe and make the most efficient use of your electricity. Find out the age of your wiring and get it checked every ten years or so, and whenever you move home.

GREEN LIGHT

If you're uncertain about your present wiring system, hire an electrician to do a safety check. It typically takes about an hour or so for the inspection. Consider any recommendations for suggested safety upgrades, but above all be sure that the existing system is safe and that you understand any limitations on its usage.

Electricity Terminology

- Electricity has its own terminology:
- The electricity you use is measured in watts – a 100-watt bulb consumes 100 watts of electricity.
- A kilowatt is 1,000 watts.
- You are billed in kilowatt hours – the amount of electricity used by ten 100-watt light bulbs, for instance, in one hour is 1 kilowatt-hour.
- An amp is an amount of electricity.
- Circuits are measured in amps.
- Voltage is electrical pressure.

Your Wiring System

- In the UK a national safety standard for electrical installations was established in 2005.
- It is recommended that domestic systems should be inspected by a competent electrician approximately every ten years.
- The inspection will alert you to possible overloads, any risks of fire, defective work, deterioration and lack of earthing or insulation.
- The electrician will compile a report detailing any steps you need to take to bring your system up to standard.

FUSES & CIRCUIT BREAKERS

Protect yourself by becoming familiar with your wiring and circuit breakers

The wires in your house are sized to carry a certain amount of electrical current. Too much current, and wire can overheat and cause a fire. Fuses and circuit breakers limit how much current can travel through wires by shutting down the circuit. They are the main safeguards of your system. Without them, you could plug in a dozen small appliances in your kitchen on a circuit designed to run just one or two, and the current would keep flowing until the wire became red hot.

If an appliance develops a fault or demands too much current from the circuit, the breaker trips or a fuse 'blows' or 'burns out', and the flow of the current stops. Circuit breakers and fuses act like on/off switches that have to be reset (circuit

Fuse Box and Fuses

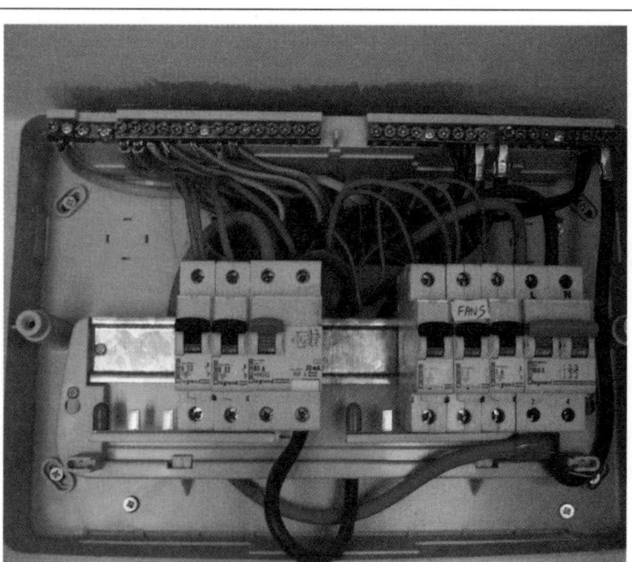

- A fuse in an old-style fuse box contains a short length of wire of the appropriate strength for each circuit; if too much current passes through it, the wire melts and breaks the circuit.
- Fuses are rated by the amperage that passes through them – 15 amps, 20 amps, etc. – which determines the size of the wire they can protect.
- A fuse will last indefinitely until it's overloaded with more current than its circuit can safely handle.

Consumer Unit and Circuit Breakers

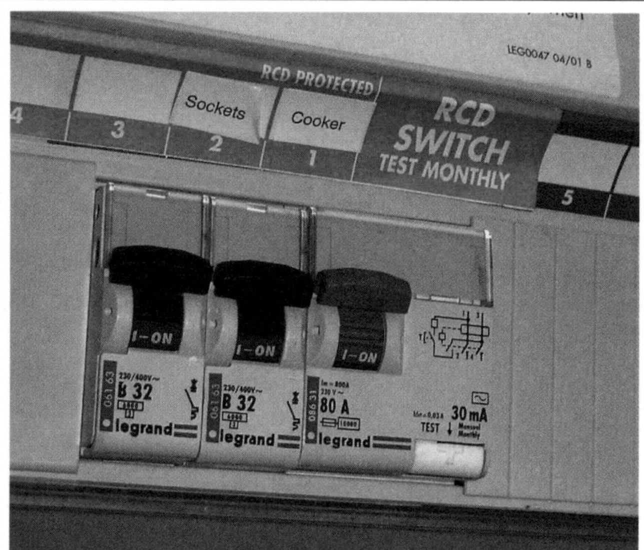

- A modern consumer unit has circuit breakers that 'trip' to stop the flow of electricity in an overloaded circuit.
- A circuit breaker can conveniently be reset and used indefinitely, unlike a fuse, which needs replacement after it burns out. The fault that caused the circuit to break must be corrected, however.
- Fuses and circuit breakers are rated to protect particular sizes of wires .
- Circuit breakers are found in earthed electrical systems.

breaker) or replaced (fuse). You must never, ever change a fuse or circuit breaker with one of larger amperage because the power keeps shutting down on a particular circuit. The wires, circuit breakers and fuses are designed to work with each other. If you tamper with this a fire can result, which often isn't covered by insurance. So be sure to understand and work correctly within your particular system.

RED LIGHT

Fuse boxes may be perfectly safe provided each circuit has the correct fuse in it, but a past resident may have replaced a low-amp fuse with a higher amp fuse, and this is a fire hazard. Except for large appliance loads, circuits that supply power sockets are normally protected by 30 amp fuses or 32 amp circuit breakers.

Using Electricity Safely

- Get your system checked every ten years and updated if necessary.
- Turn off any appliances that are not in use, particularly at night.
- Check sockets regularly to ensure that they are not overheating or scorched.
- Check flexes for signs of wear and make sure they are securely attached to the plugs, particularly with appliances that are subject to repeated movements such as vacuum cleaners.
- If you are using an adaptor to plug in several appliances, check that the total current used does not exceed the rating of the adaptor.
- If a fuse blows or a circuit breaks, the last item plugged in or switched on should not be plugged in again before it has been checked for faults.

Resetting a Circuit Breaker

- At the consumer unit, look to see which breaker has tripped – it won't be lined up with the other breakers.
- Push the circuit breaker into a complete 'OFF' position and then push to 'ON'. It will click when it goes on.
- If the circuit broke when you switched on an appliance you may be aware of the source of the problem. Otherwise, check all appliances on that circuit for faults.

SAVING ELECTRICITY

Keep electricity usage low – and your electricity bills even lower – with a few simple tips

Energy conservation is now a major issue, both globally and locally, and with some minor adjustments and a bit more awareness of our electricity use, every household can cut back, save money, and give a stressed infrastructure a break. Get into a daily, weekly or monthly routine to help reduce your usage of electricity and the size of your bills.

There are obvious things you can do every day to conserve electricity – turn off lights when they're not needed, run the washing machine and dishwasher only with full loads, cook several meals at once in a heated oven – but there are also less obvious habits. Doing an energy audit of your home and lifestyle will surprise, inform and guide you to new

Electronic Equipment

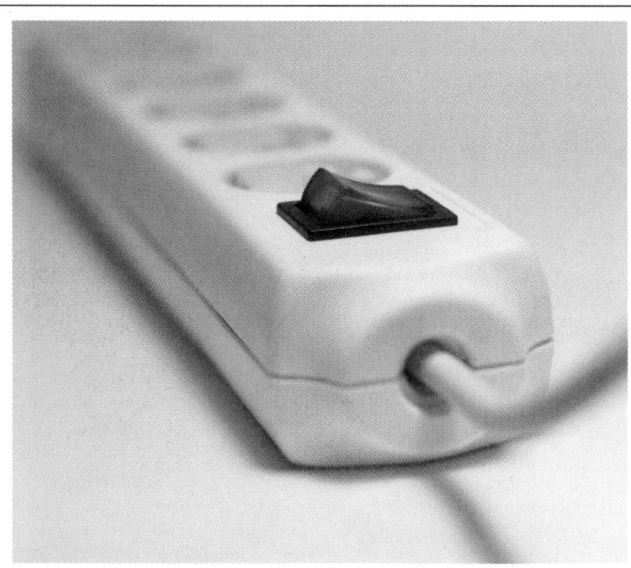

- The numerous electronic devices in the average home continue to consume power when left on standby, but this usage can be minimized.
- Shutting a PC off at the power socket will stop all electronic activity; newer models can handle many on/off cycles without damaging the hard drive.
- Use the 'sleep' mode during the day if you are not using a computer for a while, for added energy savings.
- Turn off TVs and mobile phone chargers at the socket when not in use.

Energy Efficient Light Bulbs

- A compact fluorescent bulb (CFL) replaces a standard incandescent light bulb.
- Energy efficient light bulbs use about 75 per cent less energy than standard incandescent bulbs and last up to ten times longer.
- While a CFL can cost more than an incandescent bulb electricity savings over the bulb's lifetime can far outweigh its initial cost.
- Lights fitted with dimmer switches require a special kind of CFL.

considerations regarding your energy-using habits and consumption. All those computers and entertainment devices still require electricity if you leave them on standby. And dropping the temperature of your heating thermostat by as little as one degree a month, and getting used to a slightly cooler house, can bring considerable savings. Every little bit adds up.

MAKE IT EASY

Keeping lighting usage down is great, but you can't live in the dark. Install timers and attach them to low-wattage lights for both security and safety if family members have to get up in the middle of the night. Automated systems for multiple devices programmed with a PC are available as well.

Energy Rating

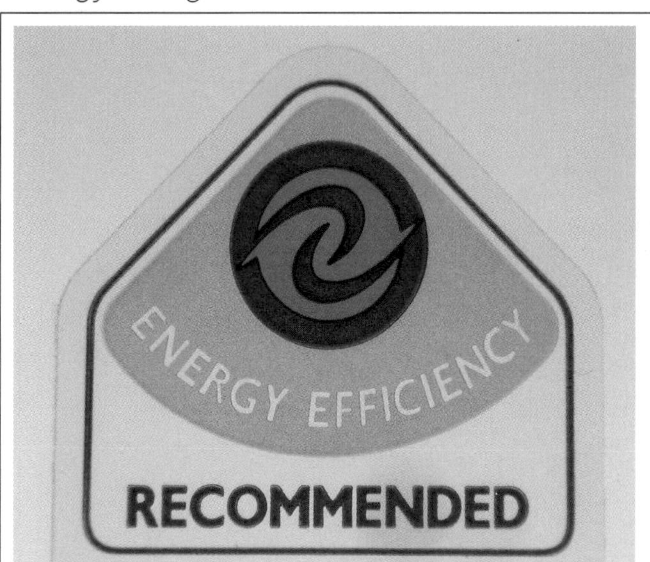

- When you're buying new domestic appliances it makes sense to choose the most energy efficient models you can find.
- Manufacturers of fridges and freezers, washing machines, tumble dryers, dishwashers, electric ovens, air conditioners, lamps and light bulbs must display the EU energy label on all products sold in the EU.
- The label rates the product according to its energy efficiency, from the least (G) to the most efficient (A). For some appliances the system is extended to A++.

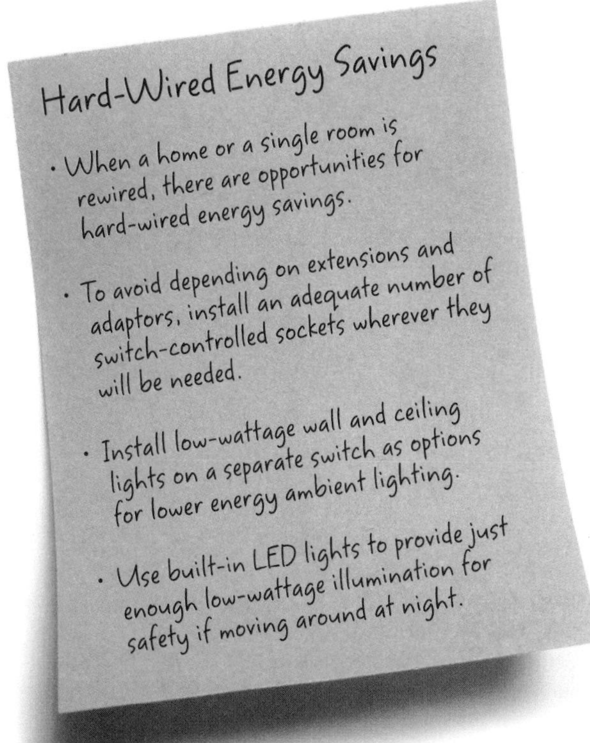

Hard-Wired Energy Savings
· When a home or a single room is rewired, there are opportunities for hard-wired energy savings.
· To avoid depending on extensions and adaptors, install an adequate number of switch-controlled sockets wherever they will be needed.
· Install low-wattage wall and ceiling lights on a separate switch as options for lower energy ambient lighting.
· Use built-in LED lights to provide just enough low-wattage illumination for safety if moving around at night.

LAMP, FLEX & PLUG REPAIR

Before throwing out your radio, light or other device, try repairing it

When it comes to repairing lamps, flexes and plugs, take a lesson in frugality from our grandparents and great-grandparents: try a repair first before you throw it away. A common repair with small electrical devices is replacing a worn flex or a broken lampholder. Hardware stores stock replacement plugs, which are easy to fit provided you understand the colour coding of the wires and ensure that you use the correctly rated fuse for the appliance.

Rewiring a lamp or light fitting can be a bit trickier – some disassembly is involved, and you don't have a lot of extra room to work – but if it is a valuable or antique lamp, or just one you like, it's well worth doing. If you feel this task is

Rewiring a Lamp

- New flexes, plugs and lampholders are available from hardware and lighting shops.
- By spending just a few pounds, you can restore a lamp to full use.
- Replace all the parts in an old lamp; don't try to keep the old lampholder unless it's in perfect condition.
- If the bulb isn't lighting, unplug the lamp and try pulling up on the brass tab at the bottom of the lampholder – it needs to make good contact with the bulb for it to work.

Repairing an Extension Lead

- If an extension lead gets worn or damaged, you can salvage it by cutting off the worn part of the wire and reconnecting either the plug or the socket to the remaining sound wire.
- It's preferable, though, to have switched sockets installed wherever you need to plug in appliances, to eliminate the need for extension leads.
- Extension leads for occasional use, for example with power tools, must be of the correct rating for the appliance and should be fully unwound during use to avoid overheating.

beyond you, take it to your local electrical supplier or a specialist lighting shop and ask them to replace the fitting.

A worn extension lead can be given a new life by cutting away the damaged area and installing a plug on the undamaged part. This repair will result in a shorter lead but it is safer than taping over torn insulation (which should be avoided).

YELLOW LIGHT

Use an extension lead only if there is no available power socket, and check that it is fitted with the correctly rated fuse. The cable should not be stretched taut. If it has to cross a pathway or other area where people will walk, reduce the risk of tripping by covering the lead with a rubber protector strip.

Replacing a Plug

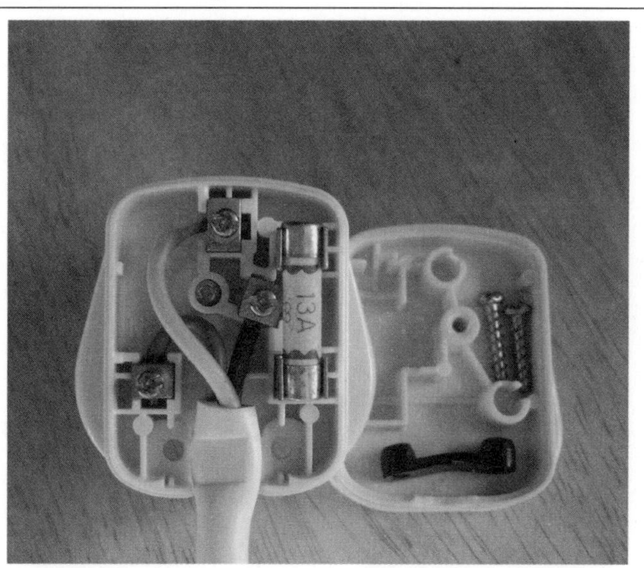

- Always replace cracked or damaged plugs.
- All three-pin plugs are sold fitted with a fuse, usually 13 amp, which is suitable for appliances such as heaters and hair dryers.
- For a lamp or other small-load appliance, such as a radio, the fuse in the plug should be replaced with a 3 or 5 amp fuse as appropriate.
- Tighten the screws in the cable grip so that it holds the lead securely, to prevent any pressure on the lead pulling on the connections to the pins.

Avoiding Damage

- Always pull a plug out of a socket by holding the plug, never by yanking on the lead.
- Don't exceed the maximum recommended wattage for a lamp when fitting a light bulb.
- Never run an electrical lead under a rug or carpet – the insulation can rub off, and a fire can start under the right conditions.
- Don't overload extensions and multi-way trailing sockets.

RENEWABLE ENERGY

Decide if the biggest renewable energy installations in history will work for you

Renewable energy is energy generated from any resource that is naturally replenished, including sunlight, wind, tidal energy and geothermal heat.

In one form or another renewable energy has been utilized for centuries. Water-powered wheels and wind-powered pumps go back thousands of years. Solar energy, the most promising for residential use, was captured by the Greeks and Romans, who oriented their buildings to capture sunlight for radiant heat in the winter but not in the hotter summer months.

Today, more renewable energy installations than ever before are showing up all over the world, some of them quite massive.

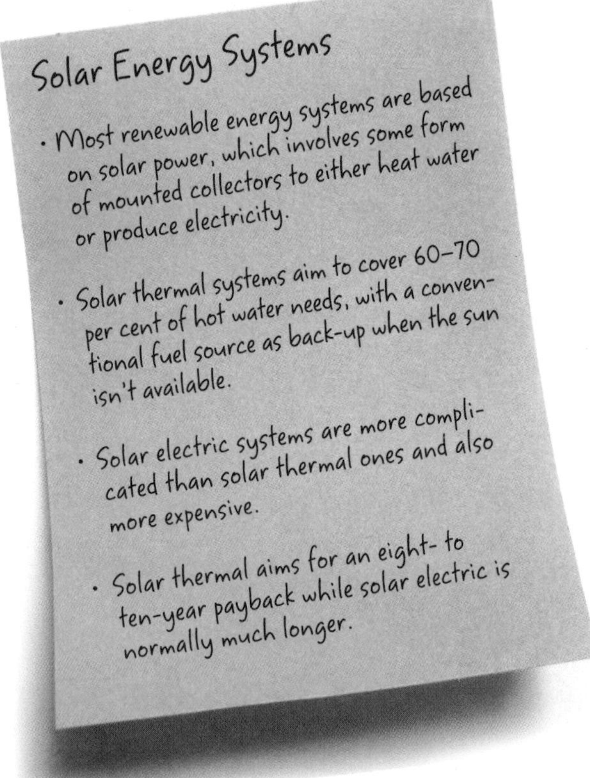

Solar Energy Systems

- Most renewable energy systems are based on solar power, which involves some form of mounted collectors to either heat water or produce electricity.
- Solar thermal systems aim to cover 60–70 per cent of hot water needs, with a conventional fuel source as back-up when the sun isn't available.
- Solar electric systems are more complicated than solar thermal ones and also more expensive.
- Solar thermal aims for an eight- to ten-year payback while solar electric is normally much longer.

Home Renewable Energy System

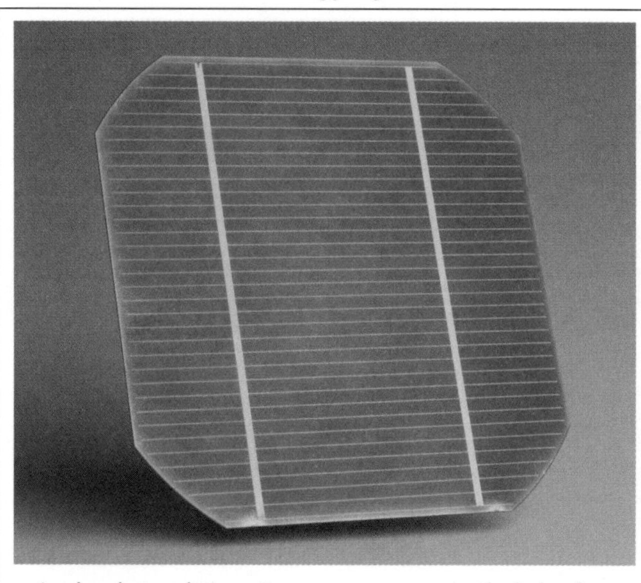

- A solar photovoltaic system includes a solar array, or series of solar collectors/panels, components to convert the solar energy into usable household electricity, and batteries to store power.
- This system calls for more maintenance than a conventional electricity supply and may require the help of an expert.
- In a stand-alone system (one that is not connected to the grid) surplus energy is stored in a bank of batteries, which provides a back-up in the event there is no solar power available due to bad weather.

Residential systems are becoming more reliable, better integrated, and even better looking. The EU's current target is for renewable energy to account for at least 20 per cent of all generated electricity by 2020.

Is it worth installing a solar energy system in your home? Will you ever recover the cost? Some systems can sell power back to your electricity supplier, gaining some small financial advantage. Increasingly, newly constructed homes are including solar installations. There are a lot of factors to consider, but it's definitely worth looking into.

YELLOW LIGHT

Solar electric installations require experienced contractors familiar with the components and with a track record of satisfied customers. This is not a job for any electrician or roofer. Since 2008 the installation of solar panels has been made slightly easier in the UK, because planning permission is no longer required in all cases.

Components

- A home renewable energy system starts with the home's service panel, wiring and fixtures.
- Additional components include a source of energy – usually a solar array – an inverter/charger for converting the array's DC power to AC, a battery charger for systems with battery back-up, and separate panels with their own circuit breakers.
- The system can be adjusted as conditions and power demands change for maximum efficiency.
- It's important that the system is sized properly for the amount of power required.

What to Know Before Installing

- Most climates can support a degree of renewable energy, but some locations are superior in terms of sunlight availability and temperature.
- Rooftop installations must be accurate to avoid leaks and to assure the roof can carry the weight of the array.
- Roof tiles that double as solar panels are available but do not perform as well as a separate array.
- Renewable energy installations are subject to local building and planning regulations – make sure you know what is permitted before work starts.

KNOW YOUR MICRO-ORGANISMS

Identifying unwelcome life forms in your home makes it easier to get rid of them

You're not the only one living in your house. Underneath and on top of the surface are micro-organisms, wind-blown seeds and fungi that can grow out of control. Normally, we all co-exist thanks to soap and water, good ventilation and dry conditions. But sometimes, the relationship breaks down, and you may find black stains on a bathroom ceiling or green fuzzy stuff growing on the roof. When it's really bad, you get true rot, the eating away of wet wood because of an unseen water problem. While you can't eliminate the source of spores and fungi, you can control them in your house.

All of these invisible-to-the-eye freeloaders feed off wood, paper, plaster and some paints, and they can wreak havoc

Mould

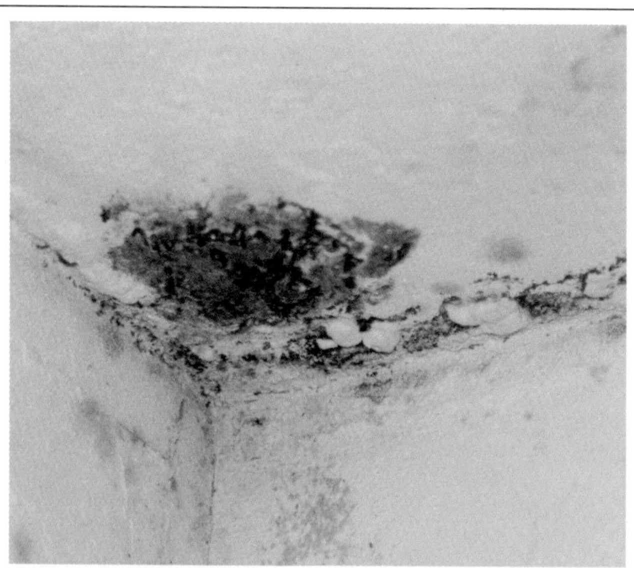

- Mould is a fungus, a type of plant that produces air-borne spores that are everywhere and survive only in moist areas while living on organic materials such as wood or wallpaper.
- You must rectify the moisture problem that supports the mould.
- Good housekeeping practices, including keeping outdoor areas swept clean, can help keep the presence of mould to a minimum.
- Various moulds, which can appear in different colours, can irritate allergies and asthma.

Mildew

- Mildew is a type of mould – the terms are often used interchangeably.
- Growth occurs in areas of high humidity, poor ventilation and warm temperatures.
- Bathrooms are a favourite for mildew growth, and the only effective cure is good ventilation after cleaning and removing any existing mildew and sealing the surfaces it grew on.
- Synthetic fabrics resist mildew, but cotton, linen, rayon, silk, wool, leather, paper and wood do not.

in your home. On roofs, if moss gets an anchor hold it never lets go. Wet or dry rot cause structural damage and must be addressed. In extreme cases of interior mould, your health can be endangered and the mould may need to be professionally removed.

Understanding these biological menaces will help you eliminate them and protect your home from future problems.

YELLOW LIGHT

Be sure to wear protective gloves when scrubbing away mould and mildew. You don't want to chance a skin reaction to the fungi nor expose yourself to the strong soaps and bleach used during the cleaning. If you're especially sensitive to the spores, an appropriate respirator might be needed as well.

Moss

- Moss is a plant without a normal system of roots, stems, and leaves that lives in moist locations and is spread by airborne spores.
- The edges of wet roofing felt can attract moss, and as it grows, the material stays wetter longer and can deteriorate.
- Moss is very hardy and survives drought conditions as well as freezing temperatures.
- When moss is found in lawns, it's an indicator of overly wet conditions, too much shade, acidic soil or poor drainage.

Dry Rot

- Dry rot is a fungus that aggressively attacks timber in buildings. Despite its name, it requires damp conditions in order to thrive.
- The fungus breaks down the cell walls in the wood and weakens them, leaving wood soft and powdery.
- Dry rot is capable of spreading through walls between plaster and brickwork, so it may be necessary to strip back plasterwork to treat the problem.
- The moisture that fostered the rot must be controlled to prevent future infestation.

INTERIOR MOULD & MILDEW

A good cleaning and ventilation are your main weapons against these pesky fungi

The terms 'mould' and 'mildew' are often used interchangeably for nasty green stuff you never want to see again. In fact, they are both fungi, micro-organisms spread by spores. In the outside world, they're a good thing, as they help to break down organic material. Inside, however, they're an unsightly nuisance at best and a health concern at worst to those sensitive to them. Both like wet, warm environments and food – walls, ceilings, fabrics and carpet – all of which if sufficiently damp can support mould and mildew life.

The obvious candidates for mould and mildew are poorly ventilated bathrooms and kitchens. Any unseen damp area due to a leaking roof or pipe can support fungal growth.

Cleaning Interior Mould

- Fill a bucket with water and add some all-purpose cleaner and a cupful of household bleach; wear rubber gloves to scrub and rinse the affected areas.
- After destroying mould, prevent its return by installing better ventilation or repairing a leaky pipe if necessary.
- Never paint or wallpaper over mould or mildew without cleaning and killing it first – it will eventually work its way through to the surface.
- Allow shampooed carpets to dry out thoroughly (wet carpet is an ideal breeding ground for mould).

Heat and Ventilation

- Controlling interior temperatures and humidity levels throughout the year goes a long way toward controlling mould and mildew growth.
- Cupboards on uninsulated exterior walls have a higher humidity level in cold weather – leave their doors open to keep air circulating.
- Observe your windows for mould growth in the winter, and consider using a dehumidifier to reduce window condensation.
- Be selective about storage in a cold cellar – textiles and books can become mildewed under the right conditions.

A good cleaning with hot water and a strong cleaner/bleach solution will remove most mould and mildew, but you must correct the conditions that allowed them to grow as well. Cleaning cures the symptoms but doesn't cure the cause. A solution could be a simple matter of turning the heat up higher during the winter months or installing a ventilation fan (or using an existing fan more often and for longer periods of time).

MAKE IT EASY

Keep a squeegee or extra towel in the shower to wipe down tile walls after showering. This helps the grout dry out faster and diminishes the chance for mould to grow. As a plus, your shower is easier to clean when you do your weekly house cleaning, and the sealant around the shower will last longer.

Extractor Fan

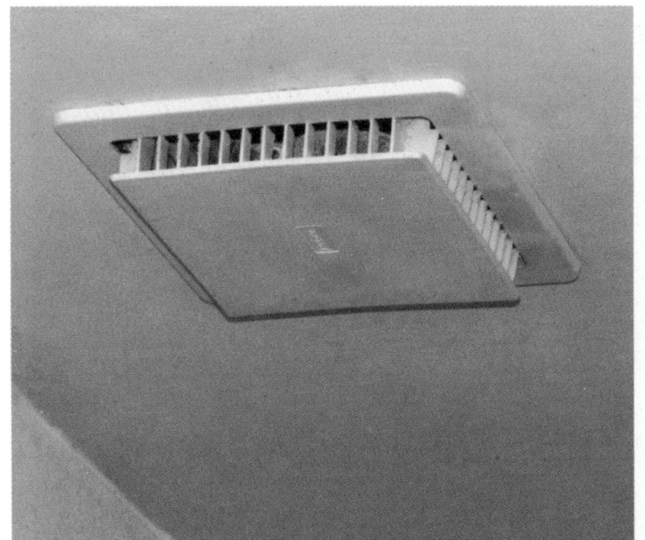

- A large-capacity bathroom fan will remove moisture fast and is especially effective if set on a timer.
- Any ventilation fan must be ducted to the outside, either through the roof or an exterior wall.
- Whole-house ventilation systems are timer-controlled to initiate air exchanges on a user-determined basis.
- Before installing a fan, confirm whether your existing wiring can be used or whether a new circuit will be required.

Painting a Wall

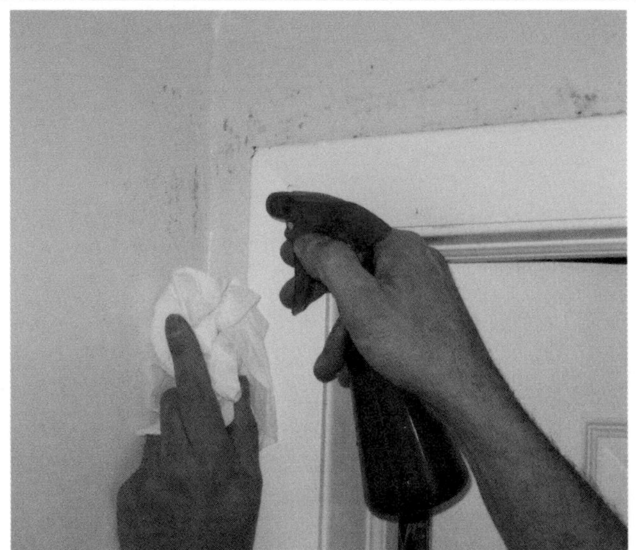

- Thoroughly clean any mouldy surface before repainting to prevent the mould from growing under the new paint.
- Many new paints formulated for exteriors, bathrooms and kitchens contain fungicide to resist mould and mildew growth, but always check with your supplier before purchasing.
- Some authorities advise against painting any areas a child could suck on with paint containing fungicide.
- Inexpensive paints and those containing linseed oil are susceptible to mildew.

EXTERIOR MOULD

Mould can damage the outside of your house, so remove it when you see it

As much as mould likes living inside, it mainly exists outside on the surface of plants. As spores are released, mould finds all kinds of new homes, including wooden decking and weatherboarding. Why decking? It's often not maintained especially well, and the typical coating of stain – and its fungicide – isn't long-lasting. As the spores land, all the exposed wood is more susceptible to the fungi. Decking in damp climates or overshadowed by trees is even more inviting. Regular sweeping and scrubbing with a mild household cleaner go a long way to keeping mould at bay.

Timber cladding can be susceptible to mould growth, too, especially when it's on a shady wall. Shrubs and bushes planted

Outside Spores Growth Conditions

- The air outside is full of spores and plenty of places for them to land and multiply in temperatures ranging anywhere from 5 to 40°C.
- Exterior wood that's shaded and/or damp is a likely mould-breeding area – remove or trim any overhanging plants, and the mould should dry up with sufficient sunshine.
- Mould fungi do not structurally attack wood; they do affect paint finishes and general appearance.
- Be sure any exterior paint you apply has added fungicide if mould is a problem.

Planting

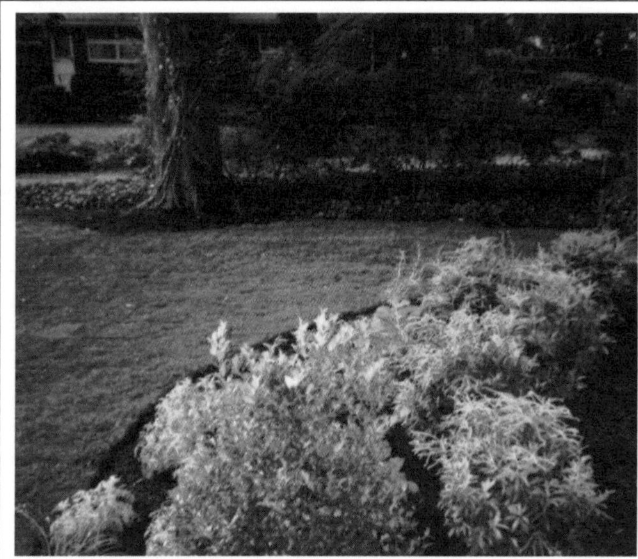

- Plants growing too close to a house, especially in shady conditions, will not allow enough heat and light to dry out wet woodwork such as window frames.
- Consider leaving at least 45 cm between the plants and the house.
- Prune back any tall bushes or shrubs or replace them with shorter plants.
- Be sure the ground around the house slopes away from it and that no soil touches any wooden parts of the structure.

close to the house can add to the problem. Some quick work with secateurs to cut back the plants and spot scrubbing on the wall should help control the problem.

Exterior mould starts slowly but can grow if left alone. It's more than an unsightly problem; it can destroy paint and, unless it's cleaned off and eliminated, it will affect future repainting as well. Catching mould early and keeping it under control can easily be part of normal yearly maintenance.

YELLOW LIGHT

Pressure washing will remove surface mould, but you can't depend on it to do a complete job. The mould often has to be scrubbed to remove it. To achieve this result with a pressure washer alone would probably require so much pressure the decking could be damaged.

Decking Maintenance

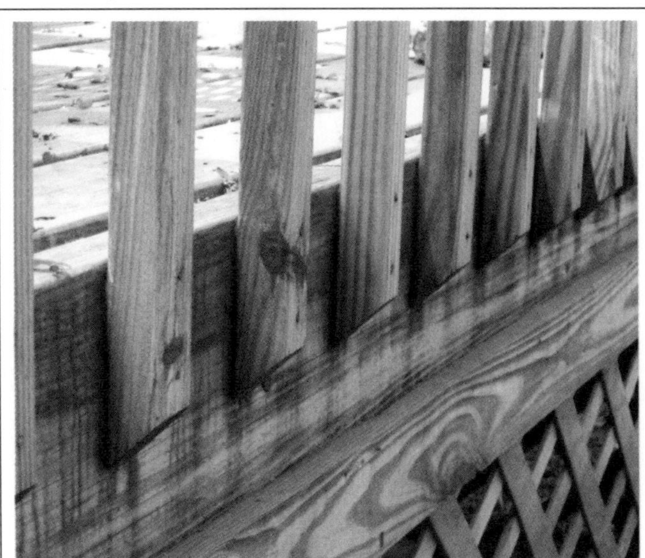

- Keep decking regularly swept so spores can't get a foothold.
- Wash decking regularly with a mild soap and water solution – a regular garden hose will do; a pressure washer isn't necessary for maintenance cleaning.
- Seal the wood once a year, before the weather turns cold, with an exterior stain or clear varnish containing fungicide.
- If decking is in poor but restorable condition, consider sanding the boards smooth so they're less likely to hold spores and water.

Cleaning Exterior Woodwork

- To clean exterior mould from walls and window-frames, add a bottle of household bleach to a 4-litre bucket of hot water and add some disinfectant cleaner.
- Scrub the affected surfaces with a soft brush, avoiding nearby plants.
- Rinse with a garden hose, again avoiding any plants.
- Repair any areas of damaged paintwork by stripping, sanding, priming, and applying two coats of new paint with added fungicide.

SERIOUS MOULD

Regularly inspect your home for mould or mould-friendly conditions to avoid unwanted health problems

In a home without ventilation or moisture problems, any mould that shows up is most likely your standard unsightly annoyance. Some people, though, are sensitive to moulds and can suffer a range of health problems. Symptoms may include a stuffy nose, running eyes, wheezing and skin irritation. More severe reactions may include fever and shortness of breath. Moulds can be particularly serious allergens for those with chronic lung conditions such as asthma.

Unless you suffer flooding, extremely high humidity, a leaking roof or other moisture problems, the chances of your home harbouring toxic moulds are slim. Vigilance is important, however, and regularly inspecting your premises

Serious Mould

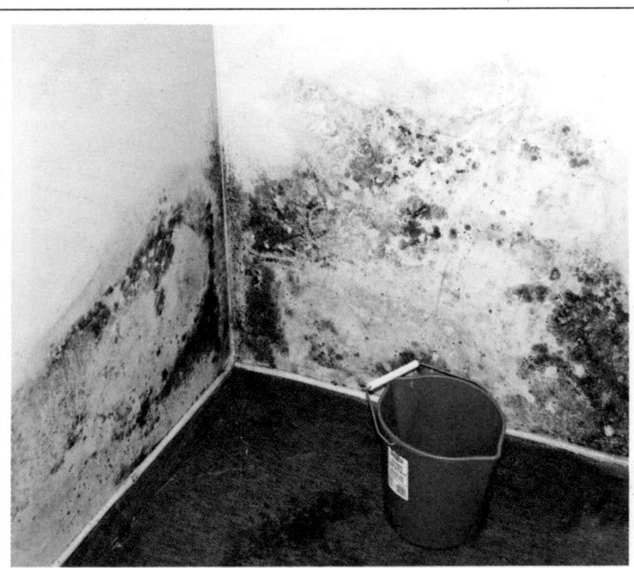

- Serious mould results from ongoing water leakage or seepage problems that go unnoticed or unattended to.
- Sure signs are softened plaster, soggy floors and large affected areas.
- Extensive mould can be a health issue for people with allergies, asthma or other lung diseases and can result in symptoms ranging from a skin rash to difficulty breathing and nausea, depending on the mould.
- If you even consider removing damaged areas yourself, wear protective clothing, gloves and a respirator.

Black Mould

- So-called black (toxic) mould produces hazardous microtoxins and can be a health risk.
- Black mould, as referred to in the media, is one of the *Stachybotrys* types of mould, shown to be harmful to humans.
- These moulds grow in wet, humid conditions and are eliminated when the wet conditions are eliminated.
- Blue, black or green stains on ceilings and walls are signs of black mould, as are brown, orange, or green stains on tiles and grout.

for any mould-friendly conditions should be on your list of things to do. If you can smell mould – it will be an earthy or musty smell – explore for the source. If you discover a major source of mould, walk away and call a remedial contractor who is equipped to remove and clean the affected area properly. After that, moisture control will be the key to preventing the mould's return.

ZOOM

The main culprit when referring to toxic mould is *Stachybotrys chartarum*, a fungus that produces toxins harmful to humans. It became known as 'black mould' in the 1990s and is said to be one of the causes of 'sick building syndrome'.

Controlling Moisture in Your Home

- Make sure air bricks and other ventilators are not blocked and fit extractor fans in kitchen and bathrooms.
- Keep lids on saucepans when cooking; open the kitchen window and shut the door to keep steam out of the rest of the house.
- Dry clothes outdoors where possible; non-condensing tumble dryers should be vented to the outside.
- Avoid bottled gas and paraffin heaters.

Hiring Professionals

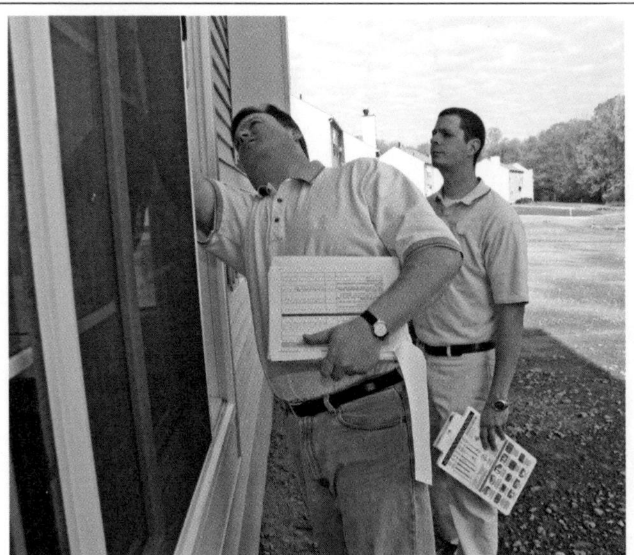

- Removing and decontaminating extensive mould aren't do-it-yourself activities.
- If mould is widespread, consult a specialist to evaluate the problem and advise on improving your ventilation.
- Find a separate, unrelated contractor to remove the mould and carry out improvements.
- Be sure the cleaning and and costs are clearly spelled out in advance as well as any warranties that apply.

WOOD ROT

Rotting wood is unsafe and must be repaired right away

The term 'rot' is tossed around too casually. Severely weathered wood that's rough and splintered after years of weather exposure is not rotted wood. Wet wood is not automatically rotted. Rather, soft wood that pulverizes into powder or disintegrates when poked with a screwdriver is considered rotted. It may be due to the presence of either wet rot or dry rot, both of which thrive in damp conditions. Rot results when certain fungi find wet wood to dine on in a damp, preferably dark environment. Fungi are selective diners when it comes to wood and prefer the cellulose or lignin – parts of wood's cell structure – depending on the fungus. As they chomp away, the cell walls weaken and eventually collapse.

Rotted Wood

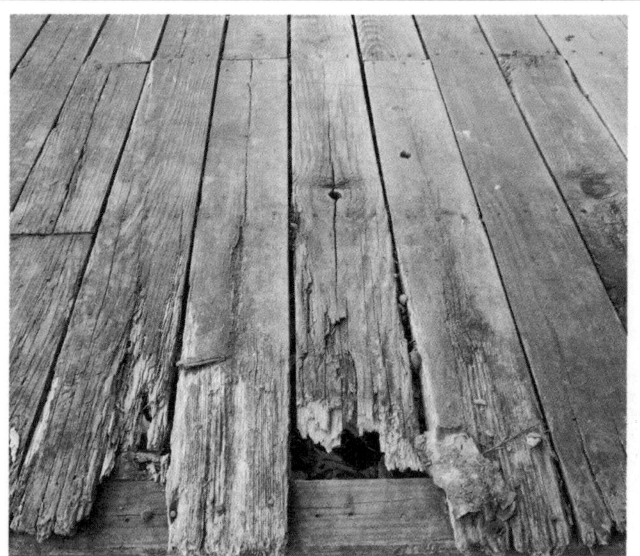

- Wood rot is found in dark, moist areas, such as cellars, and anywhere that remains damp and dirty.
- Remove all damaged wood, apply bleach or another fungicide to the rotted area, allow it to dry, and replace the damaged wood with either epoxy or with new wood.
- Use caution around rotted structural timber. Any repairs to the structure call for professional help and may require the involvement of your local building control department.

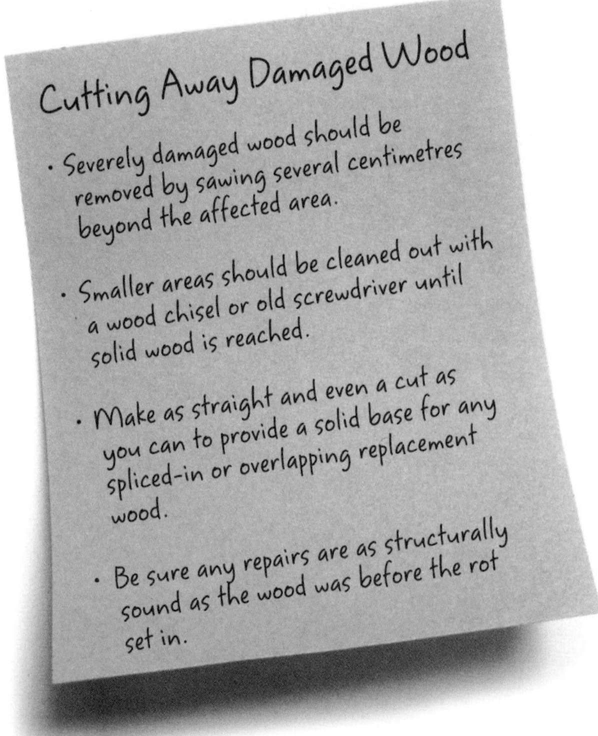

Cutting Away Damaged Wood
• Severely damaged wood should be removed by sawing several centimetres beyond the affected area.
• Smaller areas should be cleaned out with a wood chisel or old screwdriver until solid wood is reached.
• Make as straight and even a cut as you can to provide a solid base for any spliced-in or overlapping replacement wood.
• Be sure any repairs are as structurally sound as the wood was before the rot set in.

Rot manifests itself with white or brown staining and very soft wood. The worse the rot, the more damaged the wood. The first step when repairing is to stop the water problem. The rot will return as long as wet conditions allow it. The wood should then be replaced or treated and repaired with epoxy filler. Extensive rot that has infested a large section of a house calls for professional repairs.

MAKE IT EASY

You might not have any problems with rotten wood now, but it's wise to head off any future problems. Check that gutters and downpipes are intact and not leaking into the eaves or under a covered porch. Inspect pipes for leaks or corroded sections that need monitoring. Check that flowerbeds near house walls are not bridging a damp proof course.

Spraying Bleach

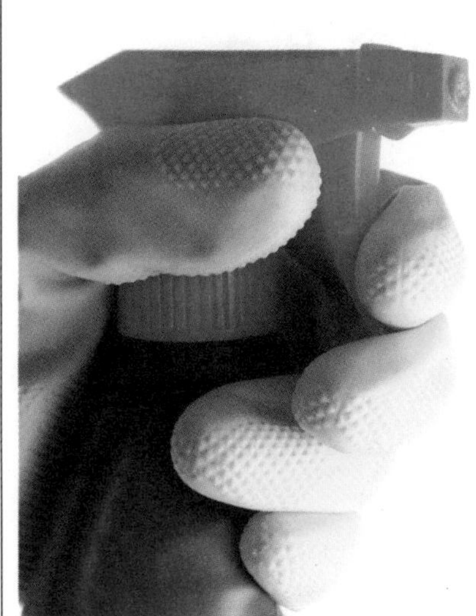

- After removing all rotted wood, spray or apply chlorine bleach (wear gloves and eye protection) or a commercial fungicide liberally over the damaged areas.
- Allow the area to completely dry before continuing the repairs.
- Drying can be speeded up with a heat gun.
- As with any water-related repair, be sure you've eliminated the leakage or exposure that caused the rot in the first place in addition to repairing the damage.

Epoxy Repair

- Small areas of rot can be repaired with any number of epoxy products available at paint and marine supply stores.
- Epoxies set very quickly – fully prepare the area before mixing the epoxy ingredients.
- Build up the epoxy in layers according to the package instructions.
- Sand or file the repaired area smooth if it's finished wood and seal with primer and paint; otherwise, concealed areas can be left with a rougher appearance.

INSTALLING A PET DOOR

A properly installed pet door allows your pets to come in but keeps weather out

A pet door provides an opportunity for your pet to enjoy a more natural environment when you are not around and eliminates the need to 'hold it' all day until someone comes home. Pet doors are convenient for both the pet and the owner and, when installed properly, minimize the cold air entering a warm home.

Pet doors are available to match pet sizes and come in a wide variety of styles. Some are manually operated – the pet pushes it open – and others have electronic locks that respond to a sensor on the pet's collar. A pet can come and go at will with either type of door. A pet door can be installed through an exterior door, window or timber wall.

Basic Facts about Pet Doors

- Purchase a door suitable for the type of installation you're doing and always read the instructions first.
- Find a door that is the right size for your pet and mount it at a comfortable height for the animal's use.
- Choose a clear door so that your pet can see any potential threats outside before going through it.
- Medium and large pet doors can be a security risk if someone is small enough to gain entry or can reach through with a stiff wire device to unlock a nearby door.

Installing the Door

Tools You'll Need
– pet door and any extensions
– template
– utility knife
– long drill bit
– jigsaw or reciprocating saw
– filler

- Choose the location for your pet door and make sure you can fit it at a suitable height for the animal.
- If you are planning to fit the door in a window or glazed door, you will probably require a glazier to cut a suitable hole in the glass.
- Alternatively, for a small window, you could have a new pane cut to size and a hole cut by your local glass merchant, following the pet door template. You can then fit the replacement pane and insert the pet door.

There are many different models, and 'tunnel' extensions are available for some brands that enable them to be fitted in doors or walls of any thickness. Properly installed, a pet door will be sealed against the weather, benefit your pet, and buy you some time if you're late returning home.

YELLOW LIGHT

Pets take to pet doors at their own pace. Don't expect yours to master the door instantly. Some take, seemingly, forever, but there are strategies to help them along. Don't assume you can neglect dog-walking duties the same day the door goes in – they'll adapt to it when they're ready.

Installing the Door (continued)

- Position the template that comes with the door, check it is level and use it to locate and mark the corners of the opening.
- Remove the entry door for easier cutting and installation. Drill a hole in each corner and cut out the opening using a jigsaw.
- In a panelled door, the gap between the pet door frame and the panel might have to be filled in with narrow strips of wood.
- Fill around the edge of the cut-out area and press the pet door into the filler to assure a good seal and to protect the wood.

Training your Pet to Use the Door

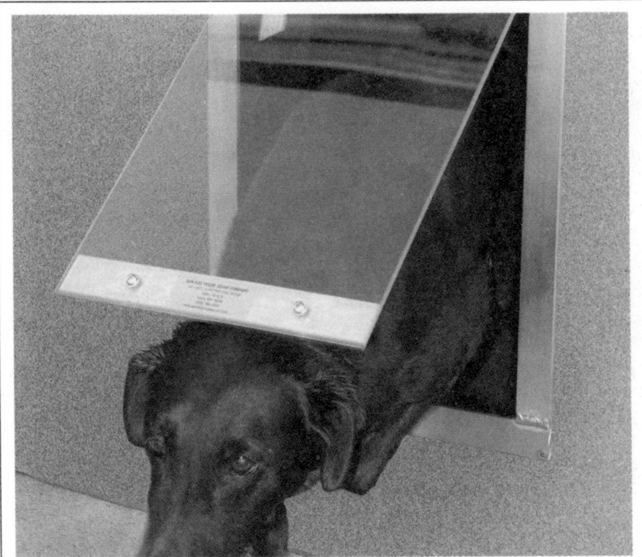

- Give your pet time to become familiar with the door. Young puppies and kittens may have trouble pushing it open at first: you can prop the door open or remove the magnet that holds it closed.
- Put the pet outside just before a meal then entice him to push the door to come in for food.
- If your cat is used to a litter tray indoors, move it close to the door, then move it outside and leave it until the cat abandons it and digs in the garden.

BIRD DAMAGE & REPAIRS

Birds can damage more than just your property – they can also spread disease – so remove them quickly

Birds, like rodents, will live wherever they can find acceptable shelter. This often means using your home to make their nests. An attic or area protected by a roof overhang makes a great shelter: it's relatively dry, concealed and close to food. However, their nesting habits can leave you with a lot of mess to clean up.

Birds also do considerable damage with their droppings, which can transmit diseases to humans from both physical contact and inhalation. Birds reproduce quickly, so you may end up with two generations if you don't get rid of them early. You might need to call in an exterminator if you find yourself up against a particularly stubborn

Birds in the Attic

- Birds will contaminate attics and any nesting places with their droppings, which are health hazards.
- Pigeons or other birds roosting in covered roof areas will stay away while you remove a nest but can return later unless the area is blocked off.
- Something as simple as playing loud music in an loft space can drive adult birds out, but be sure that none of their offspring are left behind.

Bird Removal

- Once the birds and nesting material are removed, thoroughly clean the area with an all-purpose disinfectant cleaner and bleach solution.
- Any tiles that have been damaged should be replaced and any damaged painted areas cleaned, sanded, primed and repainted.
- After removing the birds and repairing the area, monitor it for their return.
- Check other areas similar to the one they were using and block these off as well before the birds relocate.

species. Remember, they are not your friends – don't let them nest in your home.

If there is extensive damage, leave the cleaning up to a professional, who will take away any hazardous material.

RED LIGHT

Never seal up access holes used by rodents, birds, wasps, or any other animals or insects that have got inside your house until you're sure they have all been removed. Trapping them inside without an escape route will only make matters much worse. A professional exterminator will guarantee the job – call one.

PETS & PESTS

Cleaning Up the Mess

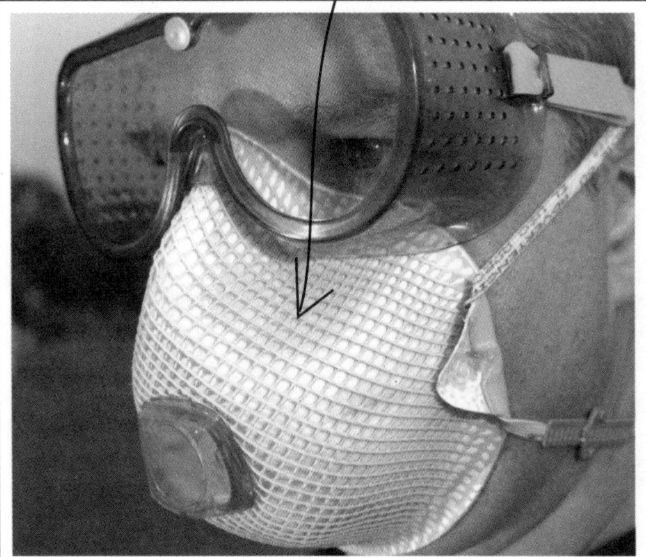

- Droppings are dangerous in both wet and dried form, but especially dry because they can pulverize during removal and become airborne and inhaled.
- Protective gear including gloves, disposable coveralls, and a respirator with HEPA filters should be worn.
- All contaminated debris should be double-bagged and disposed of.
- Extensive damage should be left to professional wildlife and pest removal experts, who will vacuum out all hazardous materials and clean the structure.

Installing Rails, Bars and Spikes

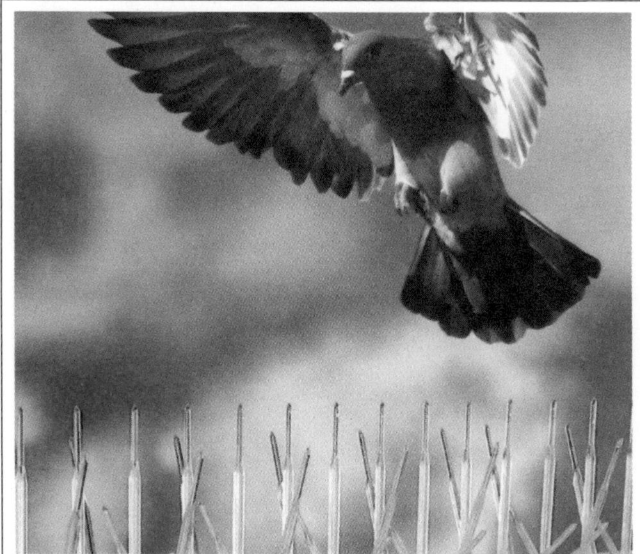

- Sealing every possible access point should keep birds and rodents out.
- A simple solution to prevent birds from returning to roosting areas under roof overhangs or porch ceilings is installing a series of wood rails or bars, spaced so birds cannot pass through.
- Another method is installing stainless steel bird spikes, which are attached with adhesive.

WASPS & BEES

It isn't enough to eliminate these insects; you have to eliminate what they leave behind, too

There are over a million known species of insects in the world, and many more that we have not yet discovered. We could not live without them nor would we want to, but you don't want to live with them buzzing inside your walls or loft, or even too close to your garden furniture. Your home makes a convenient and sheltered living area for flying squatters such as wasps and ants. All they need is a small opening through a wall or into a roofspace to get started.

Honeybees will not do structural damage, but they will leave honey and wax combs that can attract rodents and other insects that could do damage to structural timbers. It isn't enough to remove the bees; you have to find the nest,

Wasps

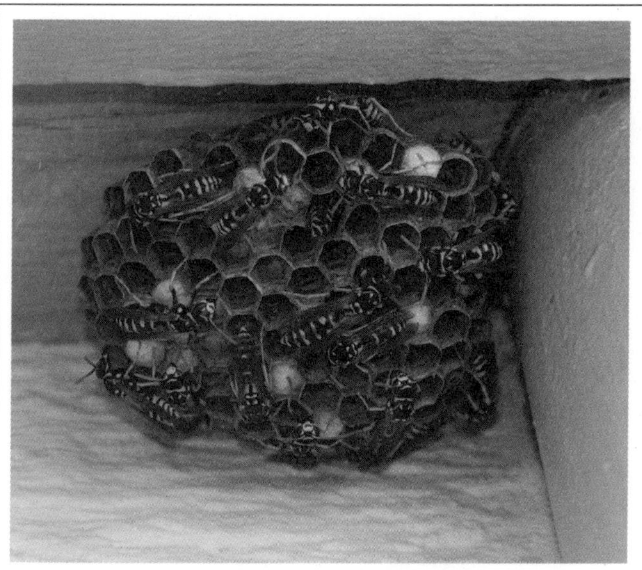

- Locate active wasps' nests during the day, but spray at night when the nest is full.
- Wasps can often be eliminated with over-the-counter aerosol insecticides.
- Their nests last one season – if they're not particularly bothersome, but in an awkward spot to remove, you might decide to leave them alone and remove the empty nest in cold weather.
- After spraying an outside nest and confirming no wasps have returned, remove with a long pole and rinse with a hose.

Insecticide

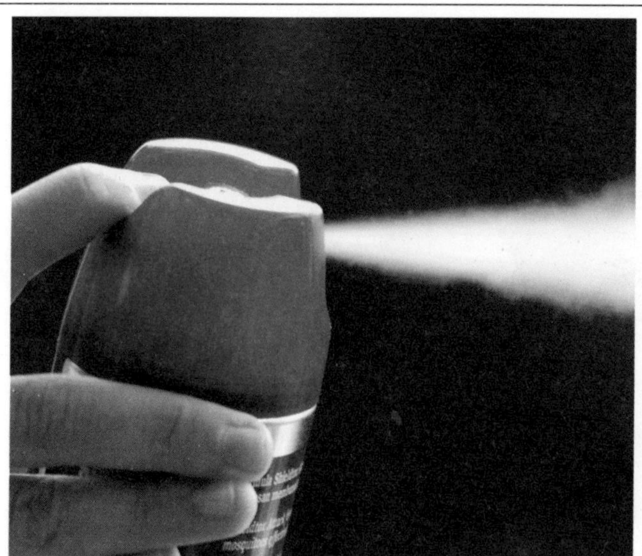

- Like any poison, insecticides must be handled carefully and used effectively.
- Read and follow label directions for your chosen insecticide and always spray from a safe distance, being sure no other people or pets are nearby.
- Always store insecticides safely where children cannot access them.
- Some sprays have an oil base and leave a residue that should be washed off any painted surfaces the next day.

remove any honey and deodorize the area. As with other home invaders, you don't want to seal off the entry point until all the insects have been removed.

Wasps don't leave honey, but they do sting. However, they will only be with you for one season. If you can live with their presence until winter comes, freezing temperatures should kill them off and provide you with time to remove old nests, which will not be reused by the insects in any event.

RED LIGHT

Wasps can be aggressive. You don't want to approach a nest during the day to exterminate it. Wait until evening when the nest is full before spraying with an appropriate insecticide. It may be wise to call in your local pest control officer to destroy the nest.

Trap

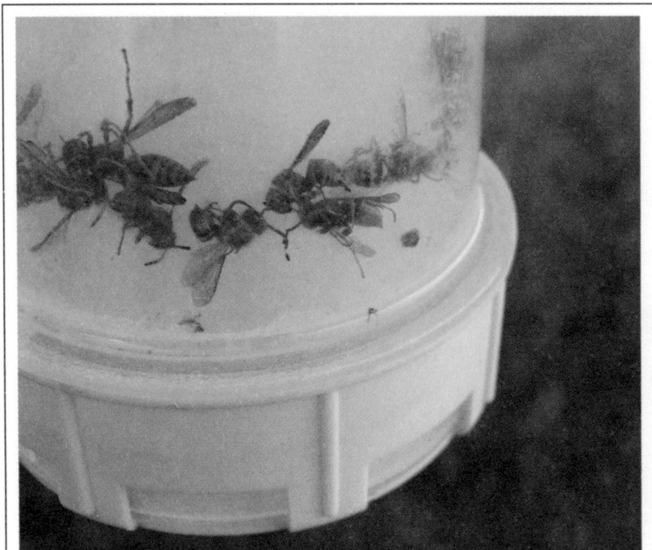

- Various kinds of trap are available that attract wasps away from your home or garden table.
- You can easily make your own traps by putting honey, jam or syrup in a few jars: the wasps will simply get stuck in them.
- Traps cannot control an entire nest full of wasps, but a few strategically placed in the garden or near open doors can be effective for nuisance wasps when you are eating.

Bees in the Wall

- Removing a honeybee colony is not a do-it-yourself job.
- Bees typically swarm in late spring, and need to be removed without being trapped inside your home.
- A member of your local beekeepers' association will probably be happy to collect the colony to re-hive it.
- Complete removal of the colony is critical to prevent damage from fermenting honey, which can attract more destructive pests.

PEST-PROOFING YOUR HOME

Keeping pests out early is easier than trying to evict them later

An ounce of prevention may be worth a pound of cure, but when it comes to keeping animals out of your house, a few boards and some screening can save you a lot of money not spent in cleaning out and repairing a damaged roof or wall space. If you haven't had any four-footed or winged visitors, the first step is to do a complete exterior inspection.

Look for any hole, opening or gap – for instance, between a pipe and the surrounding concrete foundation. Rats and mice can squeeze into impossibly small holes. Pay attention to any wood that appears to have been gnawed at or is rotted. Holes should be filled, and compromised wood should be repaired. The goal is to seal off your house completely.

Installing a Chimney Guard

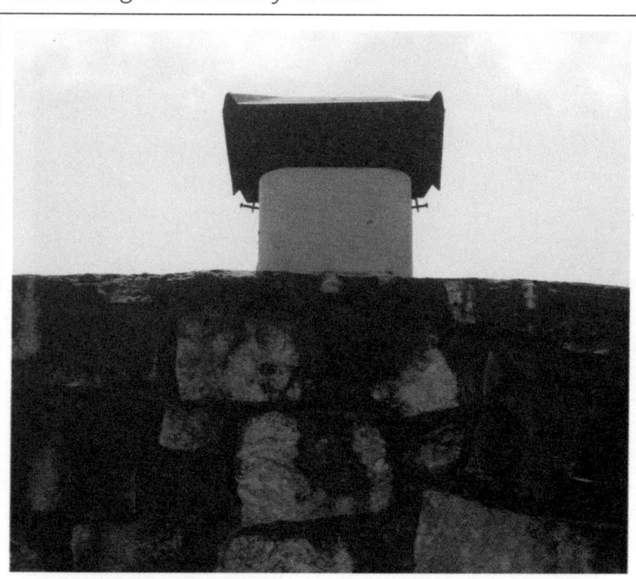

- Chimney guards protect the inside of the chimney from rain and birds while allowing the normal chimney functions to continue, as long as the guard isn't too close to the top of the chimney.
- A guard made of heavy mesh is sufficient to keep birds out.
- For easier chimney cleaning, look for a guard with a hinged top.
- When you find the type you want, check with the manufacturer that it will fit your chimney before purchasing.

Installing Screening

- Install fine-gauge chicken wire screens to cover any large gaps through which birds or rodents could access your roofspace or outbuildings.
- Aerosol spray foam works as a temporary filler in holes and gaps.
- Check for gaps at the bottom of garage, basement or back doors, and install thresholds or strips of draught proofing if needed.
- Seal any gaps between roof vents and clay tiles.

Water drainage is critical. You don't want soggy areas next to foundations or standing water under downpipes. Anything that attracts animal or insect life is fair game, including restricting access to food sources. A compost heap is a very good idea, but an open one is an invitation – don't include any cooked food scraps in the mixture.

MAKE IT EASY

Sealing off your home is an inexpensive proposition. For the price of a little exterior-grade filler, you can eliminate many if not all of the possible entry points for unwanted animals and insects. The key is being diligent and remembering that any opening presents an opportunity, so attend to them all.

Patching Concrete

- Seal up all openings with suitable materials: fill holes in concrete and replace missing mortar in brickwork.
- If appearances aren't too important, use sheet metal to cover large gaps.
- Rats and mice can squeeze into very small spaces around pipes and conduit passing through outer walls – be sure to fill and seal these.

Securing Dustbins

- Use a dustbin with a tight-fitting lid, and don't leave garbage outside in plastic bags, which will be shredded by foraging foxes or badgers.
- Be aware of food sources that will attract rodents, including pet feeding bowls and bird feeders.
- Leaving food out for any form of wildlife will also attract animals you don't want to feed.
- Collect and dispose of fallen fruit from trees in the garden if rodents are a problem.

CHOOSING THE PAINT & SHEEN

Anyone can paint, but first know what you're painting with

Walk into any paint store, and you'll be confronted with cans and more cans. They all look very similar until you start reading the labels: high-gloss enamel, quick-drying satinwood, wall paint, satin water-based, flat matt emulsion. It can be confusing when all you want is to paint a bedroom. So let's walk through what you'll need. Basically, consumer paints are either water-based (acrylic) or oil-based. Oil-based paint is more rarely used now, although there are applications it's best suited for.

For painting that bedroom, water-based paint is easier to apply than oil-based, dries faster, is more forgiving during the application, and has far less odour than the solvent in oil-based

Bathroom

- Matt paints absorb light so fewer imperfections show; they give rooms a softer feel, have less resin than glossier paints, and are less easy to clean.
- Ceilings and areas of least wear and tear are good candidates for matt paints.
- Satin and eggshell are low-lustre paints with moderate gloss, making them easier to clean than matt paints.
- Paint these finishes in bathrooms, kitchens, children's rooms and hallways: anywhere that will get a lot of hands on the walls.

Living Room

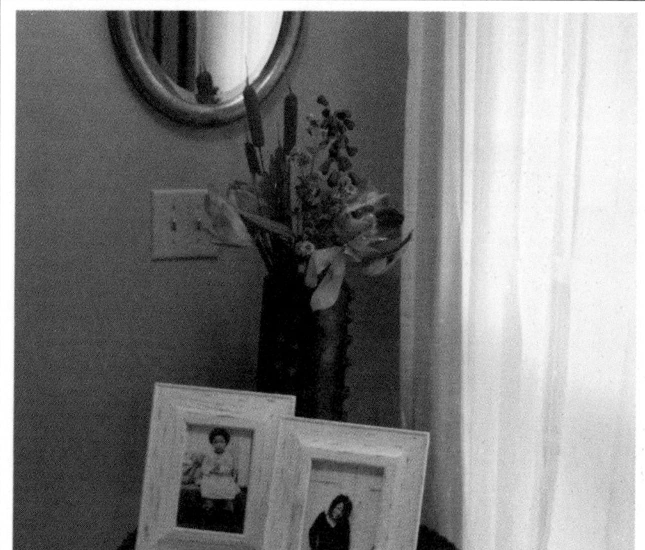

- Matt paints are easier on the eye, especially in well-lit rooms.
- Gloss paint has more resin than satin paints and stands up well to wear and tear and cleaning.
- Non-drip gloss paints are common choices for woodwork, doors and shelves in older homes and are used for repainting in these homes.
- Because of its reflective properties, gloss paint highlights a surface's imperfections, so thorough preparation work is a must before applying this finish.

paint. Paint is composed of three main ingredients: pigment that gives it colour, a binder or resin that forms the film, and a vehicle that keeps the paint in a liquid form. In water-based paint, water is the vehicle. As the water evaporates, the paint film forms to a solid finish. Other ingredients are added by each manufacturer for different purposes such as to provide stability or to regulate the drying time. A higher gloss has more binder in the paint. More pigment generally means a lower gloss and better hiding power.

MAKE IT EASY

If a surface needs regular washing – doorways, for instance, because of handprints – don't use a matt paint. High-gloss paint will show every imperfection, so consider this before applying. If you're uncertain about a colour choice, paint a small area first with a sample pot before ordering all you need.

Interior Woodwork

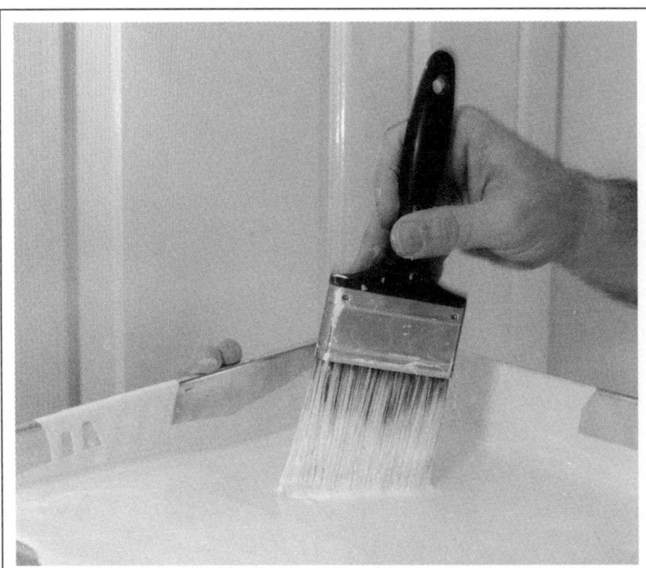

- Oil-based gloss paint is the most durable and hardest paint as it has the highest percentage of resin.
- Traditional oil-based gloss paint demands more skill from the painter applying it, has a longer drying time than water-based paint, and has more long-lasting odour.
- Experiment with gloss finish in a small area to test out the shine.
- You can always recoat a new finish with a gloss that is more suitable.

Summary of Finishes

- Matt: Apply on most ceilings and walls except those needing regular cleaning; not appropriate for woodwork; less reflective, a good finish for less-than-perfect surfaces; different manufacturers have different degrees of matt: some have more sheen than others.
- Satin and eggshell: low sheen, washable, for use in bathrooms and kitchens or any surface that needs frequent washing; also works on woodwork.
- Non-drip gloss: shiny and tough, use on woodwork and furniture.
- Liquid gloss: shiniest of all, use on woodwork and furniture.

INTERIOR PREPARATION

The best paint won't cover up a lack of preparation work

Repainting a room that badly needs it is gratifying – and the gratification is immediate. The contrast between a fresh, clean coat of lemon yellow and the dirty, scarred pine green can be startling. But bad preparation will still show through a fresh paint job. No one wants to prep, but do it anyway if you want the paint to last and to get the best results.

Preparation ranges from filling nail holes, to washing the woodwork, to extensive sanding, depending on the condition of the surfaces and the results you're looking for. If you hate old brush marks, for instance, they will have to be sanded out until the surface is smooth. If cracks in the ceiling bother you, repair them before you paint, or you'll

Washing Walls

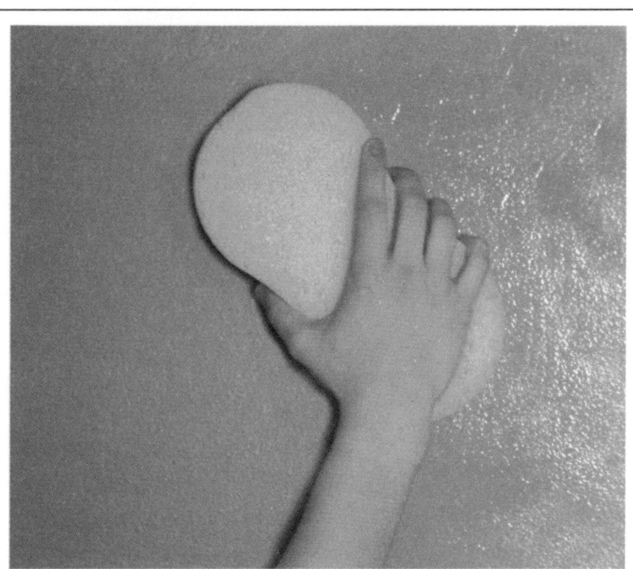

- Paint adheres best to clean surfaces.
- Woodwork should be washed with a non-foaming cleaner to remove dirt, oil and fingerprints.
- Wash bathroom and kitchen walls and ceilings with a non-foaming household cleaner as well to remove all grime and grease.
- Sugar soap is an effective traditional cleaner that removes dirt and grease and also lightly etches the surface to provide a key for painting.

Lightly Sanding Woodwork

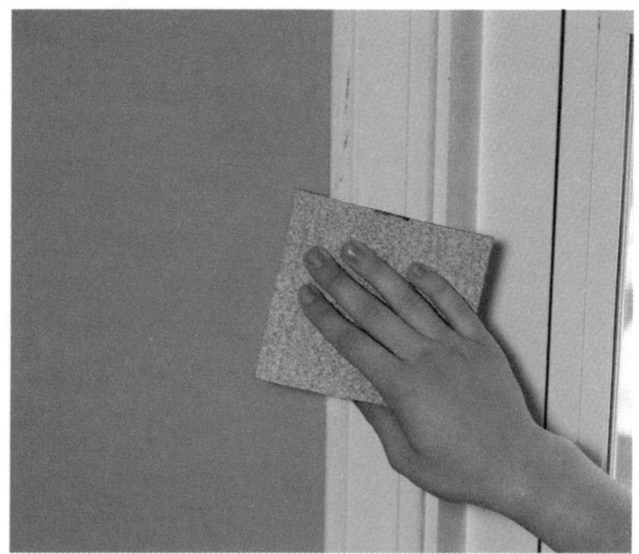

- Lightly hand-sand all woodwork to provide a better key for the next coat of paint and to smooth over nicks and gouges.
- Vacuum the dust and wipe the wood with a tack rag – a muslin cloth impregnated with resin, available from paint stores.
- Dry sanding lead-based paint will release airborne lead particles – wet sand only.
- Repair wall and ceiling cracks, fill woodwork seams, prime bare spots and fill holes, sand smooth and prime.

regret it later. Kitchen and bathroom walls and ceilings get grimy even if you don't quite notice it with the passage of time. Wash and rinse them before painting. Brass fittings with paint drips on them can either get more paint drips or be stripped, cleaned and polished, but you have to remove them first. It all takes time, but you won't regret a minute of it when you finish painting with superior results.

RED LIGHT

It's safe to assume any house built before 1960 has some lead-based paint in it. Even light sanding can spread contaminated dust. Wet sanding alone is impractical for removing deep brush marks. Special sanders with vacuum attachments plus containment procedures will be necessary for this type of preparation.

Removing Fittings

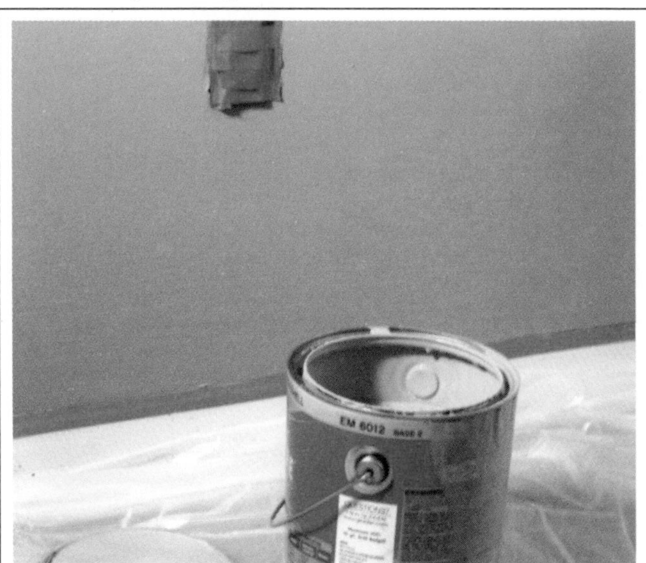

- Remove as much window and door furniture as is practical, keeping screws and fixings in a safe place.
- This is an ideal time to clean, polish and apply a clear coat of varnish, especially to old brass window and door furniture.
- With masking tape, tape off door hinges and any other fittings that can't be removed.

Plastic/Dust Sheets

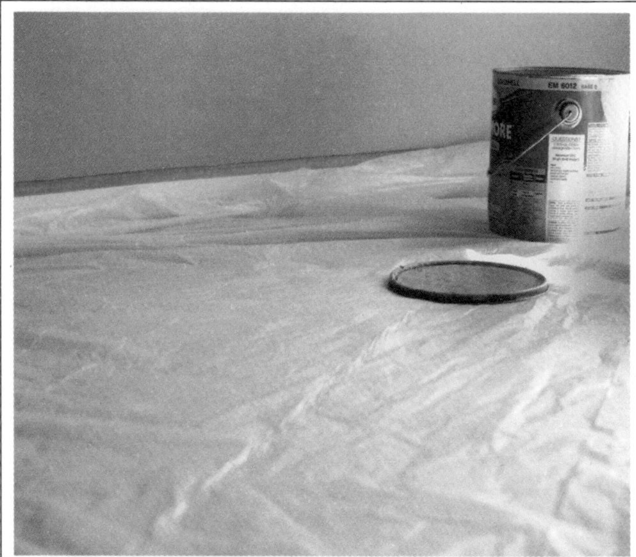

- Remove as much furniture as is practical and pile the remaining pieces on top of each other, leaving enough room to paint.
- Cover the furniture and the whole of the floor with plastic or dust sheets.
- Tape plastic around light fixtures, but keep the plastic away from the potentially hot light bulbs.
- Be sure to cover the entire area to avoid messy dripping paint.

PAINTING CEILINGS & WALLS

You can cover a large area fast with the right tools and a plan

You have a room to paint. Where do you start: the walls, the windows, the ceiling? There is some difference of opinion regarding the order you do things, but everyone would agree that the ceiling should come first. No matter how careful you are, there will be some drips and spatter from this, the highest section of a room. There was a time, before paint rollers were introduced, when all surfaces were painted with brushes from ladders and scaffolds. With today's tools, painting a room can be much less tedious.

With a roller and extension pole, you can paint most walls and ceilings standing on the floor, using a stepladder only to reach corners and angles where the walls meet each other

Painting Tips
• Fewer long strokes are better than more short ones.
• Keep plenty of paint on the roller so that it doesn't dry out, and don't try to spread the paint too far.
• Wet the roller (or brush) as often as you need to for easy movement and full coverage.
• If you need to use more than one can of paint for a single coat, mix all the paint together to avoid any variations in colour.

Start with the Ceiling

- Before rolling, use a brush to paint a wide stripe around the edge where the ceiling meets the walls.
- Using a roller fitted on an extension pole, start at one corner of the ceiling and work along the shortest direction to the other side.
- Roll a metre-square 'W' to distribute the paint and then roll in one direction.
- Some white emulsion paint contains a pink dye that allows you to easily see any missed areas while painting; as it dries the paint turns white.

and the ceiling, or to paint around light fittings. Painting with a roller gives a slight 'orange peel' texture, but it's much faster and easier than working with a brush.

The key to painting any wall or ceiling is to aim for even and complete coverage, using plenty of paint, and to avoid roller marks. Work in good light so you can see what you're doing, and take your time until it looks right.

Cutting In

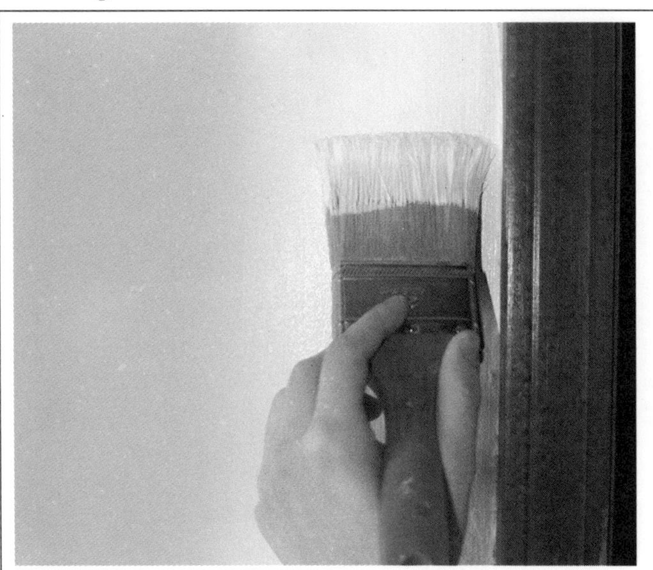

- If the walls are to be a different colour from the ceiling, allow the ceiling to dry before painting the walls, 'cutting in' where the walls meet the ceiling with a paintbrush, in each corner where two walls meet, and around all woodwork.
- Work from one corner of the wall to the other, rolling horizontally at the top and bottom and finishing with vertical rolling, maintaining a wet edge from one section to the next.
- Apply enough paint for full coverage while avoiding sags.

Cleaning Up

- Keep a roller from drying out between coats by wrapping it in a plastic bag.
- Remove as much paint as you can from your roller and brush(es) before rinsing them out.
- Clean emulsion paint from brushes and rollers with warm, soapy water, rinsing repeatedly until the water runs clear.
- Squeeze out as much water as possible then leave rollers to dry on paper towels.
- After painting with oil-based paint, clean brushes with paint thinner and throw rollers away.

WOODWORK & DOORS

Some fancy brush work will make your woodwork and doors stand out

Even though there is less woodwork than wall in most rooms, it can be more noticeable because of its glossier finish. Spray-painting leaves a beautiful, smooth finish, but it's more likely that you will paint your woodwork with a brush.

It's important to use a quality brush, and that means higher-priced. Skimping on brushes might affect your handiwork, since usually the less expensive brushes are also of poorer quality. For water-based paints, use top-end nylon brushes, not blended nylon/polyester brushes. Oil-based finishes, both paint and varnishes, call for a traditional bristle brush. The one-type-fits-all-finishes brush doesn't do a good job with any finish, only a passable one.

Brush Technique

- Paint woodwork after the walls and ceilings (unless you are decorating the room with wallpaper).
- Dip the brush into the paint no more than halfway up the bristles, tapping both sides of the brush against the inside rim of the can to remove excess paint.
- Work from the highest horizontal section of woodwork down, painting in long, even strokes.
- Brush out any drips before the paint dries.

Painting a Sash Window

- Open the window sash – the movable part – any way necessary to completely paint it and the surrounding frame.
- New wood windows with integral draught proofing call for very careful painting to avoid getting paint on the insulating strips.
- If necessary, tape off the glass to avoid getting paint on it.
- If possible, leave each window slightly open overnight – if any paint does stick after drying, you can break the bond by moving the sash.

Although woodwork represents a smaller area, it's all cut-in work and almost always takes more time than the walls and ceiling. With a careful and steady hand, you can avoid taping off the wall where it meets the woodwork and just paint freely. You'll know after you paint your first door casing whether you prefer taping or going freehand. Follow whatever is comfortable for you to get the results you want. Keep in mind that taping is time consuming, perhaps more so than the time needed to paint slowly and carefully.

MAKE IT EASY

Paint wooden windows or exterior doors early in the day so they will be dry enough to close at night if necessary. Move sliding windows every hour or so to prevent them from sticking as the paint dries, and keep moving them until the time they have to be locked for the night.

Painting a Door

- When painting doors, paint panels first, then the horizontal sections of the door, and finally the vertical sections.
- The edge of the door that opens into a room should be painted the same colour as that room's woodwork.
- Paint the top, hidden edge of the door as well – this helps prevent it from sticking later.
- If the door has multiple layers of paint, scrape or sand down the vertical edges to prevent it from sticking in the frame.

Painting a Staircase

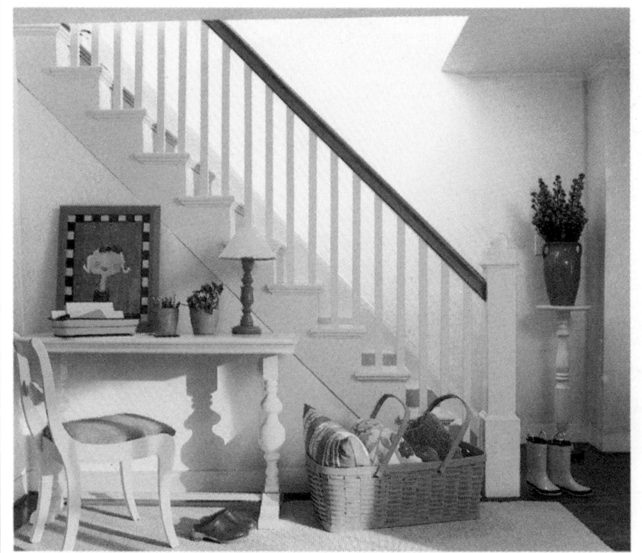

- Staircase parts include the newel posts, the handrail and the balusters or spindles; brushing them as a unit is a challenging job.
- Start on the vertical newel posts and balusters along with the bottom of the handrail, getting the finish as even as possible.
- Next, paint the top and sides of the handrail.
- If the handrail is to be stained and varnished, with painted balusters and newel posts, mask off each section before painting the other.

EXTERIOR PREPARATION

When paint has to withstand the weather, preparatory work is even more critical

Exterior paint preparation ranges from a simple wash and rinse with a hose to full-scale paint removal with sanders, heat, and chemicals. If the the original paint layer is still intact, it will often need just enough scrubbing to remove surface dirt and pollution to get it ready for repainting. But older walls with multiple layers of paint can present multiple problems: there may be areas of flaking, blisters in the paint, chipping and cracking. If the walls are rendered with stucco or a textured surface such as pebbledash, there may be cracks and gaps that need to be filled before painting.

If walls or woodwork are bearing too many layers of paint, it becomes more difficult for a new coat to stick to the old.

Power Washing

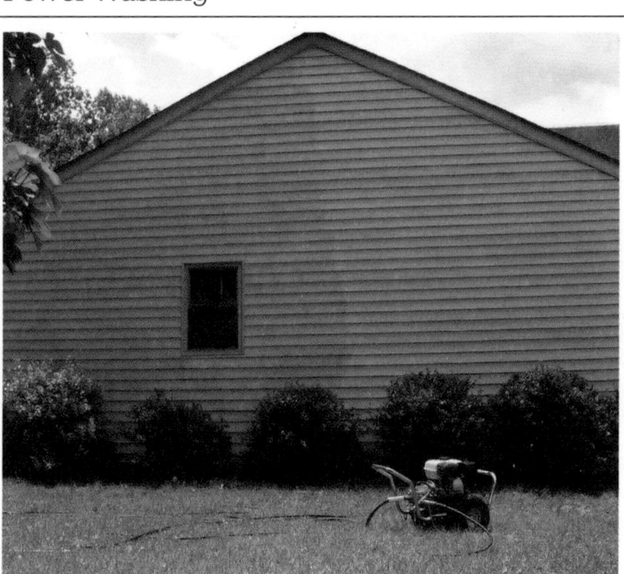

- Power washing walls may involve hiring equipment.
- Scrape off any clinging roots such as ivy and clean off any mildew separately before power washing.
- Start from the top of the wall and spray carefully, keeping the sprayer far enough from the wall so that the surface is cleaned without being damaged.
- This requires working up a ladder, which can be awkward at first due to the pressure of the sprayer. Be careful.

Scraping Paint

- Flaking, peeling and bubbling paint should be scraped and sanded off as needed and all bare areas primed.
- Older homes have a good chance of having some layers of lead-based paint, so wear protection.
- While doing exterior preparation, inspect the fabric of the building carefully for any areas of decayed masonry or rotten wood that need replacing.

Adhesion – the ability of the new paint to stick to the previous coat – is jeopardized by lack of preparation, so this step is a must. Extensive work can be messy and time consuming, but it's extremely important not to skimp on it – whether you are doing the work yourself or have hired a contractor. The most expensive paint cannot disguise poor preparation or have a long life. Exterior painting can be a big job – you want it to last.

MAKE IT EASY

As an alternative to power washing, use a car washing brush set or a telescopic pole with a scrubbing brush attachment. Some kits that attach to a hose include soap dispensers, allowing you to apply both detergent and rinsing water with the brush. Scrubbing the surface by hand can remove more dirt than power washing without the possibility of damage.

Filling Gaps

- Rub down exterior woodwork. If paint has blistered and exposed bare wood, check for any signs of rot.
- Prime any areas of exposed wood.
- Fill small cracks in rendered surfaces such as windowsills with exterior powder filler. Smooth level with the surface when filler is firm but before it sets hard.
- Fill gaps around windows with exterior-grade flexible filler, and follow the directions for curing times before painting.

Colour Selection

- Remember that your roof colour and any masonry details will affect your colour selections for the rest of the house.
- Deep colours are more prone to noticeable fading than light colours.
- Look at paint samples in bright sunlight and dark conditions as well as in average daylight.
- Instead of choosing a contrasting colour for woodwork, consider a lighter or darker shade of the wall colour.

EXTERIOR PAINTING

It's a big job, so break it up into smaller jobs

To make painting the exterior of your house more doable, break the whole project into sections and work on it during scheduled hours. You'll get it done while the weather is still warm and dry without taxing yourself.

Most houses have soffits – the wooden panels under the edges of the roof – windows and doors to paint. If your walls are also painted this is the largest area but the easiest to paint. As with interiors, start at the top and work your way down. If you have a large house, you might want to get some estimates from decorators instead of doing the job yourself.

How long will exterior paint last? It all depends on weather exposure, the condition of the building, the quality of the

Painting the Exterior

- Use a roller to paint a flat wall, using a brush to paint around windows and doors.
- On weatherboarding, brush in long, even strokes, working the paint up and into the timber edges.
- Never stop in the middle of a wall – always complete an entire section before taking a break.
- Hang your paint bucket from an extension ladder using an S-shaped hook.
- Exterior paints are available in pump-action backpack roller systems for an easier and safer job.

Painting Tiles or Shingles

- A wall hung with tiles or wood shingles is an ideal candidate for spray painting – it requires a lot of paint due to its rough surface and has a lot of spaces to fill between shingles.
- Work the paint into all three exposed edges of each tile or shingle, especially the bottom open grain of a wood shingle, which really soaks up paint.
- Watch for drips between the rows – go back and catch them before moving too far down the wall.

preparation, and the quality of the paint. To improve the odds, use quality paint with a high percentage of solids. Apply during warm, dry weather and brush on full, thick coats.

YELLOW LIGHT

Ladders can slip easily, so remember to secure any ladder, especially when you are work higher up. It's a good idea to insert a stout screw eye in an inconspicuous but secure place on the wall, to which you can tie the top of a ladder. It may be necessary to hire a scaffold tower or to have scaffolding erected to do the job safely.

Be prepared to use a lot of paint on textured finishes.

Painting Textured Walls

- Textured wall finishes are usually painted with a coarse roller with a thicker nap, or first sprayed and then rolled.
- Prime any areas that have been repaired, including newly sealed cracks, before painting.
- Modern masonry paints offer flexible, waterproof, protective finishes, and have the added benefit of filling in and sealing hairline cracks.
- Textured walls take a lot of paint: take this into account when buying materials.

Weather Conditions for Painting

- Paint on a dry day, 10–30°C, and avoid direct sunlight.
- Follow the sun around the house so freshly painted areas are not exposed to excessive heat while drying.
- Follow the paint manufacturer's instructions for temperature and shade recommendations.
- Keep in mind that these will be the best, but not always realistic, conditions to try to assure the paint will not fail.

PUTTING UP SHELVES

Adding shelves multiplies your space and makes finding the things you need easy

Think of shelving as multiplying your floor space over and over again. Without shelving, everything would be on the floor or in boxes, and horribly inconvenient to access. Put up a few shelves, and a mess of a garage becomes manageable, you're able to find your shoes in the wardrobe again, and the kids no longer have an excuse for a messy room.

The beauty of shelving is there are virtually no limits to the styles, dimensions and load-carrying ability of shelving. From the finest china teacup to a car engine, there's a shelf that will hold it safely and securely.

Aside from the shelving material – wood, metal, plastic – the shelf supports can be anything from strands of wire and

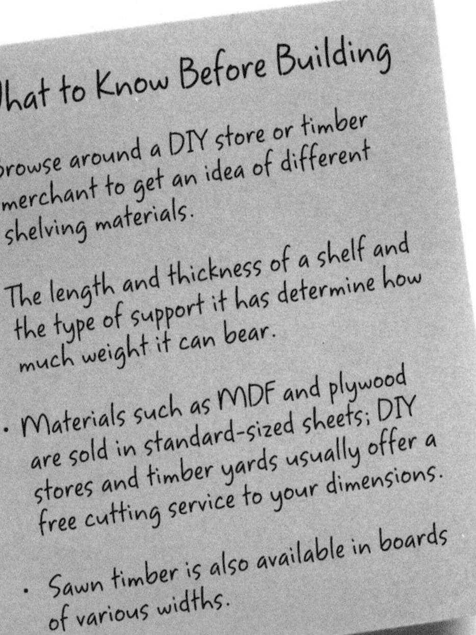

What to Know Before Building
• Browse around a DIY store or timber merchant to get an idea of different shelving materials.
• The length and thickness of a shelf and the type of support it has determine how much weight it can bear.
• Materials such as MDF and plywood are sold in standard-sized sheets; DIY stores and timber yards usually offer a free cutting service to your dimensions.
• Sawn timber is also available in boards of various widths.

Studs and Supports

- Inexpensive metal utility L-shaped shelf brackets will support any length shelf as long as they are screwed into solid walls or studs.
- The other side of the 'L' screws into the shelf.
- Metal shelving systems use slotted uprights that are screwed to the wall and take adjustable brackets, so the shelves can be installed at different levels.
- It's a simple carpentry job to make your own brackets out of short pieces of sawn timber.

cables to solid wooden posts. Hidden supports can also be used for the clean look of floating shelves, and adjustable supports allow shelves to be moved and repositioned as your storage needs change.

Shelving dimensions and the materials used govern the weight a shelf will bear, so there are some design limitations, but they are few and far between, given the materials and designs available.

ZOOM

Plywood makes excellent shelving and is less prone to bowing than engineered materials such as MDF, chipboard or oriented strand board, which are made from fine sawdust or wood chips mixed with resins, glues and binders. For all these materials, 18 mm should be considered the minimum thickness for most shelving.

Shelving Types

- Very lightweight hanging shelves to hold small items can be hung from picture hooks.
- Built-in shelves need to be constructed against solid walls and are ideal for filling spaces such as recesses beside a chimney.
- Floating shelves have hidden supports for a clean, contemporary look yet are still strong enough to support moderate loads.
- Corner shelves can be installed to make good use of unused space.

Sample Installation

Shopping list
- 18-mm MDF cut into 150-mm-wide
shelves
– 34x34-mm planed square-edged
softwood
– 80-mm steel screws and wall plugs
– 40-mm wood screws

- Each shelf should be at least 40 cm long. Mark their positions on the wall, spacing them evenly.
- Cut one support from planed timber for each shelf and to the same length.
- Screw the supports to the wall, then rest a shelf on each and screw the shelf to the support, lining up the ends.
- Cut two boards long enough to screw into the ends of all the shelves and reach the floor to provide support. Check that the shelves are level when screwing into the ends.

MORE SHELVING

Shelving kits, both pre-assembled and custom made, are easy organizers

Shelving kits, some in the form of brackets and supports only and others with the shelves also included, have been around for decades. They make sense for many installations, allow maximum flexibility and are cost effective, but do not offer the finished look of fitted wood shelving. Some finished, self-contained bookshelves offer the best of both worlds: a finished look with mounting strips or clips secured to the sides – where they're barely visible – for adjusting the location of the shelves. Old houses sometimes have custom-made shelving with nicely detailed cutouts for inserting shelves at different levels.

Wire shelving kits are a more contemporary feature. Vinyl-coated or stainless wire shelves with metal brackets are quite

Shelving Materials

- Chipboard is available plain or covered with wood veneer or melamine, which doesn't require painting and is easy to clean.
- Blockboard is engineered wood made of strips of timber glued edge to edge and sandwiched between hardwood veneers. Shelves should be cut with the core timbers running lengthways. Blockboard shelves require edging with veneer strips or moulding.
- Medium density fibreboard (MDF) is available in a range of thicknesses and weights, is easily cut to any shape and has a smooth surface for painting.

Uprights and Brackets

- Steel uprights and brackets are available in different metal finishes, colours, lengths and styles and can be purchased by the piece.
- The brackets are not always interchangeable – be sure the brackets you purchase are made for your uprights.
- Adjustable metal shelving supports are the simplest and most versatile systems available, but they do not offer an especially finished appearance.
- The key to installing uprights is to get them perfectly vertical as well as level with each other.

sturdy, but the gaps between the wires can impose a few limits as to what the shelves can hold (they're not great for thin paper files, for instance).

On the other hand, wire shelves don't accumulate as much dust as solid shelves, nor do they hold food crumbs or grains, which tend to accumulate inside kitchen store cupboards. The quality of the shelves varies, like anything else, with commercial, heavy-duty wire shelves being very good quality.

YELLOW LIGHT

Regardless of the type of shelves you install, the brackets or supports should be fastened to solid walls or wall studs for the best support. If a stud isn't available in a partition wall, various bolts, special plugs and anchors are manufactured for securing objects to plasterboard, but the shelves should be used for light loads only.

Wire Shelving

- Wire shelving kits, complete with brackets, fasteners and anchors, are sold in pre-sized sets or by length, with installation and assembly fittings sold separately.
- Modular metal shelving systems can be added to as your needs grow and may include baskets, drawers, rows of hooks and racks and wide shelves that can double as work surfaces.
- Wire shelving is convenient and fills many shelving needs, but wood shelving is more versatile.

Finishes for Shelving

- The easiest treatment for unfinished wood shelves is several coats of hardwax oil.
- If possible, finish wood shelves before installing them for ease of application.
- MDF or chipboard shelves should be sealed with paint or polyurethane if there is any chance liquids will leak on to them or if they'll be subject to regular cleaning.
- Extensive built-in shelving can be painted more efficiently with a spray gun.

CLOTHES STORAGE SOLUTIONS

Fitted bedroom furniture is big business, but you don't have to spend a fortune on storage

Wardrobes come in all different shapes and sizes, ranging from small reach-in cupboards to walk-in dressing rooms. An entire industry has evolved around clothes storage systems, expansion and organization, but you don't have to spend a lot of money to revamp and repair yours. Some wardrobe makeovers are works of art, with fine cabinetry and elegant lighting. Others are simply more thoughtfully placed shelves, rails and racks to help maximize space.

The size of your wardrobe determines the volume of clothing you can accommodate, and the design determines how much of that volume you can practically use. Installing hanging rails at different heights to hold clothes of different

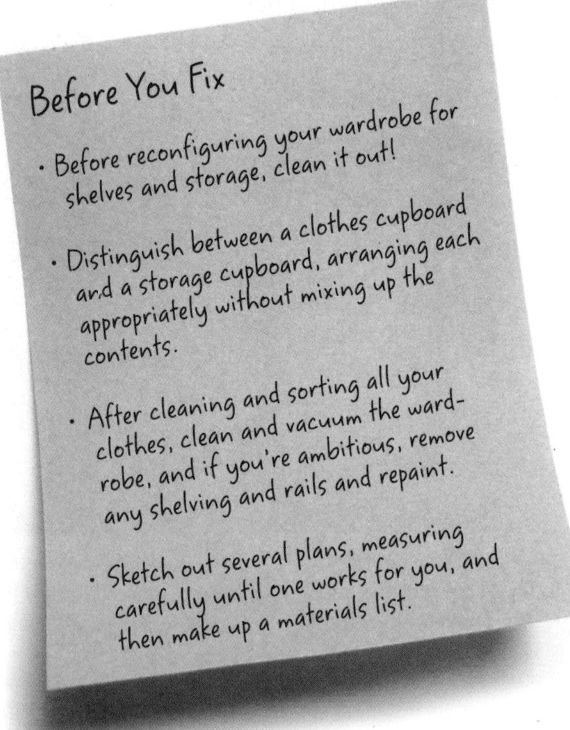

Before You Fix
• Before reconfiguring your wardrobe for shelves and storage, clean it out!
• Distinguish between a clothes cupboard and a storage cupboard, arranging each appropriately without mixing up the contents.
• After cleaning and sorting all your clothes, clean and vacuum the wardrobe, and if you're ambitious, remove any shelving and rails and repaint.
• Sketch out several plans, measuring carefully until one works for you, and then make up a materials list.

Additional Hanging Rails

- Installing multiple rails at different heights in your wardrobe can make better use of space.
- Rails require special fittings to mount them at each end, and long rails will probably need the support of an extra bracket in the centre.
- Don't paint a hanging rail; the finish will only get scratched every time a hanger slides across it.
- A metal clothes rail will resist bowing better than a wooden rod.

lengths can double the amount of clothes you can store. Built-in drawers and shelves allow you to find homes for a lot of items that might otherwise end up on the floor. And extra shelving helps you store out-of-season clothing in an out-of-the-way location.

With these practical and inexpensive suggestions, you can turn your ordinary wardrobe into an extraordinary space.

ZOOM

Consider aromatic tongue-and-groove cedar panels for lining wardrobes. Cedar is a natural insect repellent with a very agreeable scent. As the panels are exposed to air, the pores of the wood can close and restrict the cedar smell. Running very fine-grade sandpaper over the surface of the wood will reactivate the cedar oil.

Professional Upgrades

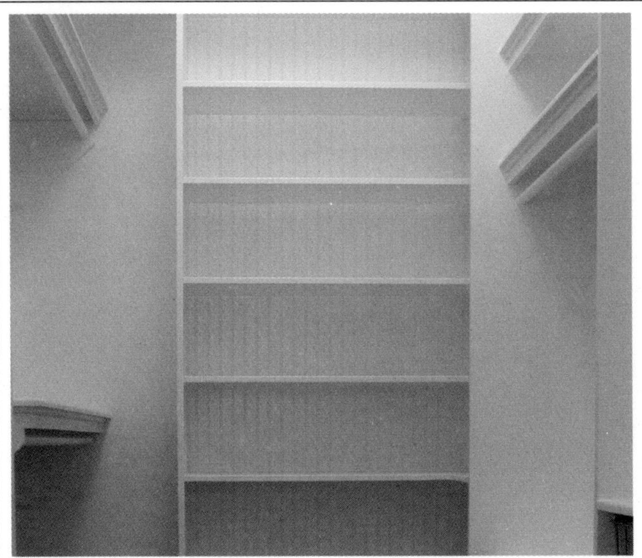

- Many companies specialize in built-in bedroom furniture. Some will design and build custom storage units that are beautiful yet expensive.
- Others provide do-it-yourself design tools and can supply modular storage units to your design.
- An online search will bring up all the bedroom storage options you could ever imagine.
- Keep a budget in mind and stick to it – the price varies greatly depending on the type of furniture, so do thorough research.

Shoe Storage

- Shoe racks range from small, adjustable shelves for a few pairs to multi-shelf shoe racks that hold dozens of shoes.
- Hanging shoe shelves are available for cupboard doors in both soft-style shoe holders and hard wire styles.
- Modular shoe racks that snap together allow for an expanding shoe wardrobe.
- The least expensive method is stacking the original shoe boxes with photos of the shoes on the side to help you find the pair you want.

GARAGE STORAGE

With new shelving and storage systems, the days of the overflowing garage are gone

Garages were once utilitarian places. Cars, lawn mowers, bikes, garden tools and boxes full of mysterious and forgotten contents packed garages in a first-come, first-stored manner. Now, entire companies are devoted to garage storage needs, including installations. Garage cabinetry can rival that found in kitchens, and garage floor finishes have come a long way from bare concrete and paints that never quite held up under the car wheels.

Upgrading your garage can be as expensive or modestly priced as you want. The main thing is to get as much as possible off the floor for convenient, dry storage and a safer garage environment (you won't trip on sports equipment if

Modern Garage Storage

- Ready-made storage systems look great but are typically more expensive than do-it-yourself storage and are limited to the manufacturer's dimensions.
- Because garages aren't subject to as much scrutiny as living areas, you don't need to produce fancy storage.
- Building a customized high-level storage unit, supported by posts, could still allow a car to park underneath.
- Make sure any items stored overhead are securely stowed so they don't fall on the car – or your head.

Modern Overhead Storage

- Heavy-capacity shelving can be supported by steel uprights attached to the ceiling joists.
- Pulley and hoist systems allow overhead storage of bulky objects such as bikes, extension ladders, and large garden equipment, with easy raising and lowering.
- Commercial overhead shelving is designed to fit above garage door tracks without interfering with the operation of the door.
- Overhead storage requires strong supports and shelving – it's wise to buy a commercial system rather than making your own.

it isn't lying all over the floor). At the most basic level, a good cleaning and sorting goes a long way towards organizing a garage. Painting the walls and ceiling (whether they're dry lined or not) and then preparing and painting the floor will brighten up any garage at low cost.

Wood boards or planks can be pre-cut at a timber merchant to any width for custom shelving. Shelving can run up close to the ceiling to store those rarely used but must-keep items. With some planning and good execution, you might even be able to put your car in your garage again.

MAKE IT EASY

Consider how far you want to take your garage storage before you begin installing anything. Do you want a finished look with painted shelves, or an industrial-style metal system? Would cupboards be better than open shelving? Complete systems that you can put up yourself are available at DIY stores.

Hanging Equipment

- Bicycles, sports equipment and garden tools can be hung on walls or ceiling using hooks and brackets.
- Think about who will use the equipment and check that it can be hung up and removed by children or shorter people.
- If bikes are hung on a wall, attach strips of carpet first so the tyres don't mar painted surfaces.
- If you need more readily accessible equipment, get freestanding racks that rest against a wall, requiring no fasteners.

Wood Shelving

- A 2240x1220 mm plywood or blockboard sheet can be cut in half lengthwise to make two shelves wide enough for bulky items.
- Mount them on 44x94 mm wall-mounted supports, and use the same timber to make vertical side supports.
- If the vertical supports rest on a concrete floor where moisture may be present use treated timber or coat untreated timber with wood preservative.
- When in doubt, add more supports.

WORKBENCH

Build a workbench for additional storage and for a clean, professional look for your workspace

Every home needs a workbench. Where else can you store your tools, repair the vacuum cleaner or paint a chair you found at a car boot sale for £1? A workbench doesn't have to be huge; even 120 cm in length will do, but it does have to be sturdy. Typically, a workbench is built out of solid timber, including the top, so it can withstand hammering and general abuse. More elegant ones can be finished off with scraps of hardwood flooring, but this is mostly for show.

A workbench can be elaborate, with built-in drawers and cupboards, or a basic four-legged affair with room for storage boxes underneath. Metal industrial workbenches, designed more for assembly work, come with various arrangements of

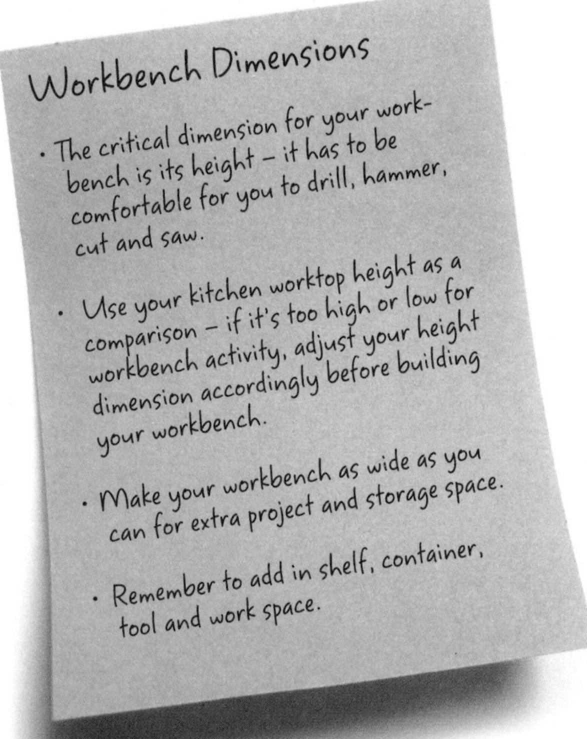

Workbench Dimensions
• The critical dimension for your workbench is its height – it has to be comfortable for you to drill, hammer, cut and saw.
• Use your kitchen worktop height as a comparison – if it's too high or low for workbench activity, adjust your height dimension accordingly before building your workbench.
• Make your workbench as wide as you can for extra project and storage space.
• Remember to add in shelf, container, tool and work space.

Simplest Workbench

- The simplest workbench is made from two sawhorses and a sheet of plywood.
- Most ready-made wood sawhorses are too short for comfortable workbench activity – they're constructed as supports for planks or sheets of wood being cut with a saw.
- Local timber merchants sometimes construct their own sawhorses and can make you taller ones for a reasonable price.
- Folding sawhorses are appropriate for a workbench that will be used for light work; they fold up for easy storage when the job is finished.

shelves and drawers as well as pre-wired sockets that plug into a standard wall socket. Typically these are somewhat narrow, but they can be a bargain if you can find one at a sale and need only a small workbench.

Building a workbench is a good exercise in beginning carpentry. The materials are inexpensive, so an incorrectly cut board isn't anything to worry about. You can even use old or scrap timber, which keeps it out of landfill and gives you something useful at the same time.

MAKE IT EASY

If you have the space, consider going longer rather than shorter with your workbench. It can always be used for storage, future projects and multitasking.

Basic Corner Workbench

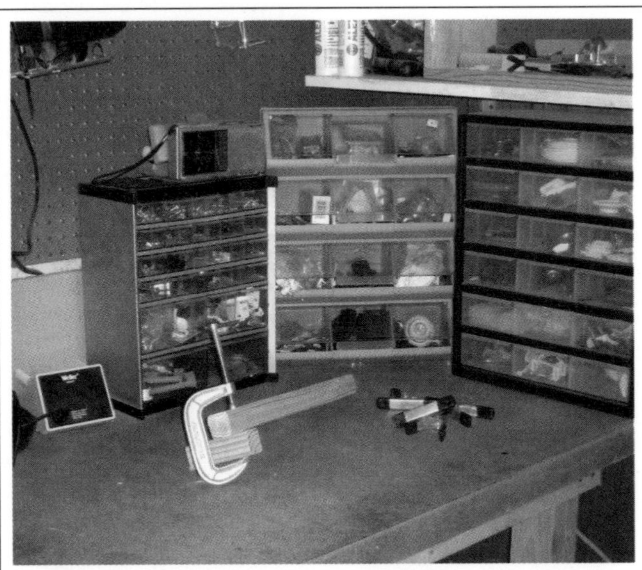

- Building a workbench in a corner of your workspace provides you with two walls for supporting the top and for hanging tools.
- Workbenches should be built near a power socket and have plenty of light for safe working conditions.
- Construct your workbench with screws rather than nails if you're uncertain its location will be permanent.
- Exquisitely made workbenches can be ordered online – they're beautiful but expensive.

Workbench Tops

- The stoutness of the workbench really depends on its intended work load.
- Traditionally, workbenches have thick, solid timber tops to withstand heavy pounding.
- If you expect to do only lighter tasks, a plywood or even a chipboard top will work adequately.
- As time goes by and your workbench top gets too beaten up for your taste, it can always be covered again with another layer of plywood or 18 mm boards for a new appearance.

KITCHEN ISLAND

Whether movable or fixed in place, an island is a great kitchen addition

Modern kitchens are a marvel. They are larger than ever and contain every appliance imaginable. As the 20th century developed, the kitchen evolved from a room solely for preparing food that would be eaten in a separate dining room to the mixed-use gathering place it is today. We prepare food, eat it and entertain, all in the same room.

Kitchens in newer homes are usually very open, with their own dining areas, and usually adjoining a family room. Older homes that have not been remodelled normally have closed kitchens with a doorway into the dining room. Either design can benefit from an island addition, but a separate kitchen must be large enough to accommodate it without being cramped.

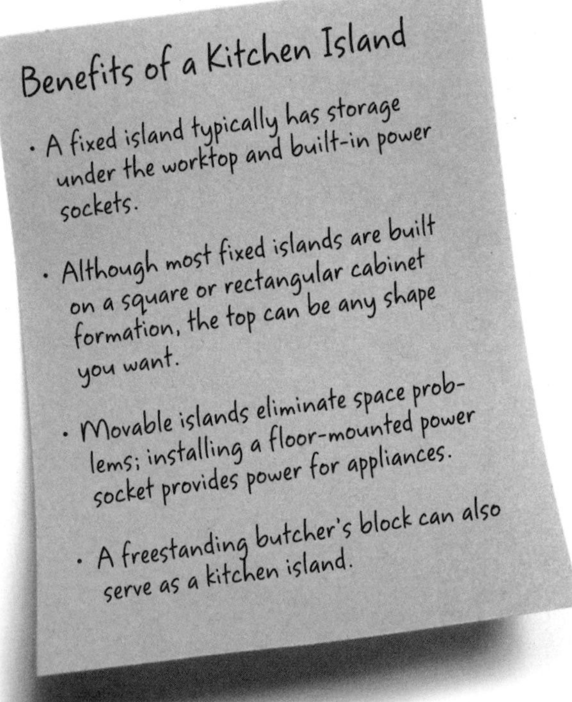

Benefits of a Kitchen Island

- A fixed island typically has storage under the worktop and built-in power sockets.
- Although most fixed islands are built on a square or rectangular cabinet formation, the top can be any shape you want.
- Movable islands eliminate space problems; installing a floor-mounted power socket provides power for appliances.
- A freestanding butcher's block can also serve as a kitchen island.

Ready-made Islands

- Movable kitchen islands on casters, both with and without storage space, are available at a range of prices.
- For the ultimate in portability, a folding kitchen trolley provides a solid work surface when needed and folds away easily.
- Catering suppliers offer commercial stainless steel work stations as another alternative to an island.
- Custom-sized butcher's block worktops are a food-friendly alternative for fixed islands that also act as chopping boards.

An island can contain a hob and maybe an oven, and a second sink, or it can be solely for storage with a worktop for food preparation and eating. You can build a simple island with a butcher's block top or choose from a range of freestanding islands with different features and prices. The advantage of a wheeled island is portability: you can move it out of the way when you need to, and you can take it with you if you move house. If your cupboards and worktops are completely full, an island offers easy expansion.

YELLOW LIGHT

A fixed island should be far enough away from other cabinets and major appliances to allow for traffic flow and not hinder doors opening towards the island. Wheelchair access is also a consideration for some households. Recommendations vary, but you should reckon on a minimum of 120 cm clearance.

Freestanding Islands

- Cut out and tape a paper or cardboard template of your proposed island to the floor to get a feel for it as a workspace.
- Include any bar stools or chairs in your measuring as they will have to be walked around as well.
- A kitchen island's worktop does not have to match the rest of the kitchen – consider a contrasting material or one that's lower maintenance.
- Sturdy antique furnishings can be adapted as interesting movable islands.

Special Considerations

- If you want a sink or gas hob in an island, appropriate drainage and gas pipework will need to be installed.
- For galley-type or other limited-space kitchens, fitting a worktop extension may be a better way of gaining extra working space.
- An extension typically folds against the cabinet at the end of the worktop using a piano hinge, opens up and locks in place when needed.

ENERGY PRIMER

Learn daily habits to cut the cost of energy used in your home

When it comes to energy, we are well supplied. We have bountiful electricity, heating and hot water from reliable sources. Do we waste some? Of course, it's unavoidable; no system is perfectly efficient, but there are ways to conserve energy and cut down on our spending.

Often it's simply a matter of turning off a device we're not using – a light, the television, a ventilation fan – instead of ignoring it. Other times it's a matter of degree: how warm or cool do we need the room temperature, how many lights do we need to perform a task, and do we really need an electric can opener instead of a hand-operated one?

Using and Losing Home Energy Sources

- Most home energy use goes towards providing heat.
- We heat water and the air, and all of our appliances create heat while they're running.
- Much of the electricity consumed by an incandescent light bulb becomes waste heat from the hot filament.
- Heat rises and most is lost through the roof, particularly if your loft is inadequately insulated; it's also lost through ill-fitting windows and doors.
- Insulation under the ground floor stops draughts and keeps your home warmer.

Typical Losses

- In a typical British home, about one third of the heat produced by central heating is lost.
- Most heat loss is through the roof, but warm air also leaks through windows and doors, through the walls and through the ground floor.
- Timers on heating systems and individual thermostats on radiators can cut down on unnecessary heat generation.
- While insulation is important, a certain level of ventilation and air exchange is needed for a healthy indoor environment.

Adjusting to a slightly cooler home by lowering a thermostat one degree a month, or insulating a hot water tank properly is not a lifestyle-bending change. Awareness is the key. Instead of continuing old habits, examine them and decide which need changing and which deserve to get booted out altogether. One approach is to limit how much you allow yourself to spend each month on energy and then find ways to meet your budget.

MAKE IT EASY

Not sure where to start in evaluating your energy usage? There are professional energy auditors who, for a fee, will test your house for heat loss, check your boiler and examine past energy bills. Your gas or electricity provider may also conduct audits for free or for a small cost.

Heating Water

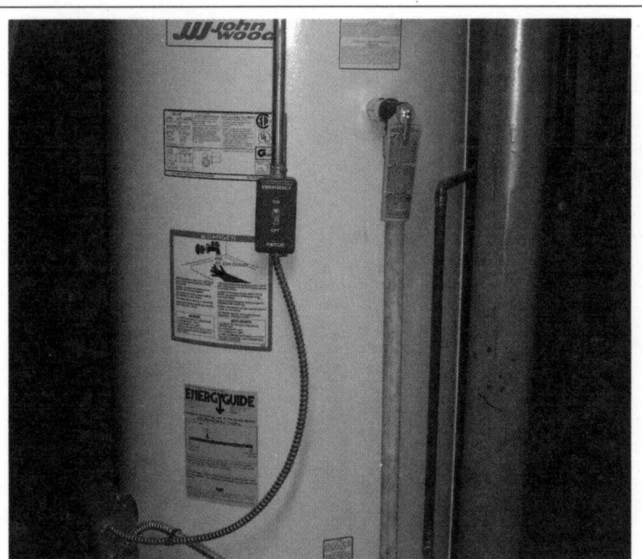

- Water heating is the largest energy user in homes after central heating.
- If you use a regular condensing boiler (or immersion heater) to provide your hot water, your storage tank should be sized to match your hot water usage – too big a tank wastes energy.
- A combination condensing boiler provides hot water only as it is needed, without the standby energy losses associated with storing hot water in a tank; this can save you money.

Everyday Energy Saving

- Modern dishwashers are water efficient, but you should avoid running the machine with anything less than a full load.
- Wait until you have a full load before using your washing machine; modern detergents work well at low temperatures.
- Use a tumble dryer only when you must: use a high spin speed in your washing machine so clothes are nearly dry, and in good weather dry them outside.
- Take a shower rather than running a bath, but keep it short or you won't save much hot water.

REDUCING HEAT LOSS

Keep the heat where you want it – inside your home

We can't live in airtight homes. We need ventilation, but we don't need infiltration or air leakage. We can control ventilation with fans in kitchens and bathrooms, and by opening and closing windows sensibly through the house. Control draughts by filling gaps and installing draught-proofing strips around windows and doors. These are all low-tech remedies.

Some people claim that new homes can be too airtight, that they don't 'breathe' as in the good old days of less tightly constructed dwellings. New houses, however, can be designed to exchange air in a controlled, timed fashion, instead of leaking 24/7 as older houses often do through their walls, windows and roofs.

Double Glazing

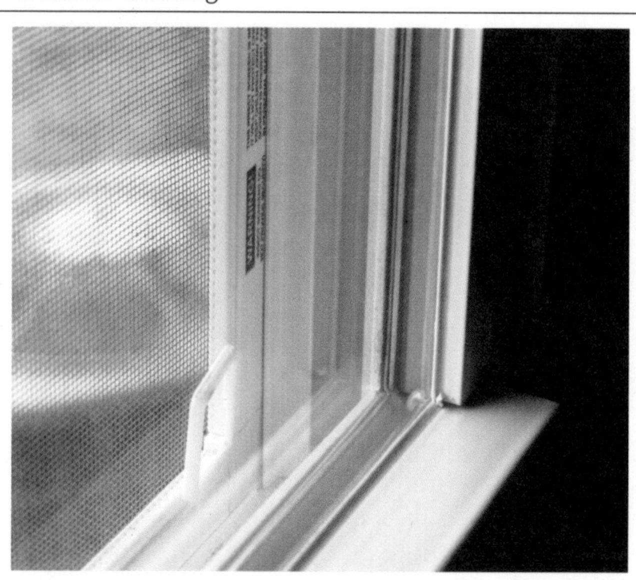

- A lot of heat can be lost through older windows with ill-fitting frames and single glazing.
- A double-glazed window has two panes of glass (or three in triple-glazed units) sealed together with an inert gas between the panes.
- Secondary double glazing can be fitted to existing windows to cut down draughts and reduce heat loss, but often spoils the appearance of the windows.
- Thick lined curtains help to cut down some heat loss on cold winter nights.

Loft Hatches

- Loft hatches should be both insulated and draught proofed around their perimeter.
- In addition to insulation, lofts need adequate ventilation to prevent excess heat build-up and to allow moisture to escape.
- In hot weather, self-powered solar fans do not require wiring to ventilate hot spaces such as conservatories; this is an excellent use of solar energy.

New houses or old, most can use some inspection for air leakage. Even insulated roofspaces should be reconsidered, as insulation standards have changed over the years. If the job seems overwhelming, break it down and do one task – draught proofing, for instance – at a time. Saving energy doesn't need to be complicated.

MAKE IT EASY

Many older homes have open fireplaces, while newer fireplace installations may have glass doors to prevent heat from going up the chimney when the fire is not lit. Keep the damper closed in an old fireplace, while remembering to open it when you have a fire, or install a tempered glass door in your fireplace.

Filling Gaps

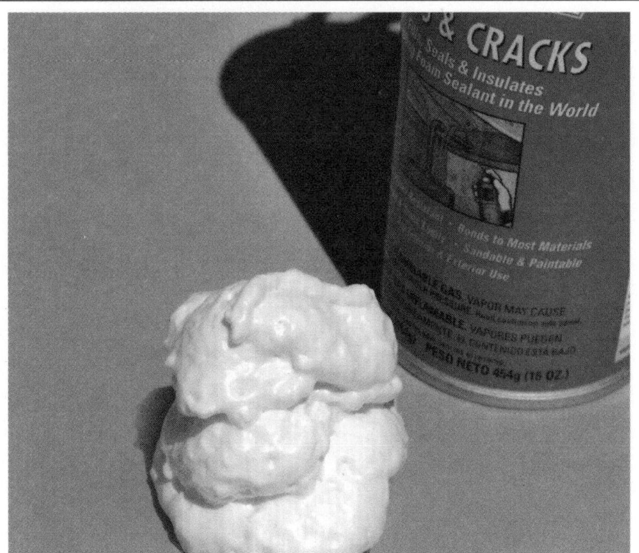

- Inspect the exterior of your house for large gaps.
- Fill these spaces with paintable, exterior aerosol insulating foam and paint the foam after it cures.
- Examine areas where corners or dissimilar materials meet, such as a concrete foundation and wooden walls.
- Never block airbricks installed to ventilate underfloor spaces.

Fireplace Doors

- If you have a gas fire with a pilot light, consider shutting it off for the spring and summer months.
- A gas pilot light uses very little gas, but you can save a few pounds by turning it off.
- Relighting some fireplace pilot lights can be tricky – be sure you know how to do yours.
- Heat-resistant, tempered fireplace doors are both a safety feature and an energy saver and can be fitted to older fireplaces.

DRAUGHT PROOFING

A range of draught-proofing materials will seal up even the leakiest openings

Wherever you have an operable door or window, you are bound to have some air leakage. If you didn't, the opening would be so tight you wouldn't be able to open the door or window. Old wooden window frames are the worst offenders. They were installed on-site, and no two installations were exactly the same. New windows are installed as finished units, assembled according to uniform specifications in a factory, resulting in tighter tolerances and less air infiltration.

Old windows will almost always benefit from some type of draught proofing, while modern windows, depending on their condition, might need their draught proofing replaced. Newer homes have draught proofing around exterior doors but

Self-adhesive Draught Proofing

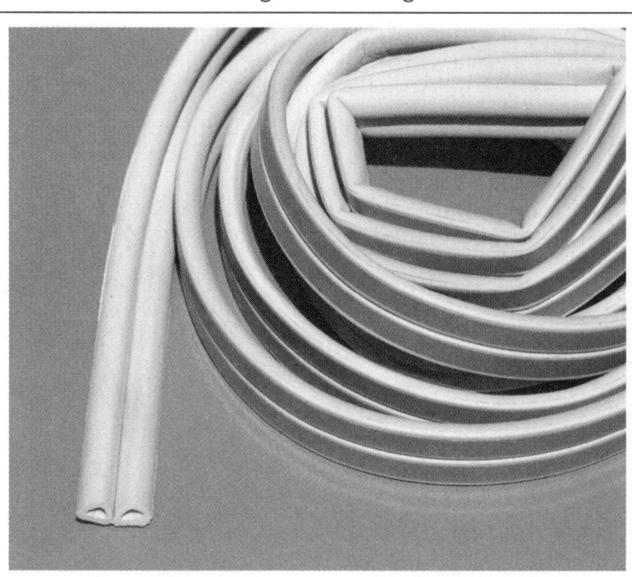

- There are multiple draught-proofing options for every application, but some are much easier to paint around than others.
- An improper installation or the wrong kind of strip can prevent a door or window from completely closing and forming a tight seal.
- Avoid felt strips – there are superior vinyl and rubber alternatives.
- Wooden external doors with self-adhesive vinyl draught proofing regularly have gaps; check yours for any improvements needed.

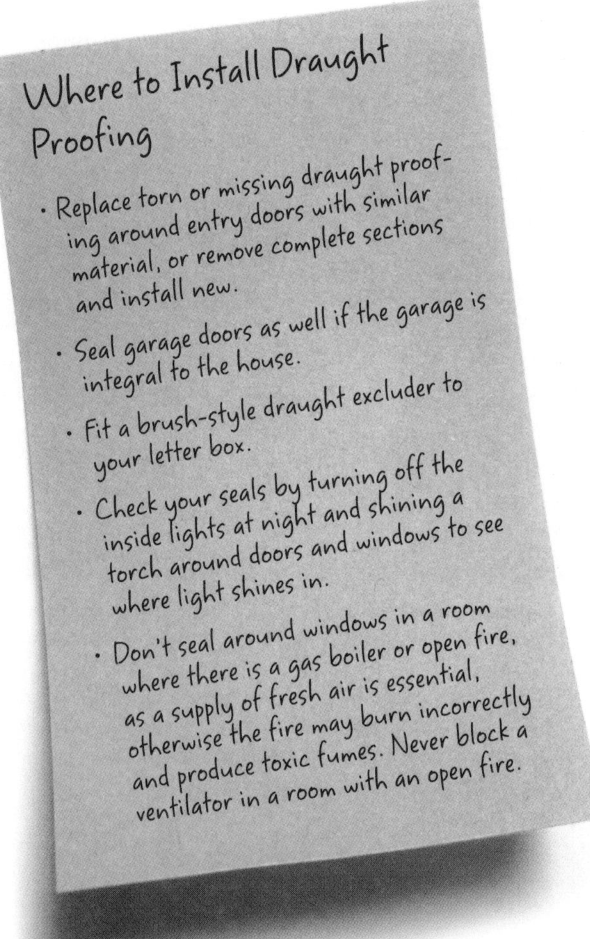

Where to Install Draught Proofing
• Replace torn or missing draught proofing around entry doors with similar material, or remove complete sections and install new.
• Seal garage doors as well if the garage is integral to the house.
• Fit a brush-style draught excluder to your letter box.
• Check your seals by turning off the inside lights at night and shining a torch around doors and windows to see where light shines in.
• Don't seal around windows in a room where there is a gas boiler or open fire, as a supply of fresh air is essential, otherwise the fire may burn incorrectly and produce toxic fumes. Never block a ventilator in a room with an open fire.

this may not be completely effective. Look for gaps and replace the strips with something better. Sealing around sliding patio doors can be problematic depending on the type of door – wood, metal or vinyl – and the original seals. Replace worn or damaged strips with material of similar dimension that won't interfere with the operation of the doors.

ZOOM

For installation, the easiest draught proofing is self-adhesive foam, vinyl or rubber. Metal strips that require fasteners for installation are the longest lasting and require more precision when installing. Metal is also more forgiving when painting near it – paint spatters clean off more easily than off the self-adhesive products.

Metal, Rubber, and Vinyl Strips

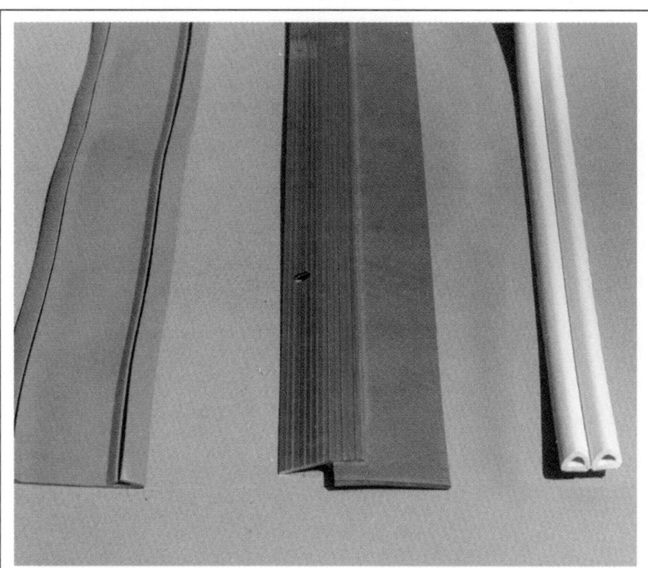

- Spring bronze metal draught proofing is extremely durable and a good option for old wooden windows and doors.
- Self-adhesive vinyl draught proofing installs and sticks well to clean surfaces and can be easily replaced.
- Vinyl windows with damaged brush-type draught proofing can be repaired using self-adhesive vinyl strips.
- Rigid metal nailing strips with rubber, vinyl, or silicone beads work when well-fastened to jambs and pressure fitted against closed doors.

Putty Tape

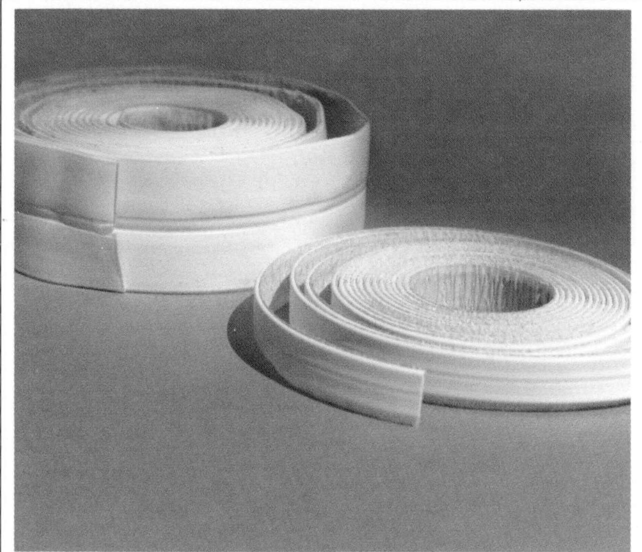

- Putty tape is an inexpensive, soft, clay-like temporary filling compound sold in multiple-strand rolls as an alternative to more permanent filling.
- The strands can be separated from the roll and pressed into gaps between windows and frames in late autumn when windows are no longer opened, and removed in the spring.
- Putty tape stays flexible, adheres to clean surfaces, fills gaps, and requires no tools for installation.
- Once the tape is installed, the window should stay closed.

ADDING INSULATION

Check to see if your house is up to national insulation standards

According to the Energy Saving Trust, if every household in Britain topped up their loft insulation to the recommended thickness of 270 mm, about £520 million would be saved on annual energy bills. Translation: insulating your loft could save you £150 per year. In addition, the environment would be cleaner because less fuel would be burned and thus emissions would be lower.

Blanket insulation is the most common and is normally made of mineral wool (fibreglass) attached to a paper or foil backing sheet. The backing acts as a vapour barrier that keeps the insulation dry. Natural sheep's wool is an alternative, environmentally friendly option.

Blanket insulation is sold in rolls, which you cut to length before installing. The rolls are wide enough to fit between

When to Add Insulation

- It's worth doing a savings analysis to decide between keeping your present level of insulation and upgrading to a higher level.
- Adding insulation to the loft is easier than adding to walls.
- Additional loft insulation can be laid over what you already have: lay it in the opposite direction, across the joists.
- Older homes may need more improvements because insulating was not a common practice until the 1970s, even in cold climates.

Loft Insulation

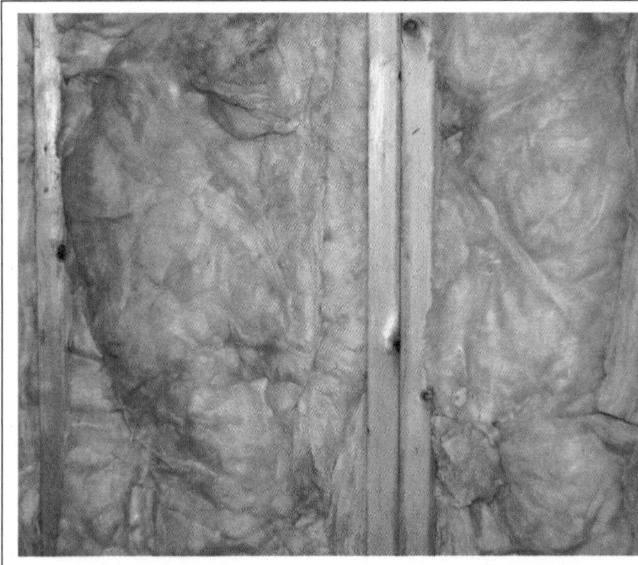

- An insulated loft prevents heat from escaping through the roof in winter.
- You can lay blanket insulation in the loft yourself. Just unroll it between the joists.
- If you want to use the loft for storage, you can lay flooring over the insulation.
- Converted lofts should be lined with rigid insulation boards fitted between the rafters of the roof.
- Remember to lag any water pipes or tanks in the loft, as effective insulation will mean they may freeze in a very cold winter.

floor joists and wall studs. The thicker the insulation, the higher its thermal resistance, or ability to keep heat from escaping. Insulation is also sold as loose fill or small bits of fibre, foam and other materials that are blown into lofts and wall spaces using commercial blowers. Insulation pays back immediately in comfort and energy savings.

RED LIGHT

When your blanket insulation is laid over a heated room – such as across a loft floor over bedrooms – it should be laid with the paper backing facing down. If you're adding additional insulation on top of an existing layer, remove the paper or use insulation without a paper backing.

Wall Insulation 1

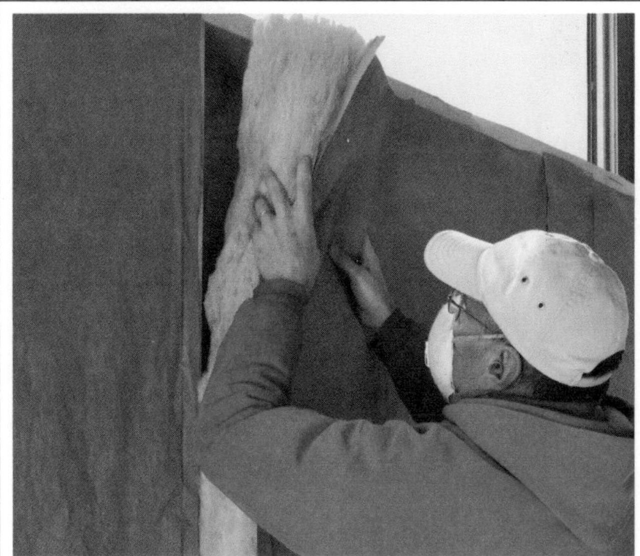

- One third of the heat lost from an uninsulated house goes through the walls.
- If you have solid walls, internal wall insulation involves fitting insulation, up to a total thickness of 90 mm, to the inside of external walls, which are then lined with plasterboard.
- Houses with cavity walls built in the last ten years are likely to have cavity wall insulation already.
- If your cavity walls are suitable for filling, the work has to be carried out by a registered installer, and is guaranteed for 25 years.

Wall Insulation 2

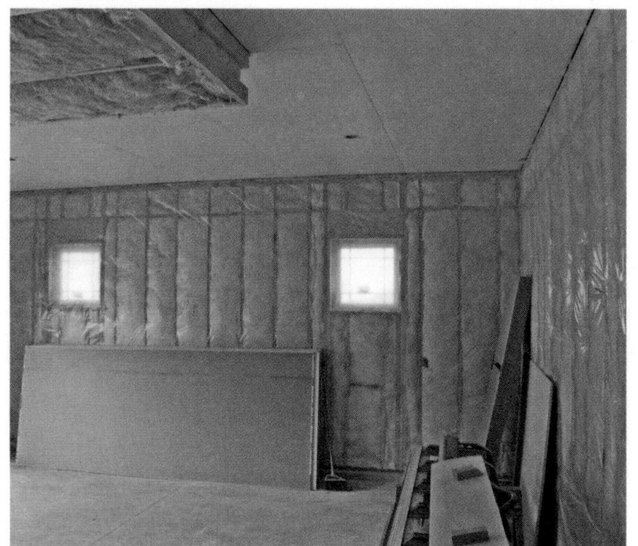

- If you use mineral wool (fibreglass), wear a protective mask and gloves while working.
- Blown insulation consists of small loose particles of cellulose fibre (made from newspapers) or mineral wool. It is fire resistant.
- The material is blown into sectioned-off areas to the recommended thickness using specialist equipment.
- Blown insulation is not suitable for DIY installation: you will have to employ a contractor.

APPLIANCES & ENERGY SAVINGS

Look for energy-saving appliances to help lower your monthly bills

Modern appliances definitely make life easier, but you don't need them to suck out all your house energy. New energy standards and ratings imposed by the European Union have led to improvements in some of the major power consumers.

Kitchen stoves offer more oven insulation than previous models and new A++ rated refrigerators use less than a quarter of the electricity they did in the 1970s. A modern energy-efficient washing machine uses less water and electricity than models manufactured a mere 15 years ago, and current tumble dryers also use less electricity.

Should you replace your appliances for the sake of efficiency? It depends on the age of the appliance you're

Install a Programmable Thermostat

- Programmable thermostats are standard in new homes and can be retrofitted to many older systems.
- The thermostat needs to be installed by an electrician.
- A programmer allows you to set times for your boiler or other heating system to come on and go off, depending on your family's needs. You can set different temperatures for various times of day, and separate timings for working days and weekends.
- Individual thermostatic radiator valves give even more flexible control.

Water Temperature

- For each 5°C reduction in water temperature, you can save 3–5 per cent in energy costs.
- A hot water temperature of 50°C is recommended for most households.
- If you have an electric water heater, consult the owner's manual for precautions for adjusting the thermostat.
- Insulating accessible hot water pipes reduces heat loss and can raise water temperature when it reaches the taps by a couple of degrees.

replacing and the amount of energy it consumes, versus the cost of a new appliance and the ongoing savings from its lower energy use.

You can further cut down electricity consumption and costs by using your appliances smartly. For instance, run only full loads of clothes and dishes and use a refrigerator to its maximum capacity.

GREEN LIGHT

Do you really need to keep your old refrigerator in the garage or basement as an 'extra'? This more than negates any energy savings you make with a new model. It's better to buy a larger kitchen refrigerator if you need the extra capacity than maintain a second one.

Water-saving Showerheads

- Showering accounts for 25 per cent of individual water usage.
- Low-flow showerheads with a flow rate of 7 litres per minute or less include aerating models, which mix air with the water, and non-aerating models.
- Another option is a shower-head with a built-in shut-off or soap-up valve, which allows the user to decrease the water flow down to a light mist or shut off completely.
- Installation is easy and requires only a wrench and some plumber's tape.

Extractor Fans

- Energy saving and extractor fans are somewhat mutually exclusive.
- You want a powerful fan that draws fumes and moisture out fast, which means it removes heat quickly, too; it's better to vent faster and for a shorter amount of time.
- Run your extractor fans only as long as you need to clear the bathroom and keep heat loss to a minimum.
- A bathroom fan timer can control and reduce excess usage.

FENCE REPAIRS

Wood fences can't stand up forever – they need help from time to time

Fences have been erected to establish boundaries ever since people began living in fixed settlements. They range from posts and rails to contain livestock, or picket fences to mark the edge of a property, to ornamental garden features.

Traditional solid fences built for privacy are popular and simple to construct: 100 mm square posts are sunk into the ground no more than 2 m apart, two or three horizontal rails are attached to the posts, and then the fence boards, frequently rough cut, are nailed to the rails. More often than not, these fences are then stained or even left alone to 'weather'.

This type of fence doesn't require elaborate carpentry skills to build, but once it's up, it requires care and feeding. Wood

Signs of a Failed Fence

- A fence falls into disrepair when the posts rot, the post holes aren't deep enough, the rails come loose from the posts, or the individual fence boards come loose.
- Unsealed fences deteriorate faster, and they often have loose boards and fasteners.
- Wood fences are expensive and time consuming to build – it makes good sense to maintain them.
- Reckon on restaining a fence every three to four years, depending on weather exposure.

Loose Fence Boards

- Loose boards can be secured with small decking screws or galvanized nails.
- If an individual board is broken or otherwise too deteriorated to secure, new ones are available from timber merchants or garden centres.
- Stain or paint any replacement boards before installing.
- Be sure the ends of all the fence boards are well sealed and none comes in contact with the ground.

fences are exposed to the weather and need to be treated like any other outdoor wood. They must be sealed regularly with paint or stain and checked for deterioration.

Picket fences are traditionally painted, providing them with better protection, if the paint is regularly renewed, than stained solid fences, which are often ignored. Given the cost and time involved to construct a fence, recoating to extend the life of a fence more than pays for itself.

MAKE IT EASY

Repainting or staining a fence is time consuming, but the task can be speeded up using a paint sprayer. An airless sprayer will paint a fence far faster than brushing, and overspray is less an issue outside in the garden than inside your house. Solid fences can be rolled or sprayed.

Reinforcing Loose Rails

- Rails that are nailed at an angle to the posts commonly come loose.
- Reinforce a loose rail by nailing a small wood block to the post; butt it up against the rail and nail the rail to the block.
- Or insert a galvanized angle iron under the rail and screw it to both the rail and the post.
- A section of timber nailed across the post and into each rail produces the sturdiest but most visible repair.

Fence Caps

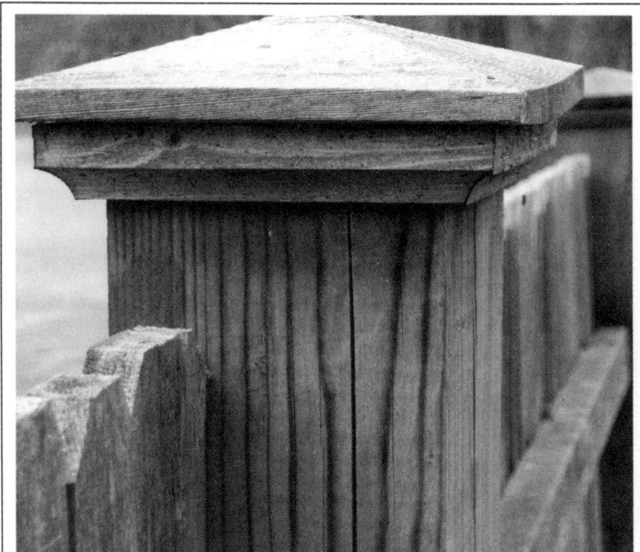

- Fence caps become loose when they remain unfinished and the nails rust and deteriorate.
- Remove loose post caps and their nails. Sand the cap's bottom side and the top of the post. Brush away dust and seal all sides of the cap with wood sealer.
- When the cap is dry, apply exterior wood glue to the top of the post, and centre the cap on it.
- Secure with two decking screws or two galvanized nails longer than the original ones.

FENCE REPAIRS (CONTINUED)

Fences in disrepair need more than restaining – posts, rails, boards and pickets can all be fixed

A properly built fence uses posts that are treated for ground contact. Timber manufacturers pressure-treat timber with chemicals that render the wood resistant to fungi found in the ground. Some pressure-treated timber is not suitable for ground contact and should not be used for fence posts, nor should untreated timber be used. In the event of rotting wood, individual posts can be replaced or supported and braced until you can fit new ones.

Rails eventually loosen if they don't have any supports to hold them or if the nails securing the rails corrode. The same is true for pickets or vertical boards. A section of a fence can either be secured with additional fixings or replaced

Leaning Fence Posts

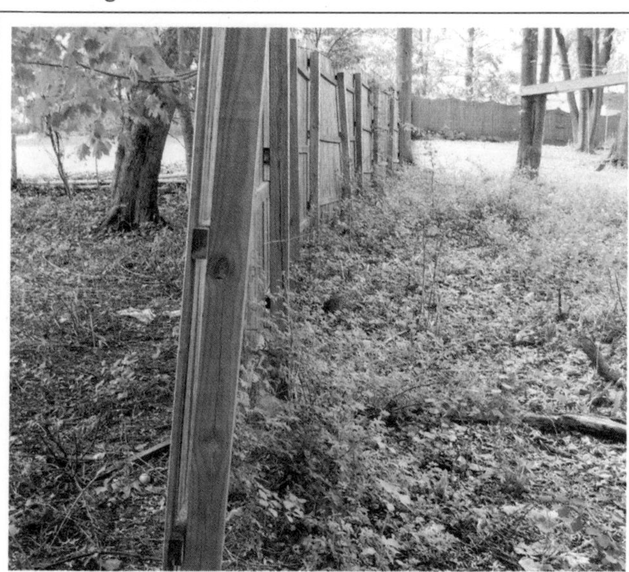

- Reinforce fence posts set in concrete slabs with brackets hammered into the concrete, to save the time and cost of post replacement.
- Rotten posts need to be replaced. If they are set in metal supports, these can be cleaned out and new posts hammered in.
- To quickly repair a leaning post, screw one end of a wire or small chain near the top of the post. Straighten the post, pull the wire tight, and attach to a pipe hammered into the ground.

Replacing Posts and Rails

- Rails may either be nailed at an angle to the posts or attached by means of metal brackets, which are nailed to the posts.
- Remove the fixings and temporarily nail a vertical batten to each pair of rails to keep the fencing upright.
- Dig out the old post and any concrete attached to it.
- If a rail end is rotten, cut out the bad section, install a new piece of rail, and secure it to the remaining rail with a galvanized bracket.

completely if necessary. This can be a problem if a picket fence is an unusual design that requires duplication. However, new standard fence panels or individual boards are commonly available at any timber yard or garden centre.

Anywhere a fence is feeling wobbly or is otherwise in need of support, brackets, blocks, cables or other means of shoring up the weak area can be installed to extend the life of the fence. As long as the repair is presentable, it's simpler than a full replacement.

YELLOW LIGHT

Treated timber is soaked in a chemical solution that will rub off on your skin during handling. Wear work gloves and a long-sleeved shirt when working with treated fence posts, and wear an appropriate dust mask to avoid breathing any sawdust while cutting the posts. Wash your hands after handling treated timber.

Digging Post Holes

- Dig post holes with a narrow shovel, a post-hole digger, a hand-operated auger, or a handheld power auger (but beware of usage hazards).
- An alternative is a metal fence post spike topped with an open metal box for securing the fence post.
- Before digging holes for a new fence, it may be a wise precaution to call your local utility companies to check the positions of pipework.

Positioning and Installing Posts

- A post hole should be at least 60 cm deep for a 2 m fence.
- The hole should also be wide enough for you to pack down your soil or concrete packing.
- The new post should be straight, lined up with its fence rails and with the other posts; if the posts are on sloping ground, it should follow the slope as the others do.
- Allow concrete to set before attaching the rails, following the manufacturer's curing directions.

DECKING REPAIRS

With some attention, decking can last for years – here's how

A lot is asked of decking. It's laid out horizontally so water can't run off and is lucky if it gets recoated every few years. It bakes in the sun and freezes in the winter. Luckily, as with any other wood structure, each damaged component is replaceable.

Decking that's seen better days but is structurally solid can always be cleaned and refinished. What if it's rough and splintered? Sanding a deck will bring it back to life and prepare it for a new finish. Decking boards that are too far gone to be saved can be removed and replaced easily enough. Not as easily replaced are the joists, the supports that the boards are nailed into. Small areas of each joist edge are exposed to the weather and usually don't directly receive any finish

Replacing Decking Sections

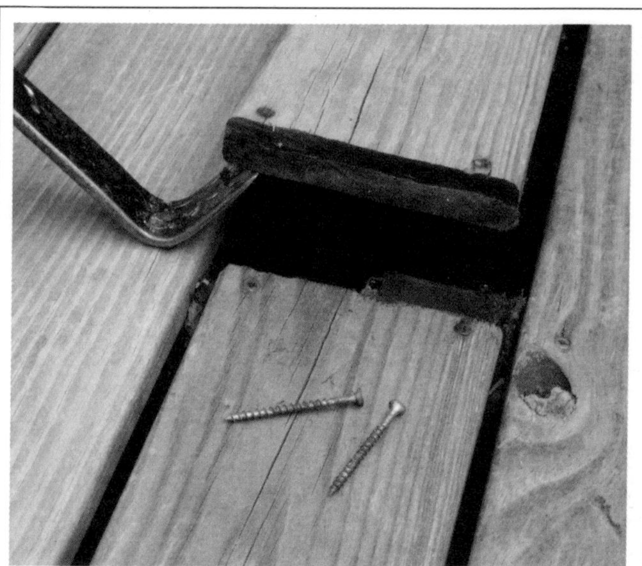

- Decking boards and rails are frequent candidates for replacement due to water exposure.
- Each piece of decking is nailed twice at each joist.
- With a large crowbar, remove any damaged boards, being sure to place a block of wood under the crowbar to avoid damaging the adjoining boards.
- Replace with wood of the same dimension and type and stain to match the rest of the decking.

Repairing or Replacing Joists

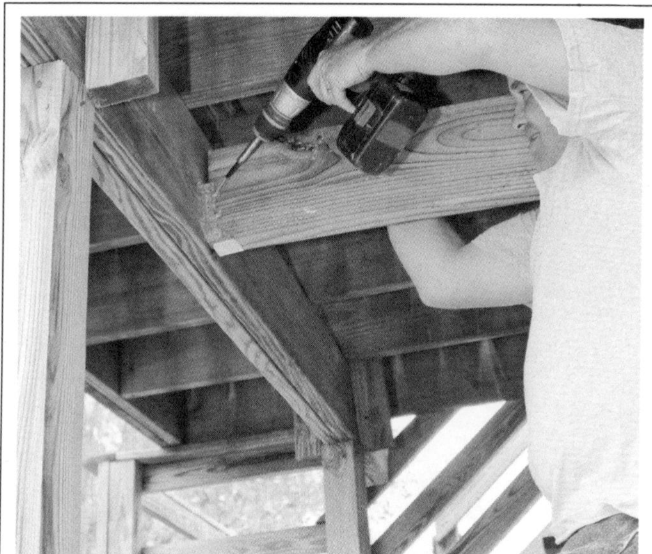

- If a section of a joist has deteriorated, cut away the damaged area with a reciprocating saw and coat the exposed wood with a preservative.
- Cut a new joist the same length as the damaged joist.
- Glue and fasten the full-length joist to the old and secure at the ends in the same manner as the others.
- If joist ends are damaged, cut away the damaged material, coat the exposed wood with preservative, and run a new joist the entire length of the old.

during recoats as they're not easily accessible. Not surprisingly, these areas can deteriorate.

Posts are also main supports but are replaceable or can have new sections spliced to them. Replacing an entire deck is expensive and a lot of work, so you might consider hiring a contractor. Refinishing and patching the neglected areas will go a long way in extending the life of your decking.

YELLOW LIGHT

Before sanding decking, punch all the nails into the boards. Often the nail heads are sticking up far enough to catch a piece of sandpaper and tear it. You'll have to punch in the protruding nails anyway after tearing your sandpaper, so save yourself the aggravation and do this first.

Firming Up Decking

- Decking gets wobbly due to age or insufficient bracing, especially in the case of first-floor decks.
- There is no limit to the amount of bracing and support you can add to a deck; more rather than less is a good idea.
- Use decking screws to secure additional braces to posts or joists to stiffen up the structure; nail or screw sections of timber between the joists as well.
- Some raised decks are built with undersized or a minimal number of posts – install additional ones for stability.

Repairing or Replacing Deck Railings

- Deck railings should be functional first and decorative second to meet safety requirements.
- The top railing is subject to deterioration and can be replaced as necessary (attach a new rail with decking screws).
- Pre-finish any replaced parts with stain or paint to match the rest of the decking.
- Replacing an entire railing and supports will update your deck and can be done in a different material, including low-maintenance metal.

OUTDOOR LIGHTING

With a little lighting, your garden becomes a lot more usable

In the summer months, our gardens become our personal playgrounds and weekend gathering spots during the daylight hours. When darkness falls, a little extra lighting allows for extra use of your outdoor space. A garden can be as well-lit as a kitchen or as subdued as a romantic restaurant, depending on your preference.

Extra lighting can also bring a sense of security, particularly for those living alone and concerned about entry doors and ground-floor windows. The types of lighting vary greatly.

Outdoor lights can be mounted on a structure, on or at the base of trees, or at any ground location. You should employ an electrical contracter to install any exterior wiring, but low

Hard-Wired Lights

- Hard-wired outdoor lights offer the brightest illumination options but are the most difficult to install.
- Wiring must meet building safety standards, and the work must be inspected and approved.
- A light mounted on a house wall can be wired to an interior circuit instead of running new wiring from the service panel.
- In addition to outdoor lights, consider adding garden power sockets for convenience.

Solar Lights

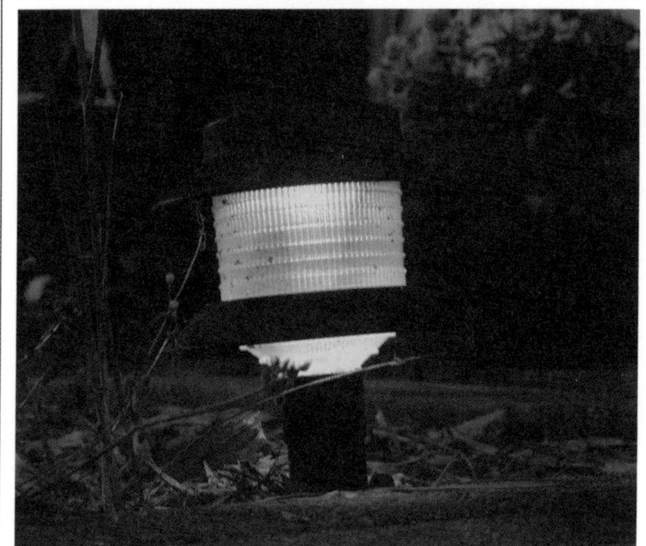

- Solar outdoor lights are the easiest to install as they require no wiring.
- A range of lights and styles is available, including path lights and spotlights.
- Other than occasionally wiping the solar panel clean, and replacing the batteries every one to three years, there is no maintenance for solar outdoor lights.
- Because they're not permanently wired, these lights can be relocated to other parts of your garden whenever you wish.

voltage garden lighting is available in a great variety of styles. Wireless solar lighting has a small solar panel that absorbs daylight, which charges an internal nicad battery. The battery powers an LED, which provides a small amount of illumination, nowhere near as much as a wired light can provide.

Which type of lighting is best? It depends on what you're trying to do. Solar lights do a good job marking paths and drives, and wired lights let you see more – an important consideration for security. Combining both types offers more options with less compromise.

YELLOW LIGHT

Consult an electrical contractor about where you can run cable and the transformers you will need. The location of your lights should be planned with the wiring layout in mind. Some layouts will be more difficult to achieve than others or be more susceptible to future disruptions (from tree roots, for instance).

Motion Detectors and Timers

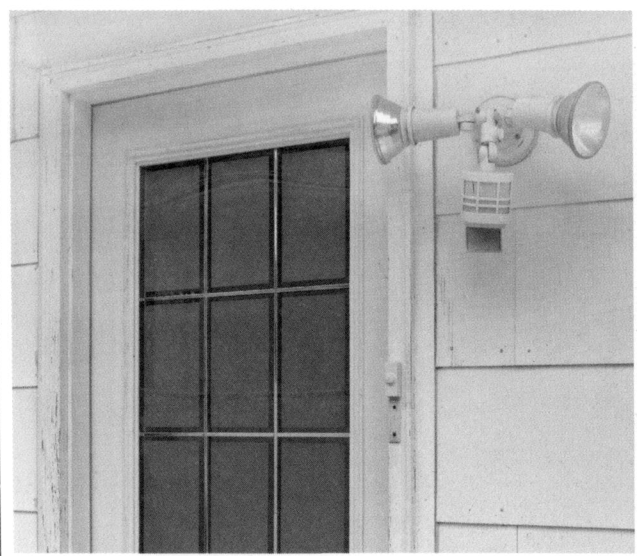

- Motion detector-activated lights allow lighting when you need it instead of remaining on all night.
- For security lights, install them high enough that an intruder can't disable the motion detector mechanism or remove the bulbs from the fitting.
- Timers allow you to control designated lighting, both indoor and outdoor, adjusting timings to changing hours of darkness.
- You can control Christmas displays or fountain pumps with timers, too.

Location of Lighting

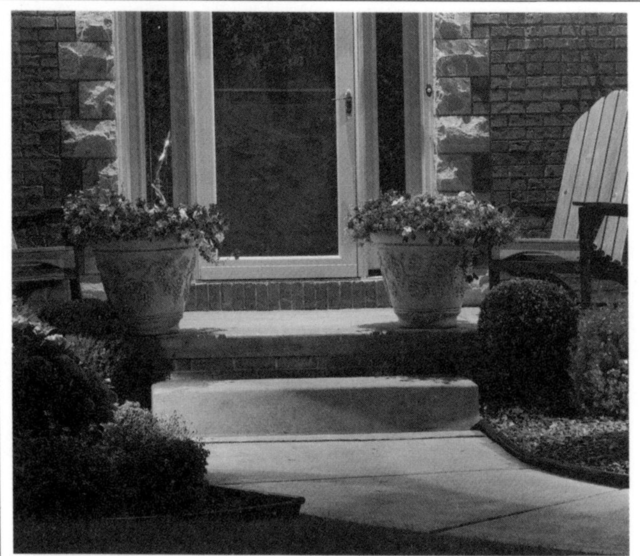

- Install lights for safety along high-traffic areas and especially near steps, which are hard to see in the dark.
- The location of your power source will affect where you install hard-wired lights.
- The type of lighting you want in any specific location will determine its design and style.
- For pure decoration, choose a focal point, such as a large tree, for additional lighting.

COMPOSTING

Why pay to have garden rubbish hauled away when you can benefit from reusing it?

Nature recycles itself. Plants die and decompose, enriching the soil. Seeds blow or drop in, and the cycle starts all over again. In an effort to improve the environment, councils have increasingly called for separating garden waste from household rubbish for large-scale composting. It's even more efficient to maintain your own compost heap at home.

What can you compost? Almost any organic material, but they're not all created equal. Leaves, weeds, grass clippings, wood (but not coal) ashes, kitchen vegetable and fruit peelings, manure from vegetarian animals, seaweed and even newspaper are all good compost candidates. The smaller the material is chopped up, the faster it will decompose.

What Is Composting?

- Composting and the general breakdown of organic material work best with a balanced carbon (dried leaves, wood chips, straw) to nitrogen (grass clippings, kitchen scraps) ratio among the pile's ingredients.
- Too little nitrogen slows decomposition while too much speeds it up and creates an odour problem, as oxygen is consumed too quickly.
- Aim for about 25 parts carbon to one part nitrogen, but don't worry about a perfect mix.
- Regularly water and turn for aeration.

Different Compost Bins

- You can make compost in an open heap, a sealed plastic bin or a fenced-in corner of your garden.
- The soil incorporation method calls for small amounts of non-fatty food waste (no meats or bones) to be mixed with soil and buried 20 cm down or deeper.
- Plastic compost bins work well to control vermin attracted to compost; they are available in tumbler models for turning the contents.
- An open wire-mesh compost bin is appropriate for garden waste.

A compost pile requires as much or as little work as you wish. A pile left alone will eventually break down, while a managed pile that you rotate and water will decompose much faster. Concerned about unsightly piles of dead stuff in your garden attracting vermin? Closed plastic compost bins are available in several styles and sizes. Set one up in a corner of the garden, save on council collections and enrich your soil at the same time.

MAKE IT EASY

Grass clippings can be recycled by leaving them on the lawn. Clippings add nutrients, help with water retention in hot weather and reduce the need for fertilizer. Short clippings work best, which can mean more frequent mowing or the use of a mulching lawn mower. Clippings can also be used on beds.

Preventing Rodents and Pests

- Keeping your compost wet and turned helps prevent rats from nesting in it.
- Limit food additions to the compost and bury them deep so they're harder for rats and other vermin to dig out.
- Consider two compost bins, one open pile for garden waste and a second enclosed bin for food scraps.
- If necessary, enclose an open bin with fine-gauge chicken wire, buried several centimetres down to prevent rats from burrowing into the compost.

Wormeries

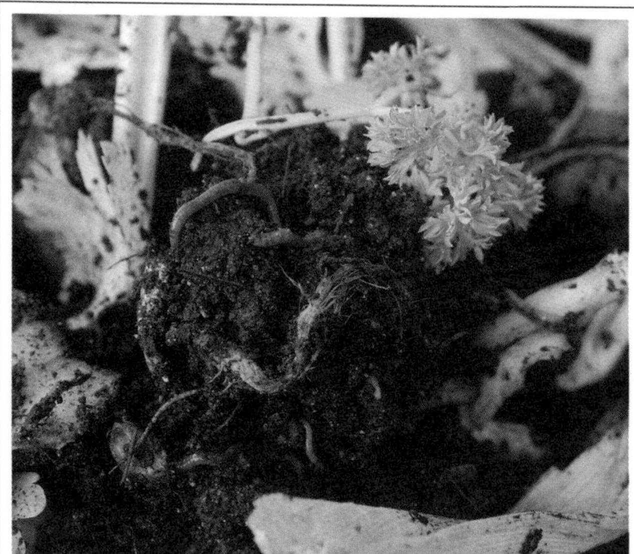

- Worm composting can take care of food waste and create rich compost.
- In an aerated plastic container, your worms can live indoors or out as long as the temperature is 5–25°C and they're kept out of direct sunlight.
- Each bin requires moistened bedding, redworms, and a supply of non-fatty food scraps, especially fruit, vegetables, crushed eggshells and coffee grounds.
- Minimal maintenance includes refreshing the bedding and removing the compost a few times a year.

RAINWATER BUTTS

Save rainwater for dry days and help the environment

According to Waterwise, the daily indoor per capita water use in the typical single-family home is 150 litres. Billions of litres of water could be saved every day if water-efficient fixtures were installed. Water butts aren't considered water-efficient fixtures, but they do indeed save water by cutting down on the demand for piped-in water. The average roof collects about 85,000 litres of rainwater each year, more than enough to water the garden when necessary.

Some rain-collection systems are nothing more than a plastic barrel into which a downpipe is inserted. Water collected between periods of rain can supplement tap water for garden and lawn use. Other more sophisticated systems include

Why Use a Water Butt?

- Rainwater is free and does not go through any processing; it's often soft water without dissolved minerals.
- Rainwater butts can be located in convenient areas for watering your garden if there isn't a tap nearby.
- Extensive collection of rainwater would keep unnecessary water out of treatment plants and decrease sewer flow during heavy storms.
- Multiple butts can be combined for increased capacity, especially during extended dry periods.

Water Butts of Any Style

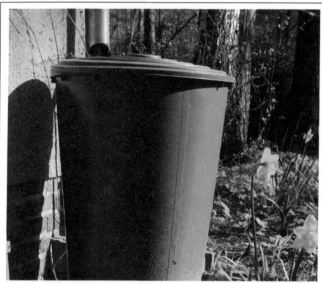

- Rainwater butts and tanks are available for purchase in many sizes and a variety of styles and designs.
- You can even make your own using a 150-litre food-quality recycled barrel, which will require a tap and an overflow control to be installed.
- Rainwater from a butt is not potable but can be used for watering indoor and outdoor plants and washing outdoor furniture, wheelbarrows, etc.
- Keep butts covered at all times to prevent mosquitoes from laying eggs in the water.

large storage tanks and filtration systems, rendering rainwater reusable for washing machines and toilet flushing and in some cases as drinking water.

Installing a rainwater butt is not complicated. They're available in a range of sizes (typically 150 litres to over 500) with taps and overflow valves. Connect a hose to each, and excess water is directed away from the butt and the house, while the remaining water is kept ready for later use. It's simple and reduces demand on your local water supply.

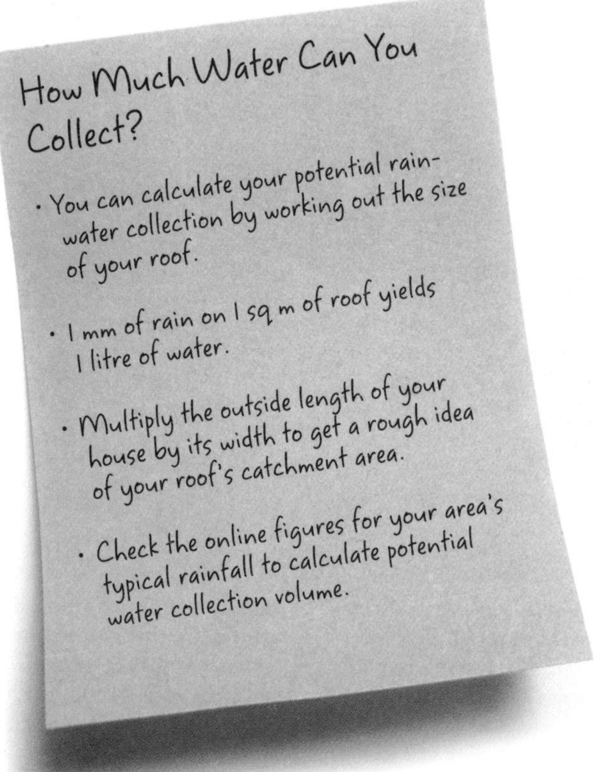

How Much Water Can You Collect?
• You can calculate your potential rainwater collection by working out the size of your roof.
• 1 mm of rain on 1 sq m of roof yields 1 litre of water.
• Multiply the outside length of your house by its width to get a rough idea of your roof's catchment area.
• Check the online figures for your area's typical rainfall to calculate potential water collection volume.

Saving Money and Water

- Water butts will not provide enough water or water pressure to water a large lawn, but can water borders and supply trickle irrigation.
- Some water companies offer information on where to purchase water butts and how to install them.
- Water butts are not always available at garden centres and DIY stores – call ahead first.
- You can also buy kits for converting or retrofitting barrels for use as water butts.

SAFETY GATES

Set these up to keep young children out of harm's way

Young kids like to wander – and they should. Everything is interesting to them. Once they become mobile, there's little that can stop them from snooping around. You want to keep them safe, of course, without hindering them too much. Safety gates restrict access but not curiosity, and they'll keep children from going into unsupervised parts of the home. They aren't substitutes for parental care and supervision, but they're a terrific parent helper.

That said, many safety gates aren't all that attractive. Different models come with different means of attaching them to walls and woodwork (some of the pressure type rubber contacts can pull paint off woodwork unless you put thin

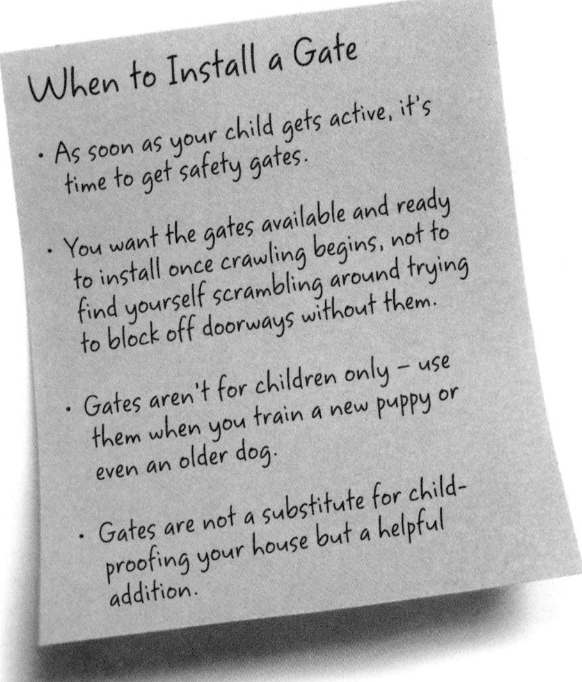

When to Install a Gate
• As soon as your child gets active, it's time to get safety gates.
• You want the gates available and ready to install once crawling begins, not to find yourself scrambling around trying to block off doorways without them.
• Gates aren't for children only – use them when you train a new puppy or even an older dog.
• Gates are not a substitute for child-proofing your house but a helpful addition.

Safety Gates

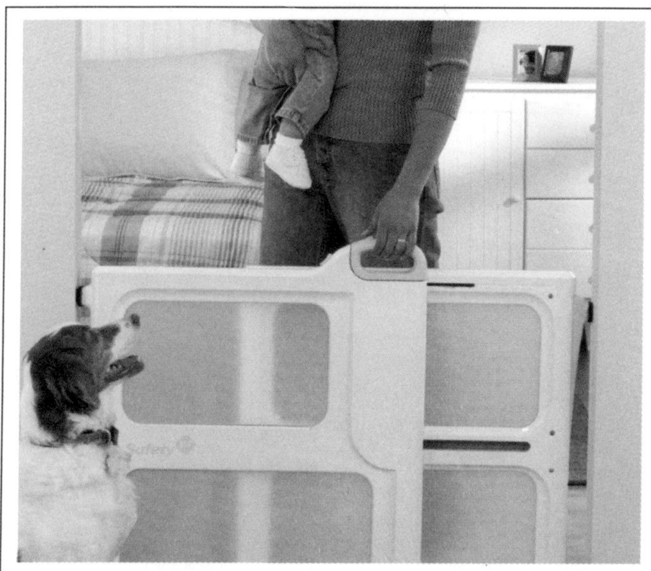

- Pressure-style safety gates are appropriate for doorways with solid wood frames. Press the rubber ends against the frame and adjust for a tight fit.
- These gates do not require any tools for installation and are expandable to fit different size openings.
- If the gate has to be moved constantly, consider fitting a screw-fixed gate instead, which is easier to open and walk through.

cardboard against the paint first). Today online sellers of baby safety products offer gates for every configuration and need, including furniture-quality hardwood models. Safety gates can also keep pets where you want them and prevent elderly people with mental impairment from leaving safe areas of the home and possibly leaving altogether.

ZOOM

Safety gates come in two categories: pressure-mounted and those with screw-in hinges for attaching to woodwork and door frames. Be sure your gate works for the intended location. Pressure-mounted gates, for example, are inappropriate for the tops of staircases, as they can be pushed over. For non-standard-size openings, adjustable gates are available.

Screw-Fixed Safety Gates

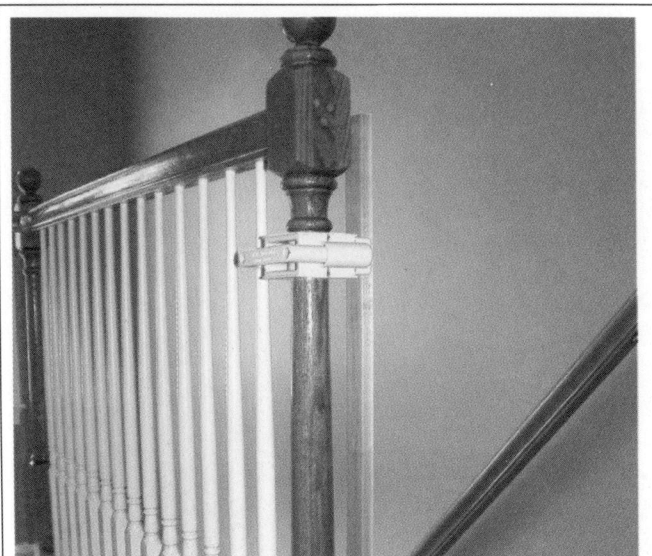

- A screw-fixed gate is secured with screws and fittings to a wall stud, post or door frame.
- At the top and bottom of staircases, these are the only safety gates considered to be secure. They should not have a lower rail you have to step over.
- When fitted at the top of a staircase, the gate should swing away from the stairs, not over them.
- To avoid spoiling the staircase with the fixings, consider tightly clamping a piece of timber to the newel post and fastening the gate to it.

Installing and Using Gates

- Install safety gates at the top and bottom of any open staircase.
- Install a gate where there are sturdy surfaces to mount it against.
- Get into the habit of shutting the gate all the time, even when your child is asleep, so that you never forget and leave it open during the day.
- Never let children see you climbing over a gate, as they will try to copy you.

WINDOW PRECAUTIONS

Make windows in your home child-safe while keeping them functional

For the most part, kids are careful around windows, but accidents happen and many children end up in hospital every year due to window-related falls.

The basics should be addressed first. Move furniture that kids might play on away from operable windows so they don't accidentally tumble out, and be sure they generally play well away from windows, even when they're closed; if you're installing new windows, consider how you want them to open (top openers are safer).

What about old windows? Double-hung sash windows open from the top and bottom. You can keep the top sashes free to provide ventilation but install a window a stop to keep the lower

Limiting Window Openings

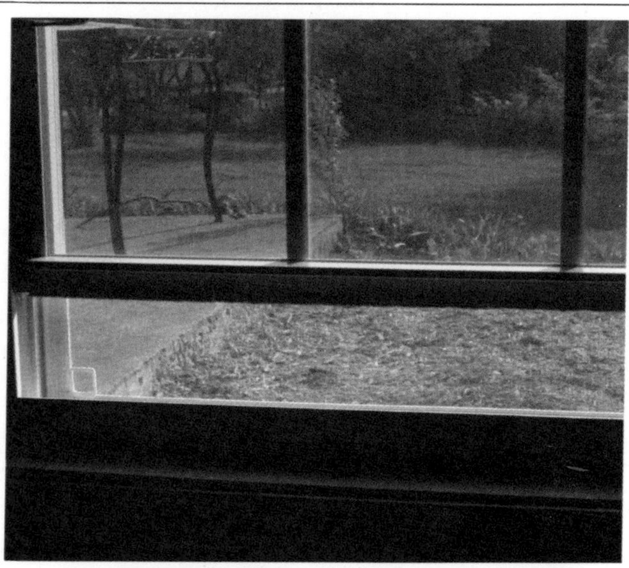

- In warm weather, be aware of open windows, which could prove dangerous for small children, particularly in tall blocks of flats.
- Where it's essential to open windows for adequate ventilation, limit window openings around children to a maximum of 10 cm.
- Windows without limiting devices should be open only when children in those rooms are under adult supervision.

Types of Guards

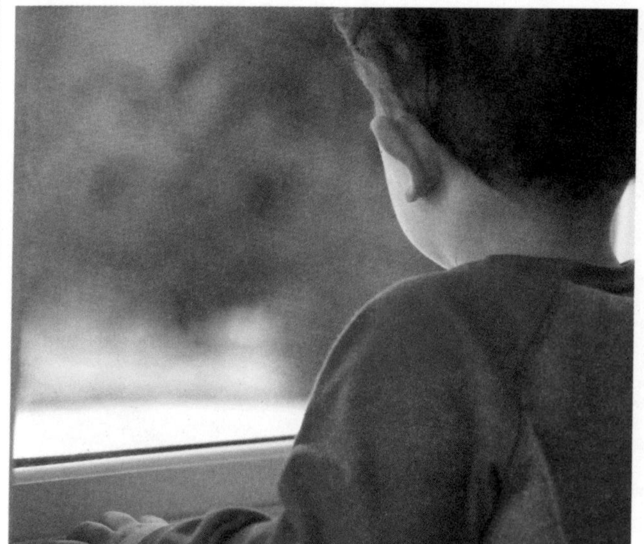

- Fittings are available that limit how far a window sash will open, while other styles are movable, allowing optional full opening.
- Casement windows can be controlled with a standard door chain lock, installed out of reach of a child.
- Interior window guards offer the fullest protection and ventilation. They need to be custom made to fit the window precisely, and the spacing between the bars should be no more than 65 mm.

sash closed, or a safety guard can be installed. Casement windows also accommodate safety guards.

Pivoting windows cannot be adapted to conventional window guards, but their movement can be limited with blocks, a door chain lock, or other fitting attached to the frame. Take the right precautions to keep your children safe.

RED LIGHT

You must be able to remove child protective guards and locks quickly should your family need to escape a fire. Older children and all adults should practise removing and releasing them. Never take the chance that a fire won't occur in your home.

Safety Locks

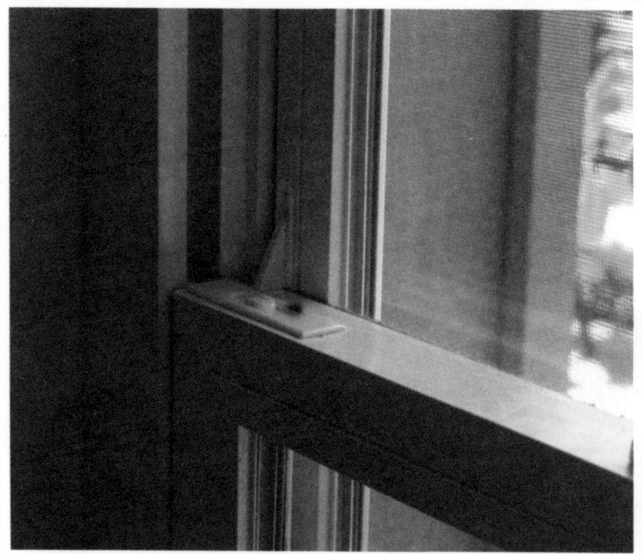

- Safety locks work on sliding windows, including sash windows, as well as sliding patio doors.
- Some ventilation locks have a movable pin or other metal section that prevents a sash from opening until the pin is moved.
- These locks are inexpensive and easy to install.
- Some styles of vent wedges adhere using their own adhesive and are meant to stay fixed in one location.

Window Blind Cords

- Window blinds whose pull cords have loops have been identified as a strangulation hazard for young children.
- Pull cords are no longer made with loops, but your home may contain older blinds that still have this feature.
- Looped cords should be replaced with free cords, tassels and tie-down devices.
- As an alternative, install cordless window coverings in children's rooms and playrooms.

ROOM & CUPBOARD DOORS

With specialized fittings, doors can remain secured while your kids stay safe

Safety latches for cupboard doors have been around for years, and are useful whether the contents of the cupboard could be hazardous to small children or you just want to stop them pulling everything out. Very young children love to empty cupboards and drawers, and some parents choose to keep one low-level kitchen cupboard available for exploration.

Locks and latches come in different styles, most of them hidden inside cupboard doors or drawers, while others lock straight through side-by-side cupboard door handles.

Locks and latches also prevent room and entry doors from accidentally being slammed on little fingers or toes. Finger guards of various types are available to prevent doors from

Protecting Fingers

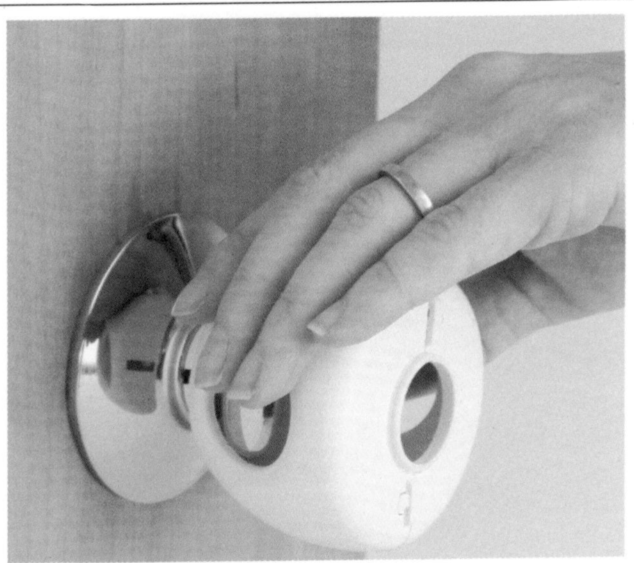

- Doorknob guards and locks prevent small hands from opening doors, but consider any elderly household members who might have trouble with these devices.
- Latches and bolts installed high on the door are out of children's reach yet manoeuvrable by adults.
- Plastic door stops and slip-on devices prevent doors from slamming into walls when opened and from damaging fingers near the door jamb when closed.
- A stop at the bottom of the door will keep it open and prevent it from closing accidentally.

Cupboard Latches

- Plastic latches that mount on the inside of cupboard doors and drawers keep both accessible to adults but not children. Some drawer latches are self-adhesive and easy to install.
- Latches allow the drawer to open slightly and then lock in place to avoid pinched fingers.
- Surface-mounted U-shaped plastic locks secure side-by-side drawer or cupboard knobs, preventing them opening.
- Self-adhesive oven and refrigerator door locks are also available.

completely shutting and slamming on to vulnerable fingers.

For bifold doors, a very simple and inexpensive plastic stop inserted at the top of the doors where they come together prevents them from opening. Locks are also available for sliding doors. If a door needs to stay open, you can fit a stop on the bottom edge to prevent movement.

Just a few simple adjustments to your doors will help prevent accidents.

RED LIGHT

Installing safety latches doesn't guarantee a child won't get past them and grab at toxic cleaners and chemicals kept in lower cupboards. Dangerous products should be kept out of reach of children. When your children are old enough to understand the dangers of these products, you can move them.

Door and Drawer Locks

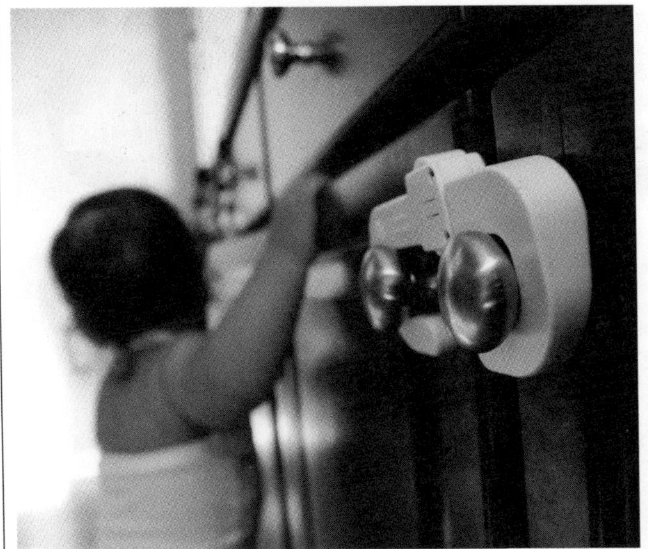

- Child safety locks are inexpensive and easy to install.
- The locks must be deterrents to children but workable by adults – this might not be the case if arthritis prevents someone working the lock easily.
- Besides storing toxic cleaning substances in higher cupboards, store breakable glass and sharp knives and scissors out of reach of curious children, too.
- Keep medicines in a locked cabinet.

Bathroom Door Locks

- Newer bathroom door locks have a button or lever to activate the locking function.
- On the outside of the door, they have a small hole in the doorknob for inserting an emergency key, or a slot for a screwdriver.
- Inexpensive emergency keys are sold separately where the locks are sold – be sure to put the key in a known place for use if your child accidentally locks the bathroom door and cannot open it.

ELECTRICAL PRECAUTIONS

Take preventative measures against electrical mishaps to ensure the safety of your family

Young children love poking fingers, pens and keys into power sockets. It's easy and inviting, when many sockets are so close to floor level. Well before your child starts to crawl, stock up on plastic socket covers and plug one into every unused socket in your home. Make sure sockets are switched off when they're not in use.

Electric flexes are another attraction, especially when babies are crawling and spend much of their time at floor level. Organizers are available for multiple flexes trailing from sound systems, computers and peripherals, etc., as well as protective coverings for any flexes running along skirting boards.

Lead Organizers

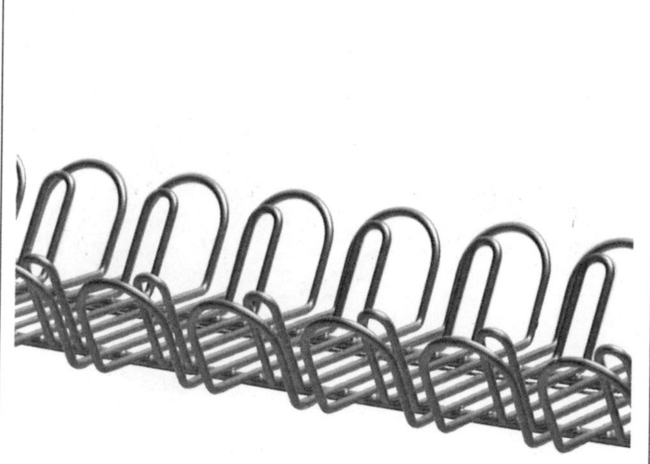

- Organizing multiple electrical leads behind computers and electrical systems benefits children and adults by keeping wires neat and safe.
- One approach is a plastic tube-type product that encases multiple leads in a neat grouping and away from small hands.
- Another product encases leads in a hard plastic container and winds them up to make them less of a tripping hazard.
- Self-adhesive plastic lead covers enclose single wires to both protect and hide them.

Securing Loose Wires

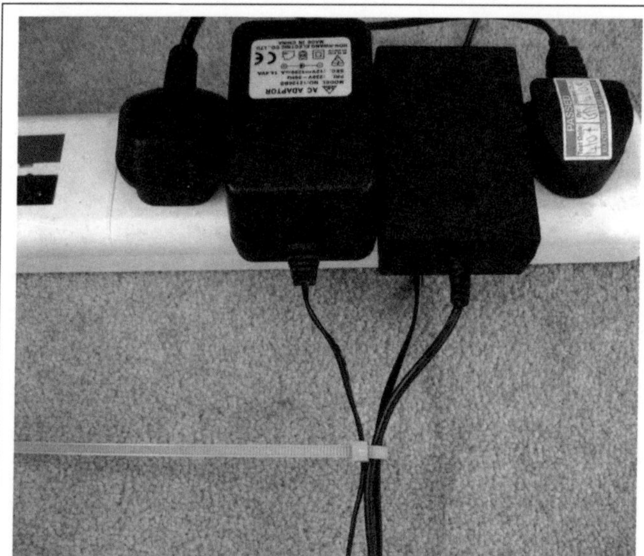

- Although not as protective as using lead covers or casings, taping or binding multiple leads together will make individual wires difficult to pull at or chew on.
- Use cable clips to secure wires to skirting boards.
- Replace any frayed or worn electrical leads for the whole family's safety.
- Never leave plugged-in kitchen appliances unattended when young children are present.

The best way to protect your children is to make sure that your electrical system is correctly installed and regularly inspected, with enough power sockets to avoid trailing wires and multiple appliances plugged into adaptors.

To stop toddlers hurting themselves by plugging in appliances such as hair dryers and tongs, make sure all your electrical equipment is safely put away out of their reach when not in use.

YELLOW LIGHT

No amount of protective devices can replace an attentive parent or guardian. Like cupboard latches and safety gates, these devices are a big help but only supplement a watchful adult. Secure your electrical installations as best you can but understand the limitations of the hardware and safety devices you install.

Socket Covers

- The most basic electrical safety devices are traditional plastic covers that you insert into each socket; they're effective and inexpensive.
- Covers should be tight-fitting so that children can't remove them.
- UK power sockets have some intrinsic safety features, but covering them makes them less interesting to curious kids.

Covers for Sockets in Use

- Protect power sockets that are in use with a hinged cover that conceals sockets, plugs and switches.
- Covers are easy to install and click shut so that small hands can't open them, but they can be quickly opened by adults.
- These are not only a safety device, but prevent kids from flicking switches and accidentally turning off equipment such as the fridge, freezer or computer.

PLUMBING SAFEGUARDS

Control the flow of water to stop messes and potential burns on children

Kids love water. It's fun to splash and interesting when it keeps coming out of a tap. Toilets are interesting, too. Push a handle, and things disappear. Toys and face cloths also disappear. As much as you want to limit water play to bath time or outside with a hose, your kids have different ideas, but you can control the water flow and extracurricular toilet usage with some readily available child-proofing fittings and devices.

A key to child safety around water inside your home is checking the water temperature. It takes only six seconds of exposure to water at 60°C to cause a serious burn, but ten minutes of exposure at 50°C. This temperature is high

Toilet Lid Locks

- Self-clamping toilet lid locks prevent the youngest children from opening the lid but not adults or older children.
- For the price of one visit by a plumber, you could buy a dozen locks or more, so they are easily worth the investment.
- Different styles are available, but some do not fit all toilets as their promotional material suggests.
- No tools are required to install toilet lid locks.

Safety Tap Covers

- Even with water heaters set to lower temperatures, children can still be injured by uncontrolled hot water coming out of a tap.
- Inflatable safety covers fit over the taps to stop children playing with the hot water tap.
- Soft tap covers also stop children hurting themselves if they fall against the hard tap.
- Cushioned bath guards protect a child falling against the edge of a metal bath.

enough for everyday purposes and more energy efficient, so set your water heater to the lower figure.

Filling up a bath or sink with the plug in presents another risk. Either can fill with water faster than the overflow protection can drain it.

Ease of exiting a slippery bath isn't a concern only for the elderly. Install grab bars for kids to use when getting out. Wall-mounted models and clamp-on styles are worth considering. It's the little things that will make the biggest impact in safety in your home.

YELLOW LIGHT

Some studies mention concern for bacterial growth if the water temperature is less than 50°C, but this applies more to people with compromised immune systems. Children have developing systems, and if this is a concern, discuss it with your doctor and balance the risks of burns versus possible water quality problems.

Grab Bars

- Grab bars or safety bars come in a variety of sizes and designs to accommodate people with different physical needs.
- Having a grab bar makes sense for anyone standing up in a slippery bath; install a long one so both adults and children can use it.
- To fasten to a tile wall, use a glass and tile drill bit for drilling the hole and stainless steel screws for securing.
- Special fittings are available for installing inside a fibreglass or acrylic shower cubicle.

Garden Hoses

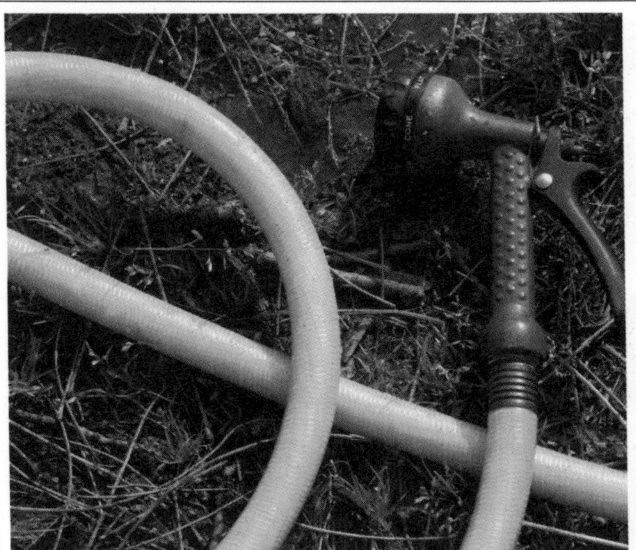

- Many hoses are made from PVC, which uses lead as a stabilizer; lead can also be found in brass hose fittings.
- Although lead levels have been reduced in recent years due to legal action against hose makers, some lead still remains and is noted on hose warning labels.
- A lead-free hose will be marked as 'Safe for Drinking'.
- Flush any hose out for a minute or two before filling a wading pool.

OTHER CHILD CONCERNS

Homes are built by and for adults – a little child orientation helps

With children, accidents happen, but the aim should be to prevent the mindless and traumatic accidents more than the bumps and bruises from normal play. Observe a child for a day, and you'll get a good idea what you have to lock up, limit access to, or ban from your kids.

Medicines can look like sweets, and junior versions can taste appealing. It's little wonder kids want to explore medicine cabinets. It's important to keep all medicines out of reach of children in a locked cabinet.

Safety gates on raised garden decks and balconies will keep toddlers from tumbling down the stairs, but check that railings around them don't have gaps large enough for a child to pass through (openings between vertical members should be less than 10 cm).

Space Heaters

- Both portable space heaters and permanently installed room heaters can get dangerously hot to the touch.
- Select a space heater such as a thermostatically controlled convector heater, in which the heating element is well out of reach.
- Look for a heater with sensors that turn it off when objects are too close or if children or pets move near.
- Use heaters on the floor only, and don't plug them into extension leads.

Video and Audio Monitoring

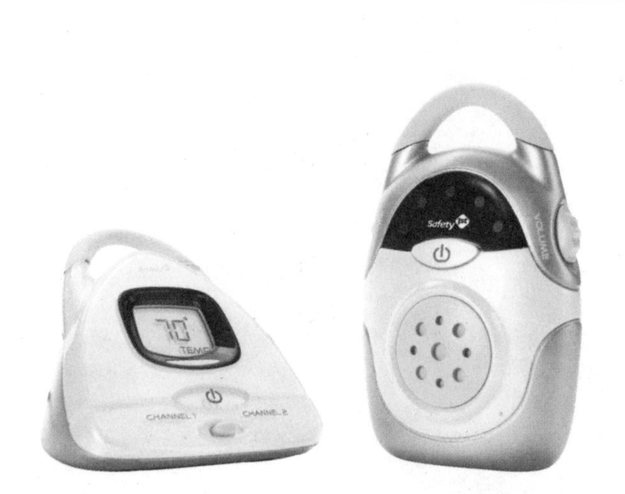

- Multipurpose baby monitors differ in built-in features, working range and price.
- Some monitors feature two- and three-way receiving, while others offer video monitoring of two separate rooms.
- Monitor size varies from very portable – about the size of a home phone – to the size of a small TV set.
- Some monitors sound alarms if a child stops moving altogether for longer than 20 seconds, and others offer night-vision features.

Baby audio monitors aren't new, but the newest generation of audio/video monitors allows you to watch a child from anywhere in the house using a monitor the size of a mobile phone. These aren't a substitute for being in the same room, but like all safety devices, they're a good supplement. Making your home safe will keep your child out of trouble and ease your fears.

Cushion Edges for Furniture

- Kids can often get hurt by sharp furniture edges, particularly small children for whom these edges are at eye level.
- Cushioning the edges with self-adhesive soft material protects your child without leaving marks on the furniture.
- No tools are required, and the cushions are removable when they are no longer needed.
- To prevent children from pulling over bookshelves and small cabinets, secure them to walls using angle brackets.

Safety and Deck Railings

- Raised deck construction must meet local building regulations.
- Railings around raised decks are a main safety feature, even for constructions that are fairly close to the ground.
- A railing must be at least 90 cm tall and should not have any gaps between any two vertical members more than 10 cm wide – this prevents babies from crawling through and falling.
- The railing must be exceptionally strong and well secured – lives can depend on it.

REFRIGERATOR

Even new, sophisticated refrigerators need some basic care and attention

New refrigerators can cost several thousand pounds, depending on the model and features, which can include ice and water dispensers, water filtration systems for these same water dispensers, multiple defrost options, and zoned cooling. At least one current model has a built-in TV that is satellite- and internet-compatible.

Regardless of the age, style or model of your refrigerator, it will need some attending to if you want it to run efficiently, but nothing more than regular cleaning and inspection. As far as repairing water pumps or replacing a condenser fan go, these can be exercises in frustration. You'll have to diagnose the problem, track down the right part and do the

Cleaning the Refrigerator

- A refrigerator works best if its coils are kept free of dust.
- The coils are either accessed through a front kick plate under the door or are located on the back of the refrigerator.
- Unplug the refrigerator or shut the power off, remove the kick plate and vacuum out all the dust, or pull the refrigerator out from the wall and vacuum the rear coils.
- Remove the back plate and vacuum the dust from the condenser fan as well.

Checking Seals

- A refrigerator door gasket has to be kept intact, clean and supple to remain an effective seal.
- Condensation on the seals suggests they are leaking and need to be replaced.
- Clean the seals monthly, after sticky spills, or when there's any presence of mould; use warm water and washing-up liquid (use a bleach-based cleaner for mould).
- When it is clean and dry, coat the seal with a small amount of petroleum jelly to keep it soft and prevent it drying out.

installation. While appliance service engineers are expensive, they are often worth it. A job like this is probably best left to a professional unless you have the time and patience to do it yourself.

ZOOM

To calculate whether a refrigerator is worth repairing, add up the call-out charge, additional labour, parts and the age of the appliance, versus replacement with a new unit under warranty that uses less energy. A new basic refrigerator will cost around £300.

You might want to wear gloves while doing this process.

Cleaning

- There's no getting around regular refrigerator cleaning if you want to avoid bad food smells and unintentional rotten food.
- Unplug the refrigerator and remove everything, storing items that must be kept cold in an insulated picnic bag and throwing out anything that even looks questionable.
- Clean inside and out with warm water and washing-up liquid – use bicarbonate of soda on stubborn spills.
- Rinse and dry all washed surfaces.

Energy Efficiency

- If your refrigerator or fridge-freezer is over ten years old it's probably using 50 per cent more energy than a new model.
- If you decide to buy a new refrigerator, look for an A++ rating.
- Defrost the freezer regularly if it's not frost-free. Both fridge and freezer run most efficiently when they are moderately well stocked.
- Arrange for the local council to collect your old fridge for safe disposal. Some suppliers offer to remove your old fridge when they deliver a new one.

DISHWASHER

While they are convenient and reliable, dishwashers do require some low maintenance

A study done at the University of Bonn is often quoted in the debate about dishwasher versus washing dishes by hand. The study found a dishwasher used less energy, water and soap than hand-washing and got dishes cleaner. One study on its own rarely settles anything, but this one seems to be unchallenged.

A dishwasher can be especially efficient and energy-saving if the dishes are not excessively rinsed – or rinsed at all – before loading them, the dishwasher is full before running it, and the dry cycle is skipped in favour of air drying with the door open after the rinse cycles are finished. Also, skipping any rinse-hold and pre-rinse cycles will save additional energy and not affect cleaning the dishes.

Checking Seals

- Dishwasher door seals can harden and crack with age, allowing water to leak.
- Wipe the gasket clean once a month with warm, soapy water, and when it is dry, rub on a small amount of petroleum jelly to keep it soft.
- Replace leaking gaskets; pull the damaged gasket out with a pair of pliers, and take it to an appliance shop for a replacement.
- Soften the new gasket in warm water and install according to the manufacturer's instructions.

Rust on Dish Racks

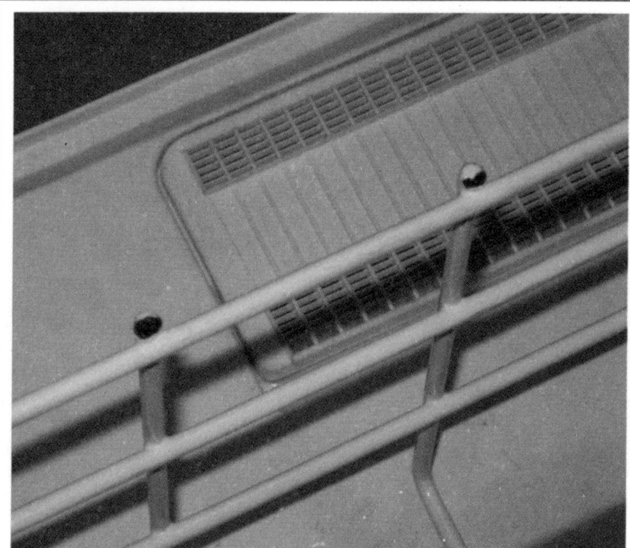

- When a dishwasher rack's vinyl coating wears out, the exposed sections of the metal rack will rust.
- Special brush-on sealants, available from appliance shops, offer only limited partial repairs, as the sealants eventually wash away.
- Wrapping small strips of aluminium foil around the rust will protect dishes resting on those spots from rust stains.
- Compare the price of replacement racks with a new dishwasher – by the time they start rusting the dishwasher is old enough to need other repairs.

Dishwashers are wonderful appliances and can have a very long life if you do some minimal routine maintenance. Like any motorized, wet environment, dishwashers wear down, especially if they are used for more than one load a day, which isn't uncommon in family settings.

Dishwashers don't need much maintenance, but periodic inspections can help keep them running. With prices starting at under £300 for a basic model, you have to evaluate whether it's worth repairing an older unit. You might find it's more cost-efficient to buy a newer, energy-saving model.

MAKE IT EASY

When replacing a dishwasher, consider whether the extra features, such as multiple cleaning cycles and electronic controls, are worth the money. These features can add to repair costs or the frequency of repairs, depending on the manufacturer and any history of warranty problems surrounding certain features or models.

Drains and Filters

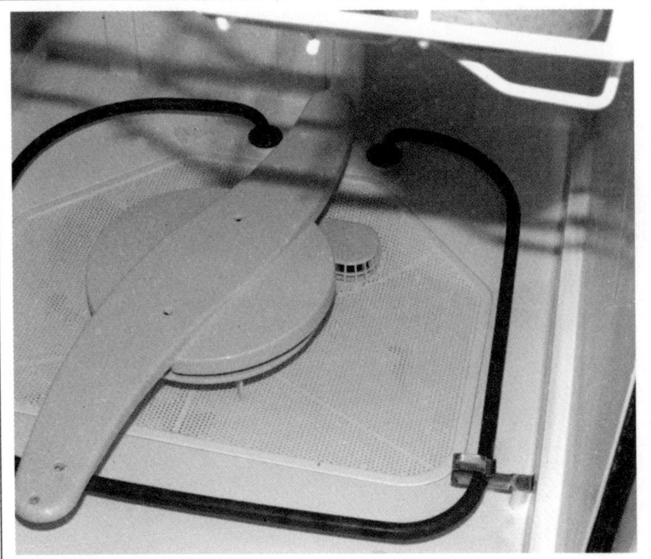

- Depending on the model and age of your dishwasher, you might have very little maintenance to do – check your owner's manual for recommendations.
- When a dishwasher fills slowly, check the water strainer, which is probably clogged.
- If it's draining slowly, look at the drain screen and remove any bits of food, broken glass, or other debris.
- Drain hoses can also get clogged – be sure to have a bucket ready when you loosen the end under the sink.

Water Sprayer

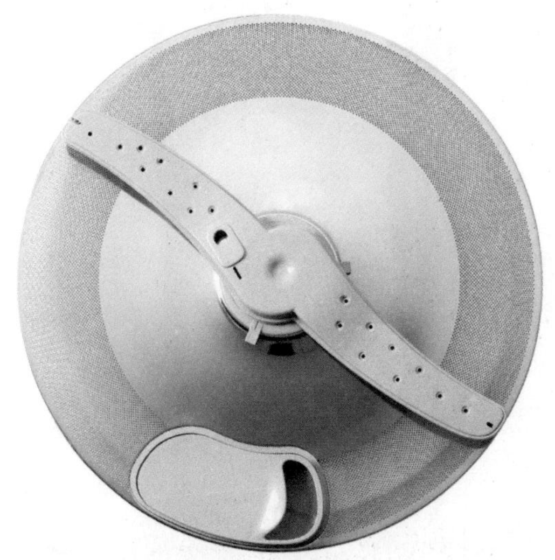

- Dishwasher water sprayers may become clogged with minerals from the water or detergent.
- Clean the water sprayer – including the upper sprayer, if present – as needed or every few months.
- Remove the unit and soak it in warm white vinegar to loosen mineral deposits.
- A spray arm is either secured with a bolt or is simply fitted over the pump and lifts off with a little bit of back-and-forth movement.

VACUUM CLEANER

Empty and check your cleaner regularly to maximize its cleaning capabilities

The first practical home vacuum cleaner was manufactured in the early 1900s by the Electric Suction Sweeper Company, which eventually became the Hoover Company. Vacuum cleaners took the drudgery out of carpet and rug cleaning. The invention of the disposable dust bag made life easier for those with allergies and made disposal faster.

Modern vacuum cleaners are light-years beyond earlier models. They're quieter, have stronger suction and larger dust and dirt storage, and come with attachments for cleaning furniture, window coverings and stairs. After years of depending on bags for dirt disposal, the bagless design has gained a lot of traction, although emptying the

Emptying the Bag

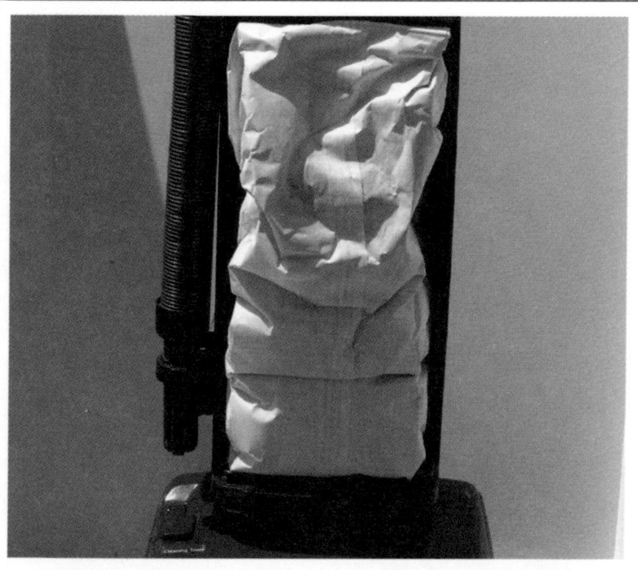

- Full bags cause the vacuum cleaner to work harder and vacuum less – empty the bag when the volume is up to the indicator line.
- It's a bit messy, but you can pull the contents out of a bag and reuse it if you're out of replacements.
- Bagless cleaners can be more expensive, but there is no additional cost in replacement bags.
- Cleaners with HEPA filters catch even the smallest particles, and are particularly useful for households of asthma sufferers.

Belts

- Belts need regular replacement, once a year or so with regular use – no tools required.
- Keep extra belts on hand in case of unexpected breakage.
- Avoid vacuuming up screws, coins, hair grips and other small objects that can damage the fan or the motor.
- Leads can fail from being repeatedly bent as they're wound up – replacing a lead can salvage a dead vacuum cleaner.

cylinder exposes the user to dust and debris.

Many a vacuum cleaner gets thrown out because it's clogged up with dust or the lead has failed. If your cleaner is picking up less and straining more, it's time for some maintenance. Observe your cleaner's performance carefully to check for any inconsistencies. These inconsistencies will point you towards any repairs needed. Regular cleanings will keep a vacuum cleaner working to full capacity without undue strain on the motor.

Brushes

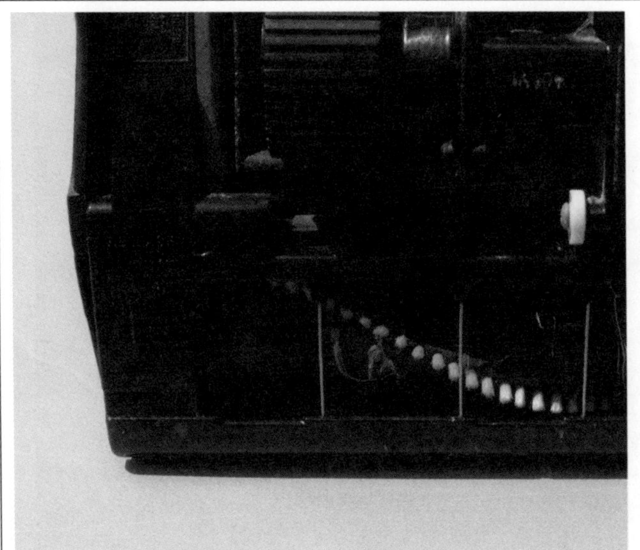

- A vacuum cleaner's brushes get tangled up with strings, rubber bands and so on – cut these away to keep the brush roller moving freely.
- Whenever a vacuum cleaner suddenly stops operating, check the fuse or circuit breaker first.
- Although upright vacuums are more popular, the advantage of a cylinder model is a larger motor available for vacuuming.
- Replace or clean any built-in filters according to the manufacturer's recommendations.

Electric Blowers

- Electric blowers are highly versatile tools that extend the life of other tools and appliances as well as performing standard chores.
- Use a blower to clean sawdust from drills, sanders and saws.
- The best way to clean out vacuum cleaner hoses, brushes and cylinders is with a blower.
- When gutters are dry, blow the leaves and twigs out instead of scooping.

SUMMER

Make this the time for holidays, barbecues and the inescapable warm weather repairs

Let's face it: If we could skip home maintenance, we would, especially during the summer. When a sunny weekend comes around, who wants to be working on the house? No one, but you don't want to be regretting it when the weather turns in the autumn and certainly not in the winter when it's far too cold to touch up the paint or repair a broken window. Pace yourself so you don't get buried by the jobs and let the summer pass you by completely.

Start with the outside. This is the time to do any wall and roof repairs while it's dry and you're not fighting wet weather conditions. You might find out after removing loose pointing that the damage is more extensive than you thought.

Paint Exterior

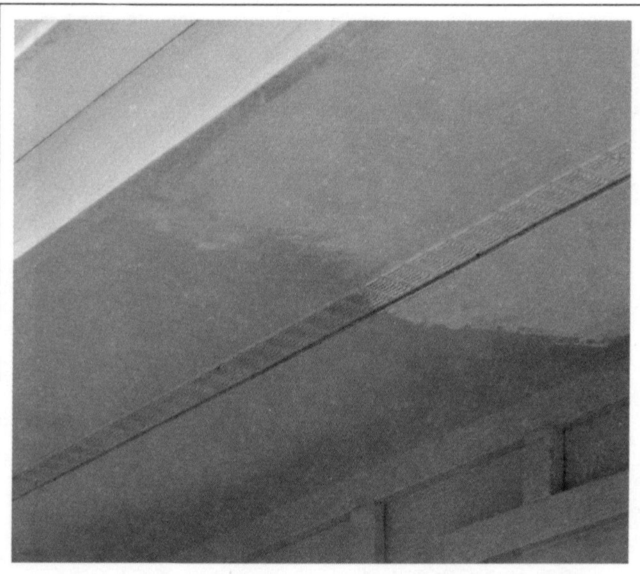

- Touch up any areas where the paint is missing, flaking or bubbling.
- Paint entire sections of wall or woodwork when touching up so the newly painted area doesn't stick out too much.
- If the entire house needs painting, schedule carefully and pace yourself so you get it done in easy stages without giving up all your free time, or consider calling a painting contractor.
- Get any painting done by early September, even if you expect a mild autumn.

Wall Repairs

- Check house and garden walls for loose and damaged mortar and bricks.
- All masonry gradually deteriorates due to exposure to the weather, particularly in the mortar joints, which eventually need raking out and repointing.
- This is a time-consuming and skilled job, and it is generally better done by a contractor.
- The pointing makes all the difference to the final appearance of the wall, so the new mortar needs to be consistent and well matched to the original.

Summer is the obvious time for painting, but it also has its limitations. Too much heat or high humidity affects both interior and exterior paints. Painting in hot sunlight can cause the paint surface to dry too fast and form a skin before the rest is completely dry, resulting in pinholes, blisters and excessive brush marks in the finish. As with any project, set up a schedule for getting the work done.

MAKE IT EASY

In hot weather, paint won't flow and level properly straight out of the can, but it can be diluted, by as much as 10 per cent if necessary, for easier application. It's tempting to paint late into the evening, but overnight dew might affect gloss paint. Stop painting about two hours before sunset to be safe.

Decking, Roof and Gutter Repairs

- If you're up on the roof replacing damaged tiles, inspect the surrounding area and replace any questionable ones as well.
- The less walking around you do on an old roof the better, since just being up there can damage tiles.
- After any gutter repairs and cleaning, run a hose to check your work and detect any additional leaks.
- Revarnish your decking for extra protection, even if there isn't a pressing need for it.

Holiday Checklist

- If you're going away during the summer, make sure your home goes on running smoothly in your absence.
- Leave keys with a neighbour, who can water plants if necessary and keep an eye on your property.
- Turn off and unplug appliances such as TVs and computers.
- Cancel any deliveries such as newspapers.
- Plug a few lamps, and possibly a radio, into timeswitches programmed to come on when it gets dark.

AUTUMN

Take advantage of the cooler (yet not cold) weather to do some maintenance around the house

Autumn is sort of a 'batten down the hatches' time after the lazy outdoor days of summer. Winter cold and wet are coming, the warm weather is heading south, and daylight is slowly disappearing. All those lovely colourful leaves are falling and too many of them are ending up in your gutters. Ignore them and your gutters are likely to overflow in wet weather. The overflow running down walls can lead to damage and create damp inside the house, and the retained water weighs down the gutters, straining their fixings and joints.

It's also time to bring in garden hoses and drain the outside pipes and taps, to avoid freezing and splitting once the weather turns cold.

Clear Leaves

- Clean the gutters thoroughly and be prepared to do it again once all the leaves are down.
- Scoop fallen leaves away from outside drain covers so that storm water can drain away quickly.
- Sweep or blow leaves off the patio and lawn and stack them in a leaf pile or put into sacks to rot down into leaf mould.

Chimney and Outside Pipes

- Inspect your chimney and get it cleaned if that wasn't done earlier in the year.
- Be sure the masonry joints on the chimney are in good shape and consider installing a chimney cap if you don't already have one.
- Before there's any danger of freezing temperatures, shut off the water to all outside taps, drain them, and put garden hoses away in the garage or shed.

In cold climates, we all spend more time indoors around the fire. You don't want to risk a chimney fire, or an electrical fire for that matter. Autumn is a good time to get your chimney swept and your boiler and other gas appliances serviced, and to do an annual safety check of all systems, including water stopcocks and smoke detectors.

YELLOW LIGHT

Carbon monoxide poisoning from boilers and other sources of incomplete combustion kills about 20 people a year in Britain, according to the Health and Safety Executive, and hundreds of others suffer serious harm. A standard boiler inspection should include checking carbon monoxide levels. Consider fitting a carbon monoxide detector, which sounds an alarm when it detects unsafe levels of carbon monoxide.

Odds and Ends

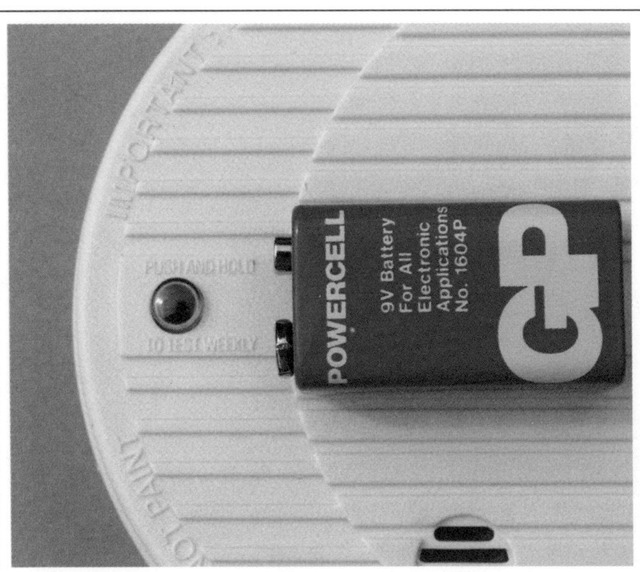

- Replace any burned-out light bulbs in outside lighting and check that motion detectors are properly aimed.
- Check that the main water stopcock is functioning and that it moves easily.
- Replace all your smoke detector batteries and test the detectors.

Safety Inspection

- With winter coming, you can expect to spend more time indoors with lights and heating systems running longer hours plus using a fireplace or wood-burning stove.
- Be sure all family members know the locations of gas, water and electricity shut-offs and how to use them.
- Lay out an evacuation plan in the event of a fire.
- Clean lint out of the tumble dryer and replace kitchen extractor fan filters.

WINTER

Winter's here, so start up some routine cold weather maintenance

If the snow is falling, it's a little late to paint the windows or clean the gutters, so here's hoping all that maintenance is finished. Winter maintenance chores are limited, but there are still some pesky tasks to attend to.

Boilers are heavily used in the winter. If yours hasn't been serviced for a year or two and you missed it during the past summer, call a service engineer now and be prepared to wait. This is the busy season for heating contractors, but you want to get it checked before it dies on Christmas Eve.

Are you prepared to be housebound for a day or two or three in heavy snow, possibly without power? Be a prepared homeowner and have non-perishable food, water, torches

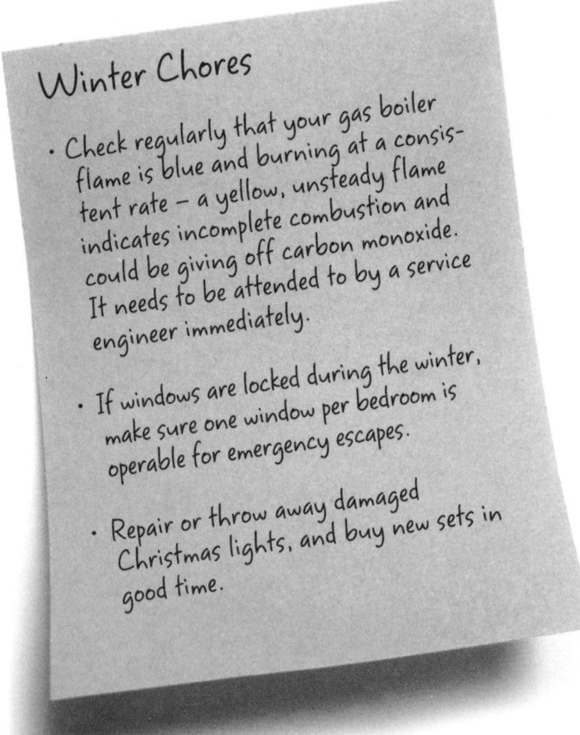

Winter Chores
· Check regularly that your gas boiler
flame is blue and burning at a consistent rate – a yellow, unsteady flame
indicates incomplete combustion and
could be giving off carbon monoxide.
It needs to be attended to by a service
engineer immediately.
· If windows are locked during the winter,
make sure one window per bedroom is
operable for emergency escapes.
· Repair or throw away damaged
Christmas lights, and buy new sets in
good time.

Car Check

- Your car works harder in cold weather, and a breakdown in the snow can strand you.
- Be sure your car has been serviced for winter driving with an antifreeze check, proper temperature-rated windscreen fluid and a healthy battery.
- Carry an extra scraper and battery cables.
- In severe winter climates, carry road salt or cat litter for traction, a tow rope and possibly a small shovel for digging out of snow.

and candles stored away in case you have to get through a period of severe winter weather.

Cold winter driving is hazardous and demanding on car batteries. Do you have a winter survival kit in your car boot? Getting stuck in a blizzard can happen to anyone, and it's not difficult to prepare for it. As with any other season, being prepared for winter weather will keep your home and life running smoothly.

YELLOW LIGHT

Wood-burning fireplaces present possible hazards. A build-up of tar in masonry and metal-lined chimneys can eventually catch fire, and hot fires can weaken chimney mortar. It's recommended that homeowners who have three or more winter fires a week should have their chimneys inspected and cleaned once a year.

Ice Dams

- If ice forms at the edge of a roof, it can cause melting snow to back up and leak into the loft space.
- Carefully clearing off snow with a snow rake or broom will temporarily ease the problem.
- Do not aggressively attack ice dams with pounding tools – there's too much risk of damaging the roof.
- When pipes freeze, open the taps and use a hair dryer, not a blow torch, to thaw them out.

Preparing for Power Cuts

- Cold weather and impassable roads can compound power cuts in the winter.
- Store some non-perishable food and bottled water, waterless hand cleaner, a torch, candles and batteries for the radio in case you lose your electricity supply for any length of time.
- Place candles inside metal bowls, baking dishes or even the sinks for safe long-term, unattended burning.
- Keep a similar kit inside your car for roadside emergencies.

SPRING

Spring brings the yearly maintenance cycle full circle – it's time to start again

You think of spring, and spring cleaning comes to mind, a fresh start now that the snow and cold are gone. You may do your own repairs or pay to have them done, but there's no way around maintenance if you want a safe, appealing place that lives up to basic expectations.

A regularly maintained house means you don't get hit with much bigger deferred problems later, so be mindful of routine check-ups. Spending a weekend in the spring on a chore list is a small price to pay to kick off a new, warmer season.

First, inspect the outside of your house for winter wear and tear. Clean the windows and woodwork to get rid of soot, grime and other seasonal gunk. Turn on the water supply to

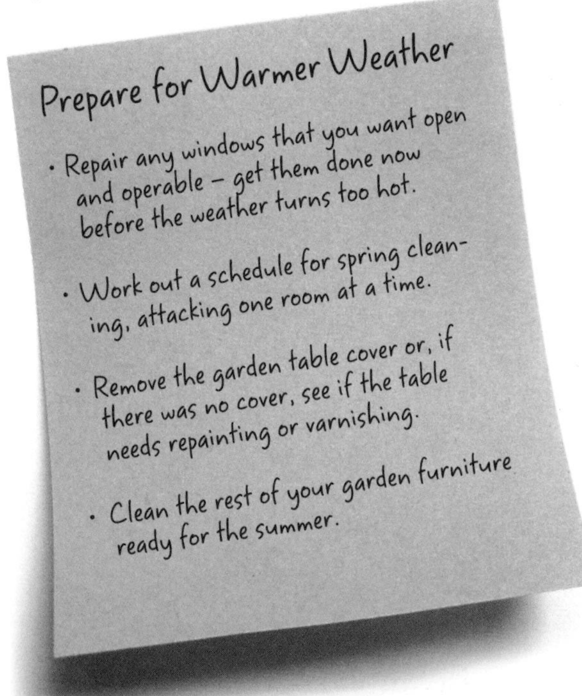

Prepare for Warmer Weather
• Repair any windows that you want open and operable – get them done now before the weather turns too hot.
• Work out a schedule for spring cleaning, attacking one room at a time.
• Remove the garden table cover or, if there was no cover, see if the table needs repainting or varnishing.
• Clean the rest of your garden furniture ready for the summer.

Cleaning Up Winter Messes

- The winter leaves grunge, and the spring is a good time to renew the outside with a scrub and wash.
- As soon as your soil starts to dry out, rake out any decomposing leaves and twigs from the garden beds.
- Clean out any fireplace ashes, screens, grates and glass doors and, if present, shut off the gas pilot light as soon as the weather is too warm for fires.
- Clean and store all winter-related items, including clothing.

outside taps. Thinking about painting in the summer? Start considering the amount of preparation, colour selection and budget for the project now. If you're not going to do it yourself, start getting estimates from decorators before they get booked for the season. Do the same with roofing contractors if your roof needs attention.

And don't forget to throw the windows open, air your home and enjoy the spring.

ZOOM

During the days of wood- and coal-burning stoves, spring cleaning was necessary to clean a winter's worth of accumulated soot. Modern heating systems have eliminated this source of grime, but spring is still viewed as a time to renew and refresh a home after it's been closed up all winter.

Exterior Checks

- Check the roof for winter damage as soon as possible.
- Check that gutters are intact.
- Check the roofspace for leaks and wet spots on the rafters or insulation, and check the roof tiles and flashing for damage.
- Masonry mortar can require repair after going through cycles of freezing and thawing – look for sandy texture, cracks between rows of bricks, and missing chunks of mortar.

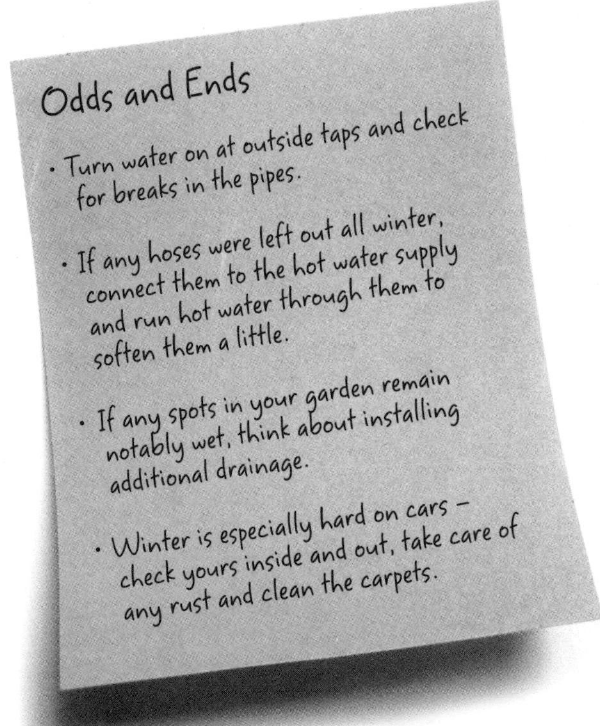

Odds and Ends
• Turn water on at outside taps and check for breaks in the pipes.
• If any hoses were left out all winter, connect them to the hot water supply and run hot water through them to soften them a little.
• If any spots in your garden remain notably wet, think about installing additional drainage.
• Winter is especially hard on cars – check yours inside and out, take care of any rust and clean the carpets.

MONTHLY

Make monthly maintenance a regular event like cooking or doing laundry

Life is full of repetition: sleeping, shopping for groceries, eating big festive meals and regretting it later. To keep your maintenance and repairs down to a manageable level, treat them the same way. Instead of waiting for problems to appear, try to prevent them arising in the first place.

As despised as 'to-do' lists are, they're better than 'absolutely must do now before the floor caves in' lists later. We accept that dishes have to be washed daily and clothes washed once or twice a week, so accepting that smoke detectors should be checked monthly isn't much of an imaginative stretch.

Having trouble following a regular maintenance list? Set up a schedule and post it on the refrigerator or as a timed

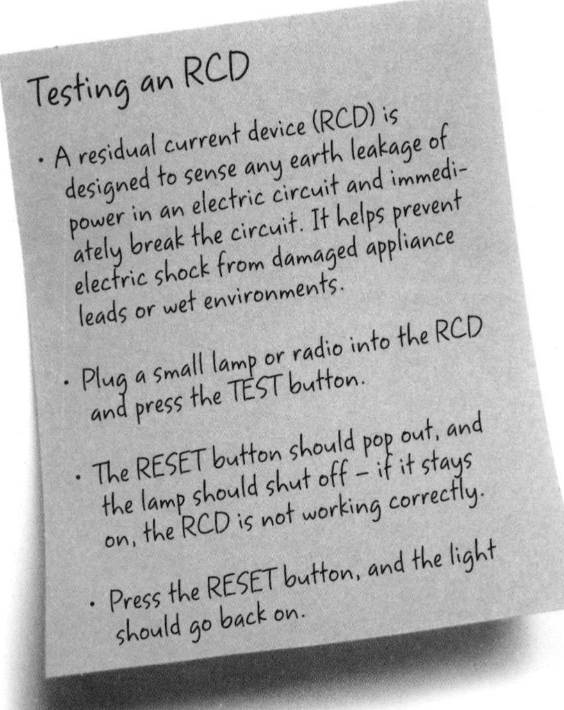

Testing an RCD
• A residual current device (RCD) is designed to sense any earth leakage of power in an electric circuit and immediately break the circuit. It helps prevent electric shock from damaged appliance leads or wet environments.
• Plug a small lamp or radio into the RCD and press the TEST button.
• The RESET button should pop out, and the lamp should shut off – if it stays on, the RCD is not working correctly.
• Press the RESET button, and the light should go back on.

Check Smoke Alarms

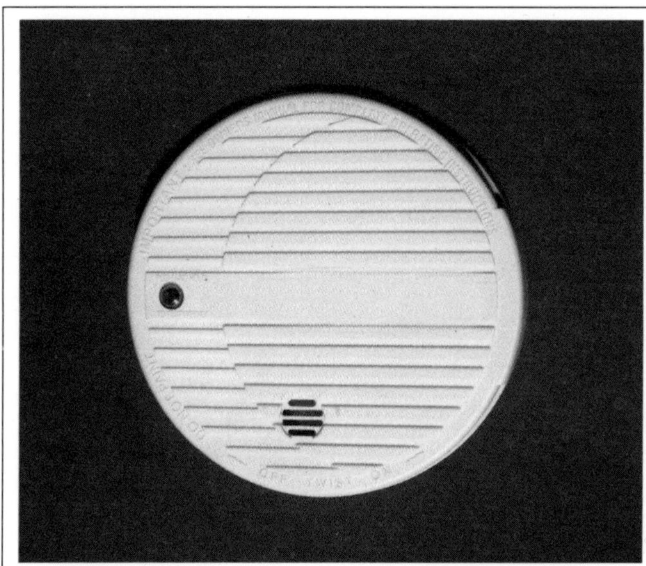

- Smoke detectors should be tested once a month by pressing the test button (do not test them with an open flame).
- If the alarm fails to sound when tested, you should replace the detector immediately.
- When a smoke detector begins randomly beeping, it usually means the batteries need replacement.
- Smoke alarms have a useful life of about ten years, at which point they should be replaced, even if they appear to be working.

reminder on your computer or wireless device. This visual reminder will help you set up a monthly routine. Make a note to check the list every month, take care of the task, and be done with it. No single task is especially onerous and is certainly easier than dealing with the consequences of not attending to it.

YELLOW LIGHT

Pouring boiling water down drains is a great way to keep them clear, but water this hot can crack moulded one-piece basin/vanity top combinations. Use a funnel inserted into these drains to pour boiling water. Never pour boiling water into a toilet, as there is some chance it could crack the bowl.

Drains

- Every drain has a trap to hold water, which acts as a barrier against sewer gases coming up through the drain lines.
- Pour water down unused or rarely used drains once a month to compensate for evaporation.
- In general, maintain drains with a bicarbonate of soda and vinegar mix, flushed down with hot water.
- Grind ice cubes and a lemon wedge in a waste disposal unit to help eliminate odours and clean away sludge.

Filters

- Clean the metal mesh filters in a kitchen extractor fan (put them in the dishwasher or leave them to soak).
- Inspect and clean tap aerators and shower heads – remove any rust particles and soak aerators and shower heads in vinegar for a few hours to break up any hard water deposits.
- If your refrigerator has a removable drain pan, remove and clean it according to the manufacturer's recommendations and vacuum the coils.

YEARLY

Once a year isn't much to ask for these important jobs

Some jobs come around only once a year – filling in your tax return and cleaning up after New Year's Eve come to mind – and they vary in importance and how much time they'll consume. If you have an open fire or a wood-burning stove, getting your chimney cleaned once a year – and inspecting it for decaying masonry and blockages caused by nesting birds – is important.

Yearly jobs tend to get done during decent weather, some in preparation for colder, wetter weather to come and others because after a year of use, dust or lint or moisture can accumulate in places you don't want it, and it's up to you to take care of them.

If you live alone, you are stuck with doing this yourself or employing someone. Otherwise, get your partner and kids

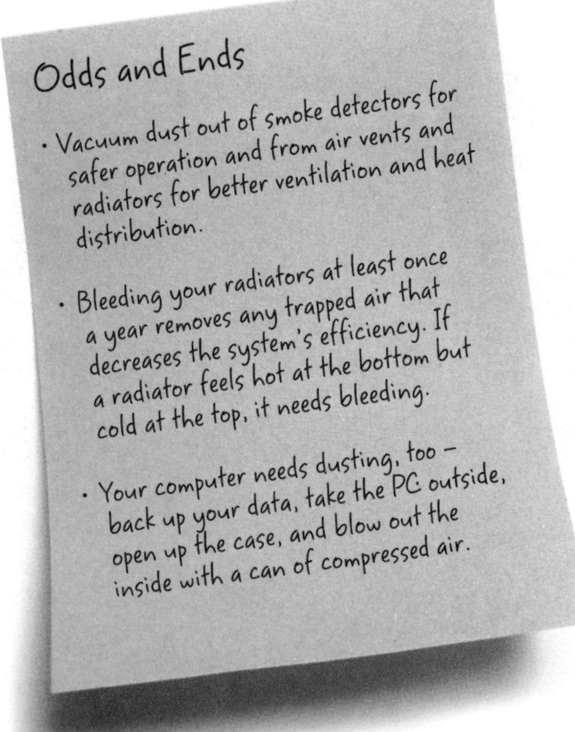

Odds and Ends

- Vacuum dust out of smoke detectors for safer operation and from air vents and radiators for better ventilation and heat distribution.
- Bleeding your radiators at least once a year removes any trapped air that decreases the system's efficiency. If a radiator feels hot at the bottom but cold at the top, it needs bleeding.
- Your computer needs dusting, too – back up your data, take the PC outside, open up the case, and blow out the inside with a can of compressed air.

Clean and Seal Tile Grout

- **Grout is a long-lasting material, but it cannot stand up indefinitely to water in shower areas.**
- **Seal tile grout once a year following the manufacturer's directions for application and drying times.**
- **If the grout has deteriorated, remove it with a grout saw or similar tool, remove any loose sealant, regrout, and then seal.**
- **Apply new silicone sealant around baths and shower trays.**

involved. Once they're old enough, children can learn to check plumbing stopcocks and the condition of bathroom tiles as well as an adult. Whether these lessons and responsibilities stick will remain to be seen, but at least you share the list of chores, and this in itself is a good lesson, although you probably don't want your eight-year-old climbing around on the roof.

MAKE IT EASY

Schedule any annual chore that may need following up with repairs by contractors well before their busy season. If you know the outside of your house needs painting, you'll have time to get quotes from more than one decorator and might even get a better price by booking early.

Inspect the Chimney

- Wood-burning fireplaces and wood stoves create tar and soot, which can build up to dangerous levels inside chimneys.
- To inspect the chimney, start from the top and check the condition of the masonry.
- Look up the flue with a strong torch and check for any build-up of soot or tar (which will appear as a shiny glaze on the walls).
- If you suspect any damage, call a chimney specialist.
- Get the chimney swept.

Get the Boiler Serviced

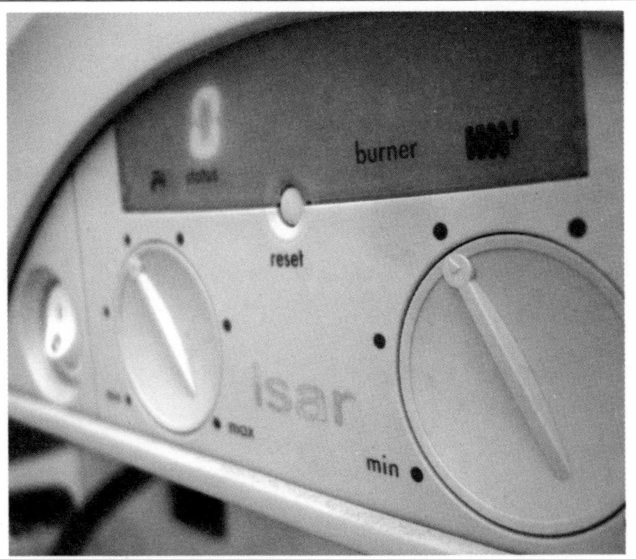

- Yearly boiler servicing might seem unnecessary, but it's inexpensive insurance, especially as a boiler ages.
- An inspection should cover function, air testing, the condition of the fire box, burners, ventilation and carbon monoxide levels.
- Check that all water shut-off valves at every fixture and the main stopcock still function properly, and inspect toilets for stability.
- Look in the cellar, loft and any outbuildings for pest and rodent infestation.

GLOSSARY

Aerator: The round screened screw-on tip of a sink tap. It mixes water and air for a smooth flow.

Aggregate: A mixture of sand and stone, and a major component of concrete.

Anchor bolts: Bolts used to secure objects or structures to concrete or masonry.

Balusters: Vertical members in a stair rail used between the handrail and the stair treads. Sometimes referred to as spindles.

Beam: A structural member transversely supporting a load. A structural member carrying building loads from one support to another.

Blanket insulation: Fibreglass or mineral wool insulation that comes in long rolls in width of 400 mm or 600 mm, to fit between joists.

Blockboard: Engineered wood material made of strips of timber glued edge to edge and sandwiched between hardwood veneers.

Blown insulation: Fibre insulation in loose form used to insulate lofts and walls.

Brace: A piece of structural timber applied at an angle beween vertical and horizontal components to strengthen the structure.

Building regulations: Community ordinances governing the manner in which a building may be constructed or modified.

Cap: The upper member of a column, pilaster, door cornice, moulding or fireplace.

Casement window: A window with hinges on one of the vertical sides, which swings open like a door.

Casing: Wood moulding installed around a door or window opening.

Ceramic tile: A hand- or or machine-made clay or porcelain tile used to finish a floor or wall. Generally used in bathroom and shower enclosures and on worktops.

Chipboard: Engineered wood material made of coarse sawdust that is mixed with resin and pressed into sheets.

Circuit: The path of electrical flow from a power source through an outlet and back to earth.

Circuit breaker: A device that looks like a switch and is usually located inside the electrical consumer unit. It limits the amount of power flowing through a circuit (measured in amperes) and shuts off the power in case of a electrical fault or overload.

Condensation: Beads or drops of water that accumulate on relatively cold surfaces, such as windows.

Conductivity: Thermal conductivity is the rate at which heat is transmitted through a material. Electrical conductivity is a measure of a material's ability to conduct an electric current.

Conduit: A pipe, usually metal, in which wire is installed.

Consumer unit: The box containing fuses or circuit breakers that distributes electric power entering the home to the various lighting and power circuits.

Contractor: A company or individual employed to perform certain types of construction activities.

Cornice: A decorative projection at the top of a wall. In interiors it usually consists of a plaster moulding at the angle between wall and ceiling.

Damper: A metal 'door' within the chimney. It is normally closed when the fireplace is not in use.

Dead bolt: A security lock installed on entry doors that can be activated only with a key or thumb-turn. Unlike a latch, which has a bevelled tongue, dead bolts have square ends.

Door frame: The surrounding case into which and out of which a door closes and opens. It consists of two vertical posts and a horizontal lintel.

Door stop: A wooden batten fixed to a door frame that stops the door swinging through when closed.

Dormer: An element of a building that projects from a sloping roof, with vertical walls suitable for windows or other openings.

Double glazing: A window made of two panes of glass with a sealed gas-filled space between them.

Downpipe: A pipe that carries rainwater down from the roof's horizontal gutters.

Draught proofing: Narrow strips of thin metal or other material installed to prevent the infiltration of air and moisture around windows and doors.

Dry lining: The erection of studs and plasterboard on a solid wall, as an alternative to traditional plaster or in order to conceal insulation, pipework etc.

Duct: A pipe of galvanized metal or other rigid material that carries warm or cool air into a room from a heater or ventilator, or stale air away from an extractor fan.

Eggshell paint: A paint made so that its surface, when dry, has some lustre but is not very glossy. Bathrooms and kitchens are often painted with eggshell paint.

Fire retardant chemical: A chemical or preparation of chemicals used to reduce the flammability of a material or to retard the spread of flame.

Flashing: Sheet metal or other material used to cover joints in roof and wall construction to protect a building from water seepage.

Flexible filler: A plastic material used to seal gaps between two surfaces, such as between a window frame and the wall.

Foundation: The supporting portion of a structure below the ground floor construction, including the footings.

Fuse: A device used to prevent overloads in older electrical circuits, or included in a plug in order to break a circuit in the event of a fault developing in an appliance.

Grain: The direction, size, arrangement, appearance or quality of the fibres in wood.

Grout: A wet mixture of cement, sand and water that flows into masonry or ceramic crevices to seal the joints between the different pieces. It is mainly used to fill gaps between tiles.

Gutter: A shallow channel or conduit of metal or PVC set below and along the eaves of a house to catch and carry off rainwater from the roof.

Gypsum plaster: Gypsum formulated to be used with the addition of sand and water for base-coat plaster.

Humidifier: An appliance designed to increase the humidity within a room or a house by means of the discharge of water vapour.

I-beam: A steel beam with a cross section resembling the capital letter I. It is used for long spans over wide wall openings, such as a double garage door, when wall and roof loads bear down on the opening.

Insulation: Any material high in resistance to heat transmission that, when placed in the walls, ceiling or floors of a structure, will reduce the rate of heat flow.

Jamb: The vertical part of a door frame or window frame on to which the door or window is secured.

Joint: The location between the touching surfaces of two members or components joined and held together by nails, glue, cement, mortar or other means.

Joint compound: A powder that is usually mixed with water and used for joint treatment in gypsum-wallboard finish.

Joist: One of a series of parallel timbers used to support floating floors and ceiling loads and supported in turn by larger beams, girders or bearing walls.

Kilowatt (kw): One thousand watts. A kilowatt hour is the base unit used in measuring electrical consumption.

Lattice: An open framework of criss-crossed wood or metal strips that form regular, patterned spaces.

Load-bearing wall: A wall that supports any vertical load in addition to its own weight.

Loft access: A covered opening in the ceiling of a top floor room that provides access to the loft.

Main contractor: A contractor who enters into a contract with the owner of a project for the construction of the project and who takes full responsibility for its completion, although the contractor may enter into subcontracts with others for the performance of specific parts or phases of the project.

Masonry: Stone, brick, concrete, hollow-tile, concrete block or other similar building units or materials.

Matt paint: An interior paint that contains a high proportion of pigment and dries to a flat or lustreless finish.

Moulding: A strip of wood with an engraved surface or decorative profile used for ornamental purposes in construction and furniture making.

Panel: A thin flat piece of wood, plywood or similar material, framed by stiles and rails as in a door (or cupboard door), or fitted into grooves of thicker material with moulded edges as part of a decorative wall treatment.

Pilot hole: A small-diameter, pre-drilled hole that guides a nail or screw.

Pilot light: A small, continuous flame (in a gas fire, boiler or stove) that ignites gas or oil burners when needed.

Plasterboard: A manufactured panel, commonly 12.5 mm thick and 1200x2400 mm or 1200x3000 mm in size, made out of gypsum plaster encased in heavy paper. The panels are nailed or screwed on to a framework of wooden battens known as studs, and the joints are taped and covered with a joint compound.

Plywood: A sheet (normally 1200x2400 mm) of engineered wood made of three or more layers of veneer, compressed and joined with glue, and usually laid with the grain of adjoining plies at right angles to give the sheet strength.

Post: A strong vertical timber usually designed to carry a beam or to support a fence.

Pressure Relief Valve (PRV): A device mounted on a boiler that is designed to release any high steam pressure in the tank to prevent tank explosions.

Primer: The first, base coat of paint when a paint job consists of two or more coats. A first coating formulated to seal raw surfaces and holding succeeding finish coats.

Putty: A dough-like material used as a filler. Glazier's putty is made of chalk and linseed oil and is used to seal glass in a window frame. Other types of putty are used to fill small holes and crevices in wood, and for similar purposes.

PVC (Polyvinyl Chloride) or CPVC (Chlorinated Polyvinyl Chloride): A type of white or light grey plastic sometimes used for water supply pipes and waste pipes.

Quadrant moulding: Moulding used to cover any gaps at the union between floor and skirting board. Sometimes called a carpet strip.

Radiant heating: A method of heating, usually consisting of a forced hot water system with pipes placed under the floor, or in the wall or ceiling.

Rafter: Timber used to support the roof. The rafters of a flat roof are sometimes called roof joists.

RCB (Residual Circuit Breaker): An ultra-sensitive plug designed to shut off all electric current, for use with appliances such as mowers and saws used in situations where there is increased risk of damp or accidental damage.

Sash: A single movable frame in a window, containing one or more lights of glass.

Sash window: A window with vertically sliding sashes. It usually refers to a double hung window, in which both the upper and lower sashes can move up and down past one another. In a single hung window only one sash is operable.

Sealer: A finishing material, either clear or pigmented, that is usually applied directly over raw wood for the purpose of sealing the wood surface.

Service panel: The box where electricity enters a home wiring system.

Shim: A small piece of scrap timber, usually wedge shaped, which is hammered behind or between other timbers to force them into position or tighten a joint.

Shingles: Wooden tiles used to cover roofs or house walls.

Short circuit: A situation that occurs when live and neutral wires come in contact with each other. Fuses and circuit breakers protect against fire that could result from a short.

Skirting board: A wooden board placed against the wall around the room next to the floor.

Socket: An electrical outlet.

Soffit: The area below the eaves and overhangs of a roof.

Strike: The pierced plate on a door jamb that engages a latch or dead bolt.

Stucco: An exterior plaster finish made with Portland cement as its base.

Stud: A vertical wood batten, also referred to as a wall stud, attached to the horizontal timbers at the top and base of the wall. Interior, non-load-bearing partition walls are constructed from studs attached to a frame and covered on both sides with panels of plasterboard.

Subfloor: The component of a floor laid over a concrete slab or floor joists, such as plywood sheet, over which the finished floor is to be laid.

Taping: The process of covering plasterboard joints with paper tape and joint compound.

Terra cotta: A ceramic material moulded into masonry units.

Tile: Small, flat, manufactured sheet of clay, slate, or other material cut to stock lengths, widths and thickness. Clay and slate tiles are typically used as roof coverings. Glazed ceramic, porcelain and glass tiles make hardwearing, waterproof coverings for walls, floors and worktops in bathrooms and kitchens, and can also be applied to outdoor surfaces such as pools and patios.

Trap: A plumbing fitting, also known as a U-bend, that holds water to prevent air, gas and vermin from backing up a waste pipe.

Tread: The horizontal surface in a staircase on which the foot is placed.

Veneer: An extremely thin sheet of wood, usually hardwood prized for its appearance, glued to a cheaper softwood or engineered wood.

Vent: A pipe or duct that allows the flow of air and gasses to the outside.

Voltage: A measure of electrical potential. In the UK the standard system supply voltage is 230 V, with a tolerance of +10 per cent and –6 per cent. Bathroom 'shaver' sockets provide low current of 110 V for electric razors and other appliances such as toothbrushes.

PHOTO CREDITS

Chapter 1
xii (left): © Vincent Giordano/shutterstock
xii (right): © photos.com
1 (left): © George Peters/istockphoto
2 (right): © Amy Walters | Dreamstime.com
3 (left): © Mark Evans/istockphoto
4 (left): © VisualField/istockphoto
4 (right): © Ryan Klos/istockphoto
5 (left): Marilyn Zelinsky-Syarto
6 (right): Danny E Hooks/Shutterstock
7 (right): © dwphotos/shutterstock
8 (left): © Lucid/shutterstock
8 (right): © Gautier Willaume/istockphoto
9 (left): © Jonathan Lenz/shutterstock
9 (right): © Olivier Le Queinec/ shutterstock
10 (left): Marilyn Zelinsky-Syarto
10 (right): Marilyn Zelinsky-Syarto
11 (left): Anna Adesanya

Chapter 2
12 (right): Courtesy of Bosch
13 (right): © Gillian Mowbray/istockphoto
14 (left): Courtesy of The Stanley Works
14 (right): Courtesy of The Stanley Works
15 (left): Courtesy of The Stanley Works
15 (right): Courtesy of The Stanley Works
16 (left): Courtesy of The Stanley Works
16 (right): Courtesy of The Stanley Works
17 (left): Courtesy of The Stanley Works
17 (right): Courtesy of The Stanley Works
18 (left): Courtesy of Bosch
18 (right): Courtesy of Bosch
19 (left): Courtesy of The Stanley Works
19 (right): Courtesy of The Stanley Works
20 (left): Courtesy of Bosch
20 (right): Courtesy of Bosch
21 (left): Courtesy of Bosch
21 (right): Courtesy of Bosch
22 (left): Courtesy of Wagner
22 (right): Anna Adesanya
23 (left): Courtesy of Bosch
23 (right): © Kingjon | Dreamstime.com

Chapter 3
24 (left): Anna Adesanya
24 (right): Anna Adesanya
25 (left): Anna Adesanya
25 (right): Anna Adesanya
26 (left): Anna Adesanya
26 (right): Anna Adesanya
27 (left): Anna Adesanya
27 (right): Anna Adesanya
28 (right): Anna Adesanya
29 (left): Anna Adesanya
30 (left): Anna Adesanya
30 (right): Anna Adesanya
31 (left): Anna Adesanya
32 (left): Anna Adesanya
33 (left): Anna Adesanya
33 (right): Anna Adesanya
34 (left): Anna Adesanya
34 (right): Anna Adesanya
35 (left): Anna Adesanya
35 (right): Anna Adesanya

Chapter 4
36 (left): Anna Adesanya
36 (right): © Dewayne Flowers | Dreamstime.com
37 (left): Anna Adesanya
38 (left): Anna Adesanya
38 (right): Anna Adesanya
39 (left): Anna Adesanya
40 (left): Kenneth Sponsler/Shutterstock
40 (right): Anna Adesanya
41 (left): Anna Adesanya
42 (left): © Misty Diller | Dreamstime.com
42 (right): © Peter Galbraith | Dreamstime.com
43 (left): Anna Adesanya
43 (right): Anna Adesanya
44 (left): Anna Adesanya
44 (right): Anna Adesanya
45 (left): Anna Adesanya
45 (right): Anna Adesanya

Chapter 5
46 (left): Anna Adesanya
46 (right): Anna Adesanya
47 (left): Anna Adesanya
47 (right): Anna Adesanya
48 (left): Anna Adesanya
48 (right): Anna Adesanya
49 (left): Anna Adesanya
49 (right): Anna Adesanya
50 (left): Anna Adesanya
50 (right): Anna Adesanya
51 (left): Anna Adesanya
51 (right): Anna Adesanya
52 (left): Anna Adesanya
52 (right): Anna Adesanya
53 (left): © Elenat | Dreamstime.com
53 (right): © Yvanovich | Dreamstime.com
54 (left): Anna Adesanya
54 (right): © Jon McIntosh/istockphoto
55 (left): © Christina Richards/istockphoto
56 (left): © Stephen R. Syarto
56 (right): Anna Adesanya
57 (left): © Christopher Hudson/ shutterstock
57 (right): © Robert Redelowski/ shutterstock

Chapter 6
58 (left): Courtesy of The Delta Faucet Company
58 (right): Anna Adesanya
59 (left): Anna Adesanya
59 (right): Marilyn Zelinsky-Syarto
60 (left): Jack Tom
61 (right): Jack Tom
61 (left): Jack Tom
62 (right): Anna Adesanya
63 (left): Jocicalek/Shutterstock
64 (right): Marilyn Zelinsky-Syarto
65 (left): Jack Tom
65 (right): Anna Adesanya
66 (right): Anna Adesanya
67 (left): Jack Tom
68 (left): Marilyn Zelinsky-Syarto
68 (right): Marilyn Zelinsky-Syarto
69 (left): © Marc Pinter | Dreamstime.com
69 (right): Anna Adesanya

Chapter 7
70 (left): Stephen R. Syarto
70 (right): Anna Adesanya
71 (left): Marilyn Zelinsky-Syarto
71 (right): Anna Adesanya
72 (left): Anna Adesanya
72 (right): Jack Tom
73 (left): Anna Adesanya
74 (left): Courtesy of Anderson Windows
76 (right): Anna Adesanya
75 (right): © David Lewis/istockphoto
76 (left): Anna Adesanya
77 (left): Anna Adesanya
77 (right): Anna Adesanya
78 (right): Anna Adesanya
79 (left): Anna Adesanya
79 (right): Anna Adesanya
80 (right): © David Park | Dreamstime.com
81 (left): © Carli Schultz Kruse/istockphoto
81 (right): Olegusk/Shutterstock

Chapter 8
82 (left): Jack Tom
82 (right): Jack Tom
83 (left): Jack Tom
84 (right): Anna Adesanya
85 (left): Anna Adesanya
86 (left): Stephen R. Syarto
86 (right): Marilyn Zelinsky-Syarto
87 (left): © VanDenEsker/istockphoto
87 (right): Stephen R. Syarto
88 (left): Anna Adesanya
88 (right): Anna Adesanya
89 (left): Courtesy of Andersen Windows
89 (right): Marilyn Zelinsky-Syarto
90 (left): © robcocquyt/shutterstock

90 (right): Marilyn Zelinsky-Syarto
91 (left): Marilyn Zelinsky-Syarto
91 (right): Marilyn Zelinsky-Syarto
92 (left): Anna Adesanya
92 (right): Anna Adesanya
93 (left): Anna Adesanya
93 (right): Anna Adesanya

Chapter 9
94 (left): Maureen Graney
94 (right): Maureen Graney
95 (left): Maureen Graney
96 (left): Jack Tom
96 (right): Jack Tom
97 (left): Maureen Graney
98 (left): Anna Adesanya
98 (right): Anna Adesanya
99 (left): Anna Adesanya
99 (right): Anna Adesanya
100 (left): © Joe Klune/istockphoto
100 (right): Jack Tom
101 (left): Jack Tom
101 (right): Marilyn Zelinsky-Syarto
102 (left): Marilyn Zelinsky-Syarto
102 (right): Marilyn Zelinsky-Syarto
103 (left): Marilyn Zelinsky-Syarto
104 (left): Anna Adesanya
104 (right): © photos.com
105 (left): © John Wollwerth/shutterstock

Chapter 10
106 (right): Kassia Gawronski
107 (right): © Serg64/Shutterstock
108 (left): Kassia Gawronski
108 (right): Kassia Gawronski
109 (right): kra/Shutterstock
110 (left): © Tom Tomczyk/istockphoto
110 (right): Courtesy of General Electric
111 (left): Kassia Gawronski
112 (left): Anna Adesanya
112 (right): Kassia Gawronski
113 (left): Kassia Gawronski
114 (right): Courtesy of General Electric

Chapter 11
116 (left): Anna Adesanya
116 (right): Marilyn Zelinsky-Syarto
117 (left): Marilyn Zelinsky-Syarto
117 (right): © Paul Senyszyn/istockphoto
118 (right): Marilyn Zelinsky-Syarto
119 (left): Anna Adesanya
119 (right): Marilyn Zelinsky-Syarto
120 (right): Stephen R. Syarto
121 (left): Marilyn Zelinsky-Syarto
121 (right): Marilyn Zelinsky-Syarto
122 (left): © Suzanne Paul | Dreamstime.com
122 (right): © Suzanne Paul | Dreamstime.com
123 (right): © Frances Twitty/istockphoto
124 (left): © Digitoll | Dreamstime.com
125 (left): © Lein de León Yong/shutterstock
125 (right): © Rick Sargeant | Dreamstime.com

Chapter 12
127 (left): Courtesy of GunDogHouse
127 (right): Marilyn Zelinsky-Syarto
128 (left): Courtesy of Joshua Jones/A All Animal Control of Tri-State @ www.aallanimalcontrol.com
129 (left): © Robeo | Dreamstime.com

129 (right): Courtesy of Bird-B-Gone, Inc.@www.birdbgone.com
130 (left): © Ed Endicott / Wysiwyg Foto LLC/shutterstock
130 (right): © TAOLMOR/shutterstock
131 (left): © Borhuah Chen/Shutterstock
131 (right): © Frank Boellmann/Shutterstock
132 (left): Anna Adesanya
132 (right): Marilyn Zelinsky-Syarto
133 (left): Anna Adesanya
133 (right): Courtesy of Rubbermaid

Chapter 13
134 (left): Courtesy of Glidden
134 (right): Anna Adesanya
135 (left): © Juriah Mosin/shutterstock
136 (left): Anna Adesanya
136 (right): Anna Adesanya
137 (left): Anna Adesanya
137 (right): Anna Adesanya
138 (right): Courtesy of Glidden
139 (left): Anna Adesanya
140 (left): Anna Adesanya
140 (right): Marilyn Zelinsky-Syarto
141 (left): © Wendy Kaveney | Dreamstime.com
141 (right): Courtesy of Glidden
142 (left): © Jack Schiffer | Dreamstime.com
142 (right): © photoslb com/Shutterstock
143 (left): Anna Adesanya
144 (left): © Frances Twitty/istockphoto
144 (right): Courtesy of Wagner
145 (left): © Lisa F. Young/Shutterstock

Chapter 14
146 (right): Courtesy of Ikea
147 (left): Courtesy of Ikea
148 (right): Courtesy of Ikea
149 (left): Stephen R. Syarto
149 (right): © Ene | Dreamstime.com
150 (right): © MaxFX/shutterstock
151 (left): © John Wollwerth | Dreamstime.com
151 (right): Courtesy of Ikea
152 (left): Courtesy of GarageTek
152 (right): Courtesy of GarageTek
153 (left): Courtesy of GarageTek
153 (right): Courtesy of GarageTek
154 (right): © Kristin Smith | Dreamstime.com
155 (left): Stephen R. Syarto
156 (right): Courtesy of Ikea
157 (left): Courtesy of Ikea

Chapter 15
158 (right): Jack Tom
159 (left): Stephen R. Syarto
159 (right): © Sunny Celeste/Shutterstock
160 (left): © Christina Richards/Shutterstock
160 (right): © Limeyrunner | Dreamstime.com
161 (left): Anna Adesanya
161 (right): © Jeffery Stone/Shutterstock
162 (left): Anna Adesanya
163 (left): Anna Adesanya
163 (right): Anna Adesanya
164 (right): © A Marcynuk/Shutterstock
165 (left): © Christina Richards/shutterstock
165 (right): © Sue Smith/Shutterstock
166 (left): © Greenstockcreative | Dreamstime.com
166 (right): Anna Adesanya
167 (left): Courtesy of Kohler
167 (right): Anna Adesanya

Chapter 16
168 (left): Claire Desjardins/istockphoto
168 (right): Marilyn Zelinsky-Syarto
169 (left): Marilyn Zelinsky-Syarto
169 (right): Marilyn Zelinsky-Syarto
170 (left): Marilyn Zelinsky-Syarto
170 (right): © Lastdays1 | Dreamstime.com
171 (left): Marilyn Zelinsky-Syarto
171 (right): Crystalcraig | Dreamstime.com
172 (left): Marilyn Zelinsky-Syarto
172 (right): Stephen R. Syarto
173 (right): Anna Adesanya
174 (left): Anna Adesanya
174 (right): Anna Adesanya
175 (left): © Lawrence Roberg/Shutterstock
175 (right): © Darleen Stry | Dreamstime.com
176 (right): © Astarfotograf/istockphoto
177 (right): © PhillDanze/istockphoto
178 (right): © Cornelia Pithart | Dreamstime.com
179 (right): © copit/shutterstock

Chapter 17
180 (right): © Dorel Juvenile Group 2008. All Rights Reserved.
181 (left): Courtesy of Safe Beginnings Inc.
182 (left): Anna Adesanya
182 (right): © Diane Diederich/shutterstock
183 (left): Anna Adesanya
183 (right): © Dorel Juvenile Group 2008. All Rights Reserved.
184 (left): © Dorel Juvenile Group 2008. All Rights Reserved.
184 (right): © Dorel Juvenile Group 2008. All Rights Reserved.
185 (left): © tiburonstudios/istockphoto

185 (right): Marilyn Zelinsky-Syarto
186 (left): Courtesy of Ikea
186 (right): Anna Adesanya
187 (left): © Alan Murphy.
187 (right): Alice Jell
188 (left): © Dorel Juvenile Group 2008. All Rights Reserved.
188 (right): © Don Bayley/istockphoto
189 (left): © Sorsillo | Dreamstime.com
189 (right): Anna Adesanya
190 (left): © Yanta/Shutterstock
190 (right): © Dorel Juvenile Group 2008. All Rights Reserved.
191 (left): © Dorel Juvenile Group 2008. All Rights Reserved.

Chapter 18
192 (right): Courtesy of Fisher Paykel
193 (left): Courtesy of Fisher Paykel
194 (left): Anna Adesanya
194 (right): Marilyn Zelinsky-Syarto
195 (left): Anna Adesanya
195 (right): Courtesy of Fisher Paykel
196 (left): Anna Adesanya
196 (right): Anna Adesanya
197 (left): Anna Adesanya
197 (right): Marilyn Zelinsky-Syarto

Chapter 19
198 (left): Anna Adesanya
198 (right): © bofotolux/Shutterstock
199 (left): Jenny Haddington
200 (left): © Suzanne Tucker/Shutterstock
200 (right): Anna Adesanya
201 (left): Anna Adesanya
202 (right): Anna Adesanya
203 (left): Jack Tom
204 (right): Marilyn Zelinsky-Syarto
205 (left): Jenny Haddington
206 (right): Anna Adesanya
207 (left): Anna Adesanya
207 (right): Anna Adesanya
208 (right): Marilyn Zelinsky-Syarto
209 (left): Anna Adesanya
209 (right): Kassia Gawronski

INDEX

A
appliances
  dishwashers, 194–95
  energy efficient, 166–67
  refrigerators, 192–93
  vacuum cleaners, 196–97
autumn maintenance, 200–1

B
bath wastes, blocked, 68–69
bees, 130–31
bird damage, 128–29
blowers, 21
bolts, 27

C
car body filler, 44
chainsaws, 22
childproofing
  electrical precautions, 186–87
  ideas for, 190–91
  plumbing, 188–89
  room and cupboard doors, 184–85
  safety gates, 180–81
  windows, 182–83
chips
  finishes, 56–57
  tile, 54–55
chisels, 19
circuit breakers, 106–7
clogs
  baths and showers, 68–69
  downpipes, 78–79
  gutters, 76–77
  outside drains, 80–81
  sinks and basins, 64–65
  toilets, 66–67
clothes storage, 150–51
composting, 176–77
contact adhesive, 33
cracks
  concrete floors, 102–3
  glass, 104–5
  plaster, 96–97
  plasterboard, 100–1
crowbars, 16
cutting tools, 16

D
damage
  broken glass, 9
  power line, 9
  roof, 8
  securing house, 10–11
  storm, 8–9
  tree, 8
decking repairs, 172–73
dishwashers, 194–95
door locks
  repairs, 10
  sticking, 92–93
doors, sticking, 86–87
downpipes
  blocked, 78–79
  leaking, 72–73
drains, outside, 80–81
draught proofing, 162–63
drawers, sticking, 90–91
drills, 20

E
ear protection, 24
electrical systems
  childproofing, 186–87
  fuses and circuit breakers, 108–9
  lamp, flex and plug repair, 112–13
  overview of, 106–7
  renewable energy, 114–15
  saving electricity, 110–11
emergencies, 3
energy efficiency
  appliances, 166–67
  draught proofing, 162–63
  insulation, 164–65
  overview, 158–59
  reducing heat loss, 160–61
ergonomics, 12–13
eye protection, 24

F
fence repairs, 168–71
files, 17
fillers, 44–45
finishes
  chipped, 56–57
  clear, 40–41
  faux, 42–43
flex repair, 112–13
flexible filler, 30–31
flooding, 2
flooring, scratches, 50–51
floors, squeaky
  initial steps, 82–83
  strategies, 84–85
fungi
  exterior, 120–21
  identification of, 116–17
  interior, 118–19
  serious mould, 122–23
  wood rot, 124–25
furniture, scratched, 48–49
fuses, 108–9

G
garage door openers, 11
gas
  appliances, 7
  boilers, 6, 7
  leaks, 6–7
  meters, 7
glass
  broken, 9

cracked, 104–5
glossary of terms, 210–13
gloves, 25
glues, 32–33
green ideas
composting, 176–77
energy efficiency, 158–67
rainwater butts, 178–79
renewable energy, 114–15
gutters
blocked, 76–77
leaking, 72–73

H
hammers, 14
hand protection, 25
hardware
filler, 30–31
nails, 28–29
sandpaper and steel wool, 34–35
screws and bolts, 26–27
tapes and glues, 32–33
heat guns, 18
holes
plaster, 94–95
plasterboard, 98–99
home security systems, 11

I
insulation, 164–65
insurance, 9, 11

K
kitchen islands, 156–57

L
lamp repair, 112–13
leaks
gutters and downpipes, 72–73
roofs, 70–71
taps, 58–59
toilets, 60–61
washing machine, 62–63
windows, 74–75
lighting
outdoor, 174–75
replacing fixtures, 1
lost head nails, 29

M
maintenance
autumn, 200–01
monthly, 206–7
preventative, 1
spring, 204–05
summer, 198–99
winter, 202–3
yearly, 208–9
marbled finish, 42
masks, 25
measuring, xii
mildew. *See* fungi
mould. *See* fungi
monthly maintenance, 206–7
moss. *See* fungi

N
nails
guns, 22
punches, 19
types of, 28–29
nuts, 27

O
oil-based finishes, 40
outdoor lighting, 174–75

P
paint
ceilings and walls, 138–39
choice of, 134–35
exterior preparation for, 142–43
exterior techniques, 144–45
finishes, 36–37
interior preparation for, 136–37
woodwork and doors, 140–41
pests
bird damage, 128–29
preventative measures, 132–33
wasps and bees, 130–31
pet doors, 126–27
pipes, leaking, 4
plaster
cracked, 96–97
holes in, 94–95
patching, 45
plasterboard
cracks, 100–1
holes, 98–99
plasterboard screws, 26
pliers, 15
plug repair, 113–14
power line damage, 9
power cuts, 3
pressure washers, 22
primers, 36

R
ragged finish, 42
rainwater butts, 178–79
refrigerators, 192–93
repairs
evaluation of, 2–3
guidelines for, 1
respiratory protection, 25
roof
damage, 8
leaks, 4, 70–71
round wire nails, 28

S
safety
gates, 180–1
gear, 24–25
glasses, 24
sanders, 20
sandpaper, 34–35
saws, 17, 21
scrapers, 17
scratches
furniture, 48–49
wood flooring, 50–51
woodwork, 46–47

worktops, 52–53
screwdrivers, 14
screws and bolts, 26–27
security, 10–11
sheet metal screws, 27
shellac, 41
shelving
building, 146–47
kits, 148–49
showers, blocked, 68–69
sinks and basins, blocked, 64–65
spring maintenance, 204–5
stains, 38–39
steel wool, 34–35
sticking
door locks, 92–93
doors, 86–87
furniture drawers, 90–91
windows, 88–89
storage
building shelves, 146–47
clothes, 150–51
garage, 152–53
kitchen islands, 156–57
shelving kits, 148–49
workbench, 154–55
storm damage, 8–9
summer maintenance, 198–99
super glue, 32

T

tape measures, 18
tapes, 32–33
taps, leaking, 58–59
tiles, chipped, 54–55
toilet
blocks, 66–67
leaks, 5, 60–61
tools, xii
basic small, 18–19
ergonomics, 12
hand, 14–15
hire, 22–23
maintenance, 13
power, 20–21
safety, 12–13, 24–25
sharp, 16–17
weight of, 13
tree damage, 8

V

vacuum cleaners, 21, 196–97
varnish, 40

W

wallpaper steamers, 22
washing machine, leaking, 62–63
wasps, 130–31
water leaks, 4–5
water stopcocks, 5
wax finishes, 41
window
leaks, 74–75
sticking, 88–89
windows
broken glass, 9
childproofing, 182–83
energy efficiency and, 160–61
securing, 10
winter maintenance, 202–3
wiring
childproofing, 186–87
fuses and circuit breakers, 108–9
lamp, flex and plug repair, 112–13
overview of, 106–7
renewable energy, 114–15
saving electricity, 110–11
wood
filler, 45
glue, 32
rot, 124–25
screws, 26
wood graining, 42
woodwork
painting, 140–41
scratched, 46–47
workbenches, 154–55
worktops, scratched, 52–53
wrenches, 15

Y

yearly maintenance, 208–9